To Roscoe Martin
with happy memories

SWORDS AND SYMBOLS
THE TECHNIQUE OF SOVEREIGNTY

SWORDS AND SYMBOLS

THE TECHNIQUE OF SOVEREIGNTY

REVISED EDITION

James Marshall

Funk & Wagnalls — New York

Library of Congress Catalog Card Number: 69–16553

Published by Funk & Wagnalls,

A Division of *Reader's Digest Books, Inc.*

Printed in the United States of America

TO *Lenore*, *Ellen*, AND *Jon*

CONTENTS

Part I

1. THE GOLDEN BOUGH *3*
2. THE "SUPREMACY" OF THE SOVEREIGN *5*
3. FIGHT OR COMPROMISE *16*
4. POLITICAL WEAPONS *20*
5. LAW *55*
6. CUSTOM *75*
7. POPULAR SOVEREIGNTY, THE SOCIAL COMPACT, AND THE WITHERING STATE *79*
8. LIBERTY AND FREEDOM *92*
9. EQUALITY *104*
10. THE POLITICAL PROCESS *115*
11. THE IDEAL OF UNITY *143*
12. DUAL AND PLURAL SOVEREIGNTY *153*
13. ETHICS AND IDEALS *160*

Part II

14. THE SOVEREIGNTY OF NATIONS *171*

15. LIMITATIONS ON SOVEREIGNTY OF NATIONS *194*

16. PRESTIGE *220*

CONCLUSION *240*

BIBLIOGRAPHY *256*

ACKNOWLEDGMENTS *270*

INDEX *273*

Part I

I

THE GOLDEN BOUGH

IN THE opening chapter of *The Golden Bough*, Sir James Frazer tells of that "strange and recurring tragedy," the succession of the priesthood of the sanctuary of Diana of the Wood, and relates that: "Within the sanctuary at Nemi grew a certain tree[1] of which no branch might be broken. Only a runaway slave was allowed to break off, if he could, one of its boughs. Success in the attempt entitled him to fight the priest in single combat, and if he slew him he reigned in his stead with the title of King of the Wood (Rex Nemorensis)." Around this tree through the day and the night a grim figure prowled. "In his hand he carried a drawn sword, and he kept peering warily about him as if at every instant he expected to be set upon by an enemy. He was a priest and a murderer; and the man for whom he looked was sooner or later to murder him and hold the priesthood in his stead. Such was the rule of the sanctuary. A candidate for the priesthood could only succeed to office by slaying the priest, and

[1] This golden tree Frazer associates with the mistletoe which some legends regard as the tree of life.

having slain him, he retained office until he was himself slain by a stronger or a craftier."

When we turn from the King of the Wood to the secular rulers of the earth, from the custom of the sanctuary to the processes of political action, the picture of the harassed priest guarding his tentative tenure will come to us again as the theme of all sovereignty. For political history is a series of tales of this kind. Again and again there recurs the story of the slaves destroying their rulers, of rulers who, realizing the hazardous nature of their sovereignty, fight to guard it. And though the sword is now often swathed in some symbolic scabbard of civilization, the war of the ruler against possible successors is as bitter as ever. For it is the destiny of the head that wears the crown that its sleep must be fitful and its days numbered.

2

THE "SUPREMACY" OF THE SOVEREIGN

IT HAS been traditional to regard the sovereign power as supreme, or at least to define it as supreme as a point of law. Such definitions may express a philosophical ideal, an archetype; but in the realm of politics, supremacy as an ingredient of sovereign power is at best a propagandist flavoring. The long line of distinguished writers and jurists who pronounced this doctrine of supremacy were grinding axes for rulers whom they served. Thus, when Bodin, in his great work *De Republica*, says: "*Majestas est summa in cives acsubditos legibus que soluta potestas*," he is talking in order to justify the absolutism of the later Valois kings and give to a personal sovereign the theoretical justification for the later claim of Louis XIV, "*L'état c'est moi.*" So too, Bracton, writing to defend the power of the English kings, tells us that *Lex* is *Rex*.

Mr. Justice Story, in his *Constitution*, written in the early nineteenth century, defines sovereignty as "the union and exercise of all human power possessed in a state: it is a combination of all power; it is the power to do everything in a state without accountability." At first blush, this sounds curious in the mouth of a man struggling to rear a young democracy. But of course in American constitutional doctrine the people as a whole were the source of such supremacy. That some could not vote and some were slaves, and that the interests of even the voters conflicted, were facts ignored in the rarefied atmosphere of constitutional theory. Story was writing of the government of the newly combined United States, states which, jealous of each other and of the Federal government, were bursting with eagerness to prove their recently won freedom from the dominion of Great Britain; inevitably he wrote of government as a superlative power. The young nation was feeling its muscles proudly and wondering at the same time whether they were sufficient to keep in line the saucy states with their doctrines of nullification. This was in the tradition of Marshall, who, with Story and other members of the Supreme Court, was building a theory of government around the principle that "a sovereign people cannot suffer derogation from the effective power of its instruments."

Austin, Bentham, Blackstone in England, and other modern writers have also held the view that the sovereign authority is supreme, that from a legal point of view it must be absolute. This absolutism exists, they urge, because, as Sir William Markby, the disciple of Austin, says: "If we once admit that all law proceeds from the sovereign body, to speak of the authority of the sovereign being limited, or of its acts being illegal, is a confusion in terms." The logic is good, but there are hollows in the premises.[1]

[1] Blackstone's idea that the sovereign is incapable of doing and even thinking evil appears absurd to us today, although in the Nazi era millions accepted the idea that what the Führer ordered was the law of the

The reply to Markby's argument is that in general the law that proceeds from the sovereign body is only such as the sovereign can enforce. If the legal sanctions, the weapons, available to the sovereign are inadequate to enforce the law, then what becomes of the sovereign "supreme" or "absolute"? He either undertakes a losing fight or remains quiescently limited. Shakespeare in *Richard II* affords an excellent example. Upon going to Ireland, Richard left his uncle, York, in charge of his realm. After Bolingbroke's rebellion got under way, York went to Bolingbroke to protest, but upon seeing the latter's armed strength, and realizing his own weakness, York spoke these lines:

> . . . If I could, by Him that gave me life,
> I would attach you all, and make you stoop
> Unto the sovereign mercy of the King;
> But, since I cannot, be it known to you,
> I do remain as neuter.

In other words, if the King's agent had had the power he would have "attached," i.e., arrested, the rebels and compelled them to kneel before the King and plead for mercy —the symbolic act of submission, an idiom of feudalism. But lacking this power, York did nothing, and left the decision of power to a later day. Here was no sovereign supremacy. Nor was this the first or the last occasion upon which a sovereign government was unable to enforce its laws and remained "as neuter."

---

land and right. However, as in the case of Blackstone, it would not occur to most people in Western Europe and the United States that middle-class norms imposed by middle-class legislators and judges on people in urban and rural slums could be wrong—though the latter may find those norms alien to them, even evil.

We shall have occasion later to discuss these theories of sovereign supremacy as a part of the political armory, but for the present it is sufficient to note that at all times there are limits to the powers of the sovereign, whether they be written or traditional constitutional limitations. Even despotism is tempered by the fear of assassination and the threat of revolution. Monarchies have been limited in some places by the practice of putting to death kings whose physical powers were failing, or, as in the powerful medieval kingdom of the Khazars in southern Russia, putting kings to death at the end of a fixed period.

Markby, the intelligent utilitarian, himself lets the cat out of the Austinian bag when he admits: "Though for legal purposes all sovereign authority is supreme, as a matter of fact the most absolute government is not so powerful as to be unrestrained. Though not restrained by law, the supreme rulers of every country avow their intention to govern, not for their own benefit, or for the benefit of any particular class, but for the members of society generally; and they cannot altogether neglect the duty which they have assumed." They dare not entirely neglect other members of society without reaping a holocaust, even if it be only in the high heels and satin waistcoats of a palace revolution. Noblesse oblige, that pretty doctrine scented with attar of roses and condescension, arises not merely from the inner drive of conscience but also from external pressure.

Just as Machiavelli advised his prince against impolitic uses of power, so Bodin warned the French king, Henry III, against certain uses of that absolute sovereignty he attached to kings. While Bodin held the sovereign to be above the law and denied that "consent plays any part whatsoever in the obligations to obey," he believed that the king's power was enhanced—not reduced—when through the Estates-General the people associated themselves with the levying of new taxes. Bodin felt the country to be antagonistic to Henry's rule and that there was some justification of this because *the people believed* their property to be threatened by new and to them onerous taxes. To Bodin, taking away property was to attack the foundation of the State. He opposed the practice of selling offices and of changing the alloy of coinage, not because the king lacked the power or his subjects the obligation to submit, but because such acts encouraged discontent and the risk of sedition. So whatever the ideal basis of sovereign power there were pragmatic limits—including sedition. Unwise uses of economic power stirred psychological counterpower which might endanger the sovereign's supremacy in effective physical force.

Law and custom, as we shall notice hereafter, are not simply the tools of rulers. They also have a restraining influence upon rulers because law and custom exert powerful arguments for the opposition; and through the force of inertia which they contain—inertia more explicitly expressed in law and more amorphous in custom—they present principles of a more enduring order than the commands of kings. The dictum of St. Augustine that "it is not for judges to judge of the law but according to the law" was applied to kings throughout the Middle Ages. The law was in general the custom of the land and Machiavelli wrote that it was sufficient for a hereditary monarch "not to transgress the customs of his ancestors and to deal prudently with circumstances as they arise, for a prince of average powers to maintain himself in his state."

In the Middle Ages, a king was deemed to be a king only if he ruled in accordance with the law, which he promised to do in his coronation oath. The oath itself goes back to the Germanic tribes; it is referred to in the Salic law as a *pactum* or agreement; it appears in the Frankish sources and early in English history. By the time of King Ethelred this oath had become stereotyped. It may be analyzed, says McKechnie in his *Magna Carta*, into three promises: "peace to God's Church and people; repression of violence in men of every rank; justice and mercy in all judgments." The oath concluded with a promise to give effect to the laws "which the common people have chosen"—which in those days signified immemorial customs or what were cited as such. Even William the Conqueror took this oath to fulfill the legal formalities of the land he had seized. "For, although one may be very strong in armed forces, yet in entering a province one has always need of the goodwill of the natives," Machiavelli observes.

One medieval writer said: "The King has a superior, namely God. Likewise the law through which he is made king. Likewise his *curia*, that is the earls and barons, since earls (commites) are so called for being as it were associates of the king, and he who has an associate has a master. And so if the king should be without a bridle, that is without a law, they ought to put a bridle on him, lest they themselves, along with him, be without a bridle." These words truly express the sentiment of the period. Natural right, the law of reason, the right of resistance justifying even tyrannicide, the social compact are the reverse of the coin on which is impressed the seal of the "supreme sovereign."

In fact the king's powers were limited in England and

on the continent by the feudal system, which gave to the barons and the Church sources of rich revenue and a dominion over thousands of the royal subjects more direct and immediate than the power of the king. The effectiveness of this feudal restraint is nowhere better illustrated than in the rebellion of the barons against the rule of John and in the denouement at Runnymede. Magna Carta was not a charter of liberty but, as McKechnie calls it, "the formal embodiment of a great mass of feudal custom." It was an attempt to limit the powers of the king by reducing to writing the vague and undeclared rights of the feudal lords and to restore some of the feudal franchises which a succession of strong kings—Henry II and Richard I—had taken away or at least impinged upon. The most interesting feature of Magna Carta bearing upon sovereign power is Chapter 61, by which John provided "security" or a lawful sanction for the rights granted by empowering twenty-five of his rebellious barons to organize a new rebellion against the king if they judged that he or his justiciar or bailiffs had broken any of the articles of the charter "if we shall not have corrected the transgressions . . . within forty days." The "community of the whole land" was required to afford active support to the committee of rebellion in subjecting the king to the law. While impractical as a sanction and subversive of peace in its legalization of rebellion, Chapter 61 was in accord with the medieval practice of *diffidatio* and repudiation of the feudal relationship upon a glaring breach of the compact by either lord or vassal. It indicates not only the power of the opposition that could compel such a declaration by a sovereign, but also the juridic background of limited sovereignty in the feudal system. Another example of limited sovereignty is the use of the symbolic attack on the king by the baronial rebellions directed against his "wicked-advisers." (See Chapter 10.)

Under Chapter 14 of Magna Carta, a council was summoned in 1221 to fix scutage, the sum to be levied by the king in lieu of military service. It assessed against the Bishop of Winchester scutage at 159 marks for his knight's fees. He refused to pay on the ground that he had dissented, and the plea was accepted by the regent. The bishop, apparently a minority of one, was thus not considered bound by the conclusions of the council. That he was not compelled to pay indicates that the king claimed no legal right to enforce this decision of his council. It also is an admission that the king (or regent) did not feel that he had the military power to collect scutage not consented to, that he did not want to try his arms in the collection of money on these terms after the rebellion against John's excessive levies.

In the United States today the sovereignty of the Federal government is limited in law by the very terms of the Constitution. Even the People, nominally proclaimed as sovereign in the Preamble, are deemed to have surrendered a part of their power. For they cannot amend the Constitution in a constitutional manner except as provided by Article V of the Constitution itself. The very statement of this principle of constitutional limitation shows the sophistry of the proposition that the sovereign is supreme because the law declares him supreme.

Two conclusions follow: (a) as a *fact*, sovereignty is never absolute and supreme; (b) even as a *legal concept* the sovereign power is limited by customs and precedents and immunities which the sovereign itself recognizes in practice, and generally in principle, on pain of rebellion. "The measure of the Czar's sovereignty," Woodrow Wilson wrote, 'is the habit of his people; and not their habit only, but their humor also, and the humor of his officials. His concessions to the restless spirit of his army, to the prejudices of his court, and to the temper of the mass of his subjects, his means of keeping this side assassination or revolution, nicely mark the boundaries of his sovereignty."

Nazi and Communist dictatorships have been subject to similar limitations. The slaughter of millions of head of livestock in Russia was the peasant's answer to collectivization for which he was not prepared. The Evangelical ministers and the Catholic Church offered substantial resistance to the Nazi program by refusing to permit their creeds to be "Aryanized" or "paganized." The corporative state in Italy had to make concessions through a concordat with the Vatican—or at least it found the alliance more valuable than a costly victory over the Church, if that had been possible. The government of Mao Tse-tung has had to slow down its "great leap forward" in response to peasant resistance.

A good working definition of sovereignty is that of Sir William Markby in his *Elements of Law*: "*The aggregate of powers which is possessed by the rulers of a political society is called sovereignty.*" This definition does not necessitate the vesting of *all* powers in the sovereign, nor does it contemplate that individuals or a body corporate are sovereign because they possess some of the powers frequently inherent in sovereignty. The Russian word *vlast* is most descriptive. This word means power, sovereignty, government; in the plural it means "the authorities."

The most that can be attributed, therefore, to sovereignty is a limited local superiority, which is never static, but is constantly in evolution, continuously see-sawing. This may vary greatly in intensity, in usage, and even in character. The rule of the Germanic kings, for example, was over a tribe or people rather than over any part of the earth's surface. The government of an autocracy, whether by a so-called absolute monarch, a dictator, or a junta, can be more compactly organized and more directly effective than a democracy which Plato contemptuously described as "a charming form of government full of variety and disorder, and dispensing a sort of equality to equals and unequals," where "subjects are like rulers and rulers like subjects." But, as will be shown later, the political process repeatedly disturbs the equilibrium of sovereignty. Power centers are real but never stable. "The Establishment" is never established but continually absorbs supporting interests and disgorges those that no longer nourish it.

Superimposed upon the day-to-day disputations of factions which haunt all rulers and pull them, now right, now left, there are always the culture, the economy, and the *mores* of the age and of the group which controls the weapons of sovereignty. They limit the freedom of action of that group itself. No sovereign in the feudal economy could have enforced a free labor market; no sovereign working in the economy of nineteenth-century finance-capitalism could have effected serfdom; though forms of peonage and serfdom (as through sharecropping) survived in rural, nonindustrialized areas of the Southern states long after slavery itself was abolished. The Federal government was unable to enforce the Thirteenth Amendment, as it was also unable to enforce the equal protection clause of the Fourteenth Amendment, against the power of anti-Negro local interests.

In his *History of the Russian Revolution*, Trotsky sums up this phase of the matter in this way: "Even the most despotic of autocrats is but little similar to a 'free' individuality laying its arbitrary imprint upon events. He is always the crowned agent of the privileged classes which are forming society in their own image." This is ancient learning. Both Plato and Aristotle believed that the ruling class *is* the State regardless of the form of the government—which is nothing less than asserting that sovereign power, stripped of constitutional adjectives, resides in some group which not only gives its character to the body politic, but creates in its own image a theory of sovereign power, however unrealistic.

3

FIGHT OR COMPROMISE

THE HISTORY of political units, cities, states, nations, alliances, and federations has been the story of battle for the achievement of this sovereignty; it has been a series of struggles for the retention of such sovereignty and the seizure of this limited "supremacy." This becomes clear in the pathological moments of history, in civil wars and revolutions, which illuminate our knowledge of the functioning of a body politic in the same manner as the study of diseased organs, the analysis of a distraught mind, and the performance of an autopsy teach the nature of the human body and its relation to its environment. Just as the knowledge of the biological properties of the cell or the electrical properties of the atom may explain the nature of greater bodies of which they are parts, so the workings of the ward politician, the manipulations of the great industrialist, the explosion of each village Hampden, and the sanctions of every household autocrat, though they themselves may not be sovereigns, portray the technique of sovereignty.

Both the sovereign and the opposition have a choice of two political techniques: They can fight or they can compromise. Compromise is frequently only the postponement of a battle, as was the case with the Missouri Compromise which did not settle but only deferred the struggle to end slavery. Compromise is resorted to only when the sovereign power does not wish to test its strength. An example occurred during the 1905 Revolution in Russia, when a crisis arose because of the strike of the workers in factories, public utilities, and railroads. Count Witte, Prime Minister at the time of the Revolution of 1905, told the tsar that he believed "there were but two ways out of the existing difficulties, either to institute a dictatorship or to grant a constitution." Upon being advised that a military dictatorship would be impossible because of a lack of troops, the tsar proceeded to issue the Manifesto of October 17, 1905, granting a constitution. When the battle lines were drawn again during the Revolution of February 1917, the tsar once more sought troops to crush it. When he learned that the armies at the front as well as the regiments in Petrograd were disaffected, he "decided to abdicate the throne which he no longer possessed." He still sought to temporize, however. He considered whether he should abdicate in favor of his son under the regency of his brother, or in favor of his brother. "He obviously dreaded to sell too cheap, and still hoped for comforting news—or more accurately for a miracle," Trotsky says in his *History of the Russian Revolution.* This time compromise was impossible. He could not sacrifice his person to preserve the sovereignty of his ruling group. So, too, President Machado, seeing that the government of Cuba was lost to him in 1933, attempted at the last moment to preserve his party's power by insinuating his Secretary of War into the Provisional Presidency. But the opposition forces were in both instances too powerful for the technique of compromise to succeed.

Compromise in government is not merely to accept part of what you want, or to accept the second best. It is also evident in the see-sawing policy of which we have examples in Soviet Russia and the United States. This is the character of Lenin's New Economic Policy, which temporarily permitted private enterprise in small commerce; Stalin's alternate cracking down on criticism and the arts, and releasing the pressure; purging and then castigating the purgers; denying sugar to the people and permitting its sale. So also President Roosevelt now condemned and now encouraged big industry; he tried to revive it through government support and the National Recovery Administration and counterbalanced these measures by support of labor organizations and the Wagner Labor Act.

The United States Constitution is a compromise between those who wanted a strong Federal government and those who insisted on the "sovereignty" of the individual states. The very process of politics involves concession to opposing factions and frequently a dragging of feet by the sovereign in implementation of the concession and even its withdrawal when the sovereign power is sufficient.

We shall have further occasion to examine the nature and functions of compromise as a part of the political process. At this point it is sufficient to recognize that one of the techniques of political action is conciliation by compromise. However, there are not only occasions when the opposition will not compromise, as in some of the instances cited above: Sometimes the sovereign need not compromise, and therefore, as a matter of good political practice, should not do so. (This assumes that there are no blunders in statecraft, that the sovereign does not compromise when strong or refuse to do so when weak. That there are blunders in statecraft is well exemplified by Chapter III of *The Prince*, in which Machiavelli analyzes the political mistakes made by Louis XII when he invaded Italy and built up the power of Pope Alexander by assisting him in occupying the Romagna; and when Louis, although he was then the prime arbiter of Italy, took the King of Spain as a partner in the division of Naples. One can open almost any daily newspaper and find current examples of cowardice, stubbornness, and folly which weaken governments. In the same chapter Machiavelli says that "a blunder ought never to be perpetrated to avoid war, because it is not to be avoided, but is only deferred to your disadvantage.") When compromise is impossible or unnecessary as a technique, there is a choice of weapons for both rulers and their subjects—or at least for some class of subjects.

4

POLITICAL WEAPONS

POLITICAL WEAPONS are of three kinds and each of these has affirmative and negative uses. There is primarily physical force, the most primitive and basic of all weapons. Then there is economic power. Thirdly there is propaganda, or the use of psychological power. In some of its phases this third weapon rests upon the potential application of physical force or economic power.

THE SWORD

It is probable that political decisions in primitive times were enforced internally as well as against other clans or tribes by a blow. At the Teutonic husting the tribesmen voted for their *dux* or on policy by raising their spears. This act was more than a vote—it was a sign that so many spears would be used to support the new leader or the cause. And so they were used, for dissenters in primitive societies were put to death or driven from the community. The ballot box and the modern voting machine are a sublimation of the husting. We must not forget that the pencil mark on the ballot and the lever of the voting machine today represent guns and clubs, that they symbolize violence as surely as did the raised spearheads of the Teutonic tribesmen. An example of this may be found in the activity of the Nazi storm troopers upon Hitler's accession to power immediately following the German elections of March 4, 1933.

In societies industrially more primitive than our own, where economic and propagandist weapons were not as powerful as they are at present, supporters were enlisted by the prestige of available physical force, and wavering followers were similarly kept in line. Thus the Emperor Wu-ti, in the third century, could truly write:

> If the sharp sword be not in your hand,
> How can you hope your friends will remain many?

And when all else fails, tyranny extends its days with the block and the firing squad that silence dissenters. The blood purge is the final weapon to sustain the threatened power of the sovereign.

Indeed, it is axiomatic that the State, and to a greater or lesser degree all social institutions, depend at some time on force or the threat of violence. John Dewey, in his *Liberalism and Social Action* (where he also intimates that revolutions can be achieved and defended against reaction without violence), tells us:

> Force, rather than intelligence, is built into the procedures of the existing social system, regularly as coercion, in times of crisis as overt violence. The legal system, conspicuously in its penal aspect, more subtly in civil practice, rests upon coercion. Wars are the methods recurrently used in settlement of disputes between nations. One school of radicals dwells upon the fact that in the past the transfer of power in one society has either been accomplished by or attended with violence. But what we

need to realize is that physical force is used, at least in the form of coercion, in the very set-up of our society.

Physical force may be used against persons in the execution of law; the death penalty may be inflicted, or a defendant may be arrested or imprisoned. The police may kill in the execution of their office; they may charge a crowd with clubs; they may hold prisoners for inquisition by the "third degree," or hold them incommunicado or in prison camps, just as the Nazis, Italian Fascists, and the Soviet Union treated their political enemies. The soldiery may be called into action to repel an invasion, to shoot a mob, or to break a strike. An enemy of the ruling group may be exiled or assassinated. On the negative side there is the refusal to grant either passports or permission to leave the country; there is the intentional failure to give protection to persons within the national borders (frequently, for example, in labor disputes, unpopular political demonstrations, and lynchings); there is outlawry; and there is excommunication, which is limited outlawry and subjects the person excommunicated to physical as well as psychological deprivations which the State will not redress.

Property may also be the object of physical force. It may be physically destroyed, or seized for taxes or in the execution of a judgment; an embargo may be placed on commerce, or property may be declared contraband and so subject to seizure and destruction. Property may also be taken for public use as by eminent domain proceedings; and the State may use its force to take property of individuals for the private profit of public utilities. And for centuries an object which caused death became a Deodand, a forfeit, a contribution to God, the king acting as his representative to receive it.

Physical force may be a weapon in the hands of the opposition, which may assassinate, kidnap, riot, or seize government or private property; it may commit sabotage against public or private property. Smuggling and dealing in contraband are also applications of force to property. These were weapons in general use by the American Colonists against Great Britain; they were weapons which defeated prohibition in the United States. Force may be negatively used too as by boycotting some public service, by striking or engaging in "passive resistance."

Passive resistance can be an economic or psychological weapon, but essentially it is force. Human bodies confront the authorities in protest. When those bodies go limp and refuse to move from where they may be blocking traffic or public buildings and are bodily removed by the police or soldiers, it is clear that this is an application of physical power by both demonstrators and police or military. It is a confrontation with the sovereign power to which eventually the sovereign power must react either with force or concessions or lose control. Passive resistance was the most successful Gandhian tactic in obtaining the freedom of India, perhaps because British public opinion would not accept in the twentieth century the violence necessary to defeat such resistance, although it did in the colonial empire in the nineteenth century. One must doubt whether such a tactic would have been successful against Stalin or Hitler.

History is crowded with examples of rulers acceding in part at least to demands backed by violence or the threat of force. A few examples will suffice. In the Middle West, the so-called "Farm Holiday" groups, comprised of farmers, prevented the sale of mortgaged farms on foreclosure, and together with the demonstrations of unemployed groups, undoubtedly helped pave the way for President Roosevelt's New Deal legislation and unemployment relief in the cities. In the United States, France, and other countries farmers have withheld their produce from the market to protest low prices. The threat of a general strike in 1925, when the British government was unprepared to meet the crisis, was directly responsible for the subsidy to the British coal industry. Although the Commune of Paris was crushed and Louis Blanc executed, the struggle of the people of Paris nevertheless did prevent the restoration of the monarchy in France and blocked the royalist coup (Legitimist or Orléanist) which Thiers was courting after the exodus of Napoleon III.

Smuggled immigrants and violence against British officials caused Great Britain to abandon the League of Nations Mandate in Palestine and made possible the creation of Israel as a nation. Great Britain's sovereignty was not worth the economic or psychological costs of suppressing the rebellion.

Law in the modern State is itself based upon force. This is nowhere more powerfully stated than by Alexander Hamilton's argument in *The Federalist* for a strong central government.

> It is essential to the idea of a law, that it be attended with a sanction; or, in other words, a penalty or punishment for disobedience. If there be no penalty annexed to disobedience, the resolutions or commands which pretend to be laws will, in fact, amount to nothing more than advice or recommendation. This penalty, whatever it may be, can only be inflicted in two ways: by the agency of the courts and ministers of justice, or by military force; by the coercion of the magistracy or by the coer-

cion of arms. . . . It is evident that there is no process of a court by which the observance of the laws can, in the last resort, be enforced. Sentences may be denounced against them [men] for a violation of their duty; but these sentences can only be carried into execution by the sword.

Although positive law is generally observed without the application of sanctions, they loom in the form of commands to pay money, in the threat of forfeiture and bodily pain, including death and imprisonment. Ultimate sanctions are forfeiture of property or office and bodily punishment, including death and imprisonment. These sanctions are applied as retribution for civil or criminal violations of duties imposed by the State. But there are also secondary sanctions, such as the imposition of a fine or the granting of a money judgment. These are secondary sanctions because in the final analysis they depend upon force applied to person or property to effectuate them. Thus, through means of court judgments, civilized men have interposed a psychological weapon to avoid wherever possible the use of force, which is costly. But by deferring force, its presence is neither dispensed with nor wholly concealed.

"If the court's judgment sets in motion the sheriff who will attach my goods," Professor Morris R. Cohen argues, "then how in the name of the empirical science of law can any one claim that it is not a command? One may as well argue that if a man, with a gun to enforce his 'judgment,' declares in my hearing, that I shall be filled with lead if I do not give him my watch, I have not received any order or command, but have only heard a judgment or prediction."

René Demogue, in *The Notion of Law*, says with respect to that idea of law which we get through experience:

It may be defined as the force which is the strongest in the last resort, the force of him who laughs last and so laughs the best, as the proverb has it. It is, therefore, hardly exact to say that law is greater than force [*le droit prime la force*], or that force is greater than law, because law without force is not law —from the practical point of view from which we are considering it at present.[1]

We shall see later that positive laws, as well as ethical rules or moral laws, have in themselves functions as political weapons, such as symbols of, substitutes for, and limitations on sovereign power. But neither those uses of law nor what Sir Henry Maine referred to as "the retreat out of sight of the force which is the motive power of law," [2] should blind us to that potential violence on which sovereign authority is sustained. For, says Ihering, "law is the well understood politics [Politik] of power."

And although the symbolic force of law is great in more advanced civilizations, and physical coercion is less frequent and necessary than in primitive society, law, as Demogue so clearly tells us, "is that which is imposed by an organized force from which there is no appeal. Law is practically a synonym for social fact imposed if need be by coercion."

GOLD AND BREAD

History shows that economic power has always been an important element of government. The Bible and other an-

[1] Citing Pascal, *Pensées*: "Thus not being able to make that which is just strong, man has made that which is strong just."

[2] *Early Law and Custom,* p. 387; where he also says: "The great difficulty of the modern Analytical Jurists, Bentham and Austin, has been to recover from its hiding-place the force which gives its sanction to law."

cient literature tell of the rich gifts brought to kings and princes whose favors had been sought and of the riches, including the farming out of taxes, which they in turn distributed to favorites. The very munificence of the gifts, one is led to believe, was intended at times as a symbol of the donor's power as often as it signified the value of the alliance which he sought. It was not only to save souls that the aristocracy built cathedrals and gave costly presents to the Church. The Middle Ages and Renaissance are filled with instances of the purchase of political support: this occurred when the Florentines agreed to pay a yearly tribute of 200,000 florins to King Ruberto of Naples for his aid to the Guelph cause against Castruccio Castracani of Lucca and his allies.

In earlier times economic power must have been more closely related to physical power because movable property was in large part in weapons and horses. Romulus, we are told, established "manhood suffrage in which all alike possessed the same weight and enjoyed the same rights." By the time of Servius the wealth of Rome had increased, and Servius instituted a census and distributed the population into classes and "centuries." There were the knights and five classes of infantry. The classification depended upon the amount of property, measured in pounds of copper, possessed by each citizen. Each class had to provide itself with arms, the wealthier having more armor and weapons than the second class, the second class more than the third, until the fifth class was reached; these carried slings and stones and no armor. The population possessing less than eleven thousand pounds were exempt from military service. (At a later date men of property could purchase substitutes when called for military service. The purchase of substitutes was the basis of medieval scutage. This purchase of substitutes was also possible at the time of the draft during the American Civil War.) Servius introduced a new system of voting in Rome, "so whilst not one was ostensibly deprived of his vote, all the voting power was in the hands of the principal men of the State." The knights voted first, then the centuries of infantry of the First Class, voting by centuries, a majority of each century casting its vote. Then, "if their votes were divided, which seldom happened, it was arranged for the Second Class to be summoned; very seldom did the voting extend to the lowest class." Property qualifications as prerequisites to voting are familiar in Anglo-American political history. Only in 1964 by the Twenty-fourth Amendment was the poll tax abolished as a prerequisite to voting in Federal elections. In the case of *Harper v. Virginia* (1966) the Supreme Court eliminated the poll tax requirement in the states.

Economic power can be utilized independently of the exercise of physical force against property.[3] No discourse is necessary to demonstrate the power exerted by sovereigns through the spoils system, whether this be applied in the crude manner of the invader who encourages his men to take what they can of the property of the natives, or in the more refined manner of Andrew Jackson and the local political leaders who dispense among their supporters public office, salaried at public cost. Then there are franchises, monopolies, benefices, bonuses, public improvements, exemptions from taxation, change of the character and emphasis of taxation and grants of credit with each of which

[3] "Sovereignty is not property, but it carries with it important economic rights which are closely related to the rights of property," R. G. Hawtrey says in *Economic Aspects of Sovereignty*.

the sovereign power can attach powerful supporters to itself. Tariffs calculated to stimulate monopolies or favor certain industries are familiar devices to the same end. A nice case in point is the sugar schedule of the McKinley Tariff of 1890. The duty on raw sugar was abolished. This enabled refiners to import at a smaller cost their raw material from the sugar-growing islands of the West Indies and Cuba, but at the same time it enabled imported sugar to compete advantageously with the home-grown crop. This situation was corrected by the grant of a bounty of two cents a pound to domestic growers. The government lost $55 million in revenue a year and obligated itself to pay about $5 million a year in bounty. Usually, however, tariffs are increased to "protect" home industry and eliminate foreign competition.

The sovereign can make or break groups of its subjects by the issuance of fiat money, manipulations of the gold exports and reserves, and changes in the metallic content of the monetary standard. The destruction of the tsarist ruble was an effective way to destroy private ownership in Soviet Russia. The ruin of the mark was a good weapon against the collection of reparations from Germany. Greenbacks and silver coinage helped to reestablish the balance between the American farmers and the financial institutions to which they were heavily indebted.

There are still other ways in which property can be destroyed by the State. Thus, in answer to the demands of a powerful press, the evangelical churches and a well-organized political movement, the Eighteenth Amendment, making the manufacture and sale of intoxicating beverages illegal, was added to the Constitution of the United States; and under this amendment statutes which made alcoholic liquors contraband were adopted. Similarly, during the Civil War, Lincoln, by his Emancipation Proclamation, destroyed property rights in human beings. This was an exercise of economic power as well as a measure of State propaganda. It may be suggested that such measures, in common with all other positive laws, require in the last analysis sanctions of physical force, and that therefore they should not be regarded as economic weapons. It is of course true that their enforcement depends on such sanctions, but the mere possibility of enforcement affected the market for breweries, distilleries, and liquors in the case of the Eighteenth Amendment, and the value of slaves in the case of the Proclamation.

The opposition also has a choice of economic weapons (some of which the sovereign itself can at times utilize, pervert, and direct), such as the strike, the boycott, the blacklist, refusal to pay taxes, smuggling, bootlegging, the destruction of government credit by the short selling of money, and refusal to grant loans. Nicholas Biddle, in his fight on the enemies of the second United States Bank, deliberately caused financial stringency. The small group which for more than a century controlled the Banque de France broke ministries through its manipulation of foreign exchange and the discount rate.

In all ages bribery has been a weapon against adverse governmental action. Bribes are of many varieties and considered to be of differing degrees of corruptness in the eyes of each society. There is the crass gift of money, universally condemned; there is the diversion of private business to the governmental official or his relatives and friends, an act which is winked at (see the practice of giving the writing of insurance policies to politicians, and the retaining of lawyer-legislators by utility and transportation corporations);

and there is the offer to a retiring official of a more or less lucrative business connection, in recompense for service rendered or to eliminate him from the field of politics. This latter practice is often not disapproved in countries such as the United States, where public service is frequently regarded not as a career in itself, but as a stepping-stone to a profitable business stimulated by the right connections. There is of course indirect bribery, such as the contribution to the political campaign of a candidate or his party. (A successful contractor in one of our great cities told me that he had never paid a bribe for a public construction contract or for the modification of any contract terms. He is a truthful man and I believe him. On further inquiry he admitted that he always made a substantial contribution to the campaign fund of the political party in power and that doubtless for that reason his financial responsibility as a bidder for public contracts could not be doubted. I was told by a distinguished office holder that he was promised a large campaign contribution by certain persons, who, upon discovering his attitude on public utility questions, withdrew their promised aid.)

The leverage which economic power supplies to physical power has been accentuated by industrial technology. As John Dewey has pointed out:

> That the competitive system, which was thought of by early liberals as the means by which the latent abilities of individuals were to be evoked and directed into socially useful channels, is now in fact a state of scarcely disguised battle hardly needs to be dwelt upon. That the control of the means of production by the few in legal possession operates as a standing agency of coercion of the many, may need emphasis in statement, but is surely evident to one who is willing to observe and honestly

report the existing scene. It is foolish to regard the political state as the only agency now endowed with coercive power. Its exercise of this power is pale in contrast with that exercised by concentrated and organized property interests.

Property is a weapon because men require goods for consumption in order that they may live. So the possessor of land can give to the serf and the possessor of the means of industrial production can supply to the worker subsistence in exchange for service. This service can be commuted to a money payment. (See the history of scutage and feudal land tenure which developed into the leasehold system of today.) Almost all service is now given for a recompense in money—the token which can be exchanged for subsistence goods. Although by reason of the decay of land economy and the greater ease of transportation, labor is freer and more liquid than in the days when it was attached to the land, property still has great power to compel service and obedience because the laborer would starve without subsistence or be forced to rely on public welfare assistance, which to many people is frustrating and humiliating. The welfare state has created out of social insurance an economic weapon to keep the very poor, the old, the sick, and the parents of children dependent upon it. This mode of protection is a modern purchase price for fealty to the sovereign.

The disparity of security between persons owning and persons employed creates power in ownership, or as Ihering puts it, "The power of property in the hands of him who has more than is needed for securing his physical necessities or even a comfortable living depends upon others having less; who, being obliged to work in order to supply what they lack, must seek in continuous employment the means of subsistence." Except in times of crisis, when those possessing economic power cannot themselves afford to pay the price for support, property cannot be divested of this power, because to fight its battles it bands together and buys with the means of subsistence the hungry and the ambitious. So the peasant revolts in medieval England and in Russia were put down by peasants. Strikes of industrial workers have been broken by other industrial workers (hired as strikebreakers) and so-called private police who in reality were often thugs. Technical advances in communication and transportation have given strength to the employers, as Willard Harris Crook has shown in his discussion of the British General Strike of 1926.

Walther Rathenau, Minister of Finance in Germany after World War I, gives an accurate picture of the relationship between economic organization and sovereignty when he says in *In Days to Come*: "The depersonalization of ownership, the objectification of enterprise, the detachment of property from the possessor, leads to a point where the enterprise becomes transformed into an institution which resembles the state in character." But this similarity of structure and functioning must not be confused with identity of situation. The power of even the largest corporation is not (with rare exceptions as in economically undeveloped countries) sovereign power. As Mr. Justice Holmes has warned us it may be degree that makes the difference.

As we have already seen, the sovereign himself requires property—that is, economic power—to dispense in exchange for support. For this he must obtain goods or money from his subjects, which he does by means of taxation or fines. Some of the most sanguinary and fundamental battles in history have grown out of the sovereign's need for this economic sustenance, and the resistance by those sections of the populace which have been called on to satisfy the needs of the sovereign maw. Examples may readily be found in the France of 1789, the American Colonies in 1775, the Thirty Years' War, the baronial wars against John, centuries of Irish history, and the story of Japan on the Asiatic continent.

It is because of this need of economic power that governments tend to favor those who have this weapon in their hands. In this connection it must be pointed out that economic power, particularly finance capital, is more rapidly mobilized than manpower for it is more apt to be of one mind and because it is more concentrated and fluid. The granting or the refusal of a loan by great banking houses can be settled upon in a few moments. A telephone call to a banker or a broker can transfer capital beyond the seas or bring it home from abroad. The manipulation of the gold standard is frequently preceded by a flight of capital. Capital can often evade tariffs and escape restrictive and standardizing legislation (as well as high labor costs) by setting up factories abroad or investing in foreign enterprise instead of functioning at home. Ford factories, as well as potatoes, transplanted from America, can become a staple of Ireland.

In Western capitalist countries, economic power has been substantially concentrated in a few large corporations and cartels controlled by a handful of persons—who are not necessarily the owners of the corporations. The historic development of this system is described by Berle and Means in *The Modern Corporation and Private Property.* They point out that there are two important aspects to this corporate concentration. The factory system which was developed by the Industrial Revolution brought workers in ever-increasing numbers under a single management, each great corporation employing more men and women in a single plant than inhabited a county a century earlier. Parallel to this concentration of labor was the "equally revolutionary" centralization of capital control, the money of many individuals being pooled, while the power to direct the use of that money was divorced from ownership through voting trusts, holding companies, or the mere complexity of otherwise disassociated stockholders acting in unison. Thus the status of worker and property owner was changed; the worker surrendering his independence and the property owner his wealth to those who controlled the policy of the corporation: its management often selected by or permitted to remain in control by the financiers of the corporation, but usually self-perpetuating through their control of stockholders' proxies. Wages are paid to the laborer for his labor and to the investor for his wealth, but realistically they rarely share in the power of management or the determination of policy. Nevertheless, in the United States, where about one quarter of the population—either through direct stock ownership or participation in a pension fund—has a financial interest in corporations, the stock-holding interest has political power to maintain the capitalist system.

"This system," Berle and Means say, "bids fair to be as all-embracing as was the feudal system in its time." Again, "The rise of the modern corporation has brought a concentration of economic power which can compete on equal terms with the modern state—economic power versus political power, each strong in its own field. The state seeks in some aspects to regulate the corporation, while the corporation, steadily becoming more powerful, makes every effort to avoid such regulation. Where its own interests are concerned, it even attempts to dominate the state." We have an example in the National Industrial Recovery Act (until it was declared unconstitutional), conceived as a means of protecting labor and increasing buying power among industrial workers; adopted to free industry from legal restraints and encourage trade associations; and administered to foster monopolies and break strikes. And no legislation having economic impact is introduced but has corporate lobbyists bearing down on legislators.

It is no wonder, therefore, that the modern government tends to woo that coquette, corporate industry, and solicit Madame Finance. It is only when depressions or wars have weakened and confused industry and finance, when their power has been weakened, that a government feels able to place limitations on their powers. This is so because it is at such times that other groups, having counter demands, become more vigorous, attach themselves to the government (the sovereign group) and compel the sovereign to listen to them. While the dominant political group is embarrassed, other interests are able to obtain concessions by the use of weapons which they are either too feeble or too contented to apply in normal times. This is part of the process of politics which will be discussed hereafter.

In historic times those who have possessed the means of production have by this very fact controlled the most powerful sovereign weapons, for they have either been the sovereigns themselves or have received in increased economic power the reward that goes to them who can supply the support which the sovereign must have for his security. And they who control production cannot only purchase physical violence whether in the form of police or mobs, but they can pay the price for propaganda; they are the patrons of the arts and sciences and as such they can muster intelligence and technical skill which grow only in human bodies, bodies which must be fed as any other human bodies and which possess the weaknesses and vices of mankind everywhere. "Coercion," says Ihering, "is effective only so long as the whip is in sight; remuneration works continually."

WORDS AND SYMBOLS

One of the principal weapons used by sovereigns or ruling classes in all ages has been that of propaganda. We find an early instance in the Books of Samuel. That prophet was displeased by the demand of the people for a king. It was not so much that he disapproved of kingship as that the popular demand implied a repudiation of the kingship of God and displaced him, Samuel, as the judge or leader of his people. And so we find that though the Hebrew word for king used in Deuteronomy means "counsellor, head, leader," the word used in Samuel connotes "potentate, tyrant."

Psychological or propagandist weapons are words and acts which are aimed to induce the hope or fear of the application of physical force or economic power; they may veil the intentions of the sovereign or decoy the subjects. There are also applications of physical force and economic power the principal purpose of which is not so much to effect a particular act as to create a symbol of something far beyond that act. As examples of the latter note the executions of Charles I, Louis XVI, and Nicholas II after they had been effectually divested of physical power; Iconoclasm during the Protestant Reformation; the destruction of the Bastille during the French Revolution, of the statue of George III during the American Revolution, and of that of Heine and others by the Nazis. Boycotts may have little economic effect but can be psychologically a potent force to rally opposition. Thus the bus boycott in Montgomery, Alabama, to eliminate racial segregation in buses became a model for the non-violent civil disobedience of the civil rights movement under the leadership of Martin Luther King, Jr., and others.

The principal purpose of propaganda, whether utilized by the sovereign or the opposition, is to avoid physical force or the use of economic weapons; or sometimes to divert them to a more favorable channel. Thus taxpayers' organizations and lobbyists of all kinds attempt to guide governments to actions favorable to their interests; and governments encourage farmers to plant larger or smaller acreage, or varied crops, and advise businessmen of trade opportunities in the different countries.

But sometimes propaganda is exercised in order to create a symbol to induce the use of physical force and economic weapons. Examples are the advocacy of the boycott against British goods in the colony of Massachusetts; a similar boycott was instigated by Gandhi in India. Instances of the martyr complex are too numerous and current among revolutionaries to require citation. The invitation to create martyrs is the solicitation of material for propaganda. The police can be goaded into retaliation with clubs, guns, or tear gas and then charged with being "Cossacks." The Tsarist government encouraged pogroms through the Black Hundreds; the planting of forged documents and *agents provocateurs* have long been used to afford sovereigns and those seeking sovereignty the occasion to take drastic action. Such an occasion was the burning of the Reichstag prior to the March 1933 election in Germany, attributed by Hitler to the Communists, who were at once persecuted. Livy recounts how the king, Lucius Tarquinius, caused swords to be "planted" in the home of Turnus Herdonius, who had proclaimed him a tyrant. "As he [the king] had not the power to get him openly put to death, he compassed his destruction by bringing a false charge." At the instigation of the king, the people later went to the home of Turnus and found the weapons, which proved to them the existence of a plot of rebellion and they killed Turnus. For political reasons charges were made against the good works of Demosthenes which was the occasion for his speech *On the Crown.*

Long before the printing press, radio, and television, rulers feared the effects of the spoken word. That was one reason why prophets were not honored in their own land. And did not Antipater propose as one of the peace terms which he offered to Athens that she surrender up to him Demosthenes, together with other orators, who had been fanning the patriotic spirit of the city against Macedonia? When Attila approached Rome in 452 there was no army to stop him. Only the Pope, Leo I, went out to meet him and after they had conferred, Attila withdrew. When, some years later, the Vandals came under Genseric, the Pope could not save Rome, but he did save the churches and the lives of those who offered no resistance. Stalin might ask with contempt how many divisions the Pope had at his command, but Khrushchev sent his "unofficial" emissary to the Pope.

It would be impossible in this discussion to devote the

space necessary to enumerate and illustrate all the psychological weapons which sovereigns and their foes have used. But mass emotions have been brought into action by moral appeals, by appeals to instincts noble, venal, and savage, by the authority of churches and wise men, by deliberate falsehoods and the stimulation of superstitious fears, by rationalizations crystallized into doctrine and dogma, by blackening the leaders of movements in truth or in falsehood, by blackmail, by dramatizing individuals and identifying causes with them, by identifying one cause with the good and another with evil. Sometimes these weapons are used in curious and *ad hominum* ways: Samson's wife appealed to him to reveal to her the answer to his riddle for the sake of his love for her; Delilah induced him in the same manner to explain the secret of his strength. Then there is the weird story told by Louis Adamic of the IWW demonstration against President Wilson in Seattle: The streets that were to have received him with tumultuous applause were lined with silent, motionless men soberly dressed in their work clothes and carrying banners of protest.

No study of political propaganda can be complete without reference to the remarkable passage on "War Propaganda" in Hitler's *My Battle*, which reads in part:

> All propaganda should be popular and should adapt its intellectual level to the receptive ability of the least intellectual of those whom it is desired to address. Thus it must sink its mental elevation deeper in proportion to the numbers of the mass whom it has to grip. If—as with propaganda for carrying through a war—the object is to gather a whole nation within its circle of influence, there cannot be enough attention paid to avoidance of too high a level of intellectuality.
>
> The receptive ability of the masses is very limited, their un-

derstanding small; on the other hand, they have a great power of forgetting. This being so, all effective propaganda must be confined to very few points which must be brought out in the form of slogans until the very last man is enabled to comprehend what is meant by any slogan.

Words are, of course, merely symbols and in political life they are built up to imitate the words of philosophy and religion and give to political issues a greatness which they rarely possess. It is almost irresistible for a withering little sovereign or a bristling little leader of a small "left" group on the floor of a parliament to conceive of himself as a godlike Agamemnon or Orestes, as a latter-day Solomon or a Lenin. When they have not aroused sufficient following or have not the resources to fight, or when the sovereign wants to justify his violence, the politicians swing great words to move the populace. At times the sovereign attaches to his acts the labels of the opposition—he grants meaningless constitutional governments or enters vapid alliances—to avoid substantial compliance.

Of course it is only through symbols that political thought and discussion are possible, and without symbols politics would be reduced to the elemental state of signs and actions. As John Dewey has said in his *Liberalism and Social Action*:

Intelligence in politics when it is identified with discussion means reliance upon symbols. The invention of language is probably the greatest single invention achieved by humanity. The development of political forms that promote the use of symbols in place of arbitrary power was another great invention. The nineteenth century establishment of parliamentary institutions, written constitutions and the suffrage as means of political rule, is a tribute to the power of symbols. But symbols are significant only in connection with realities behind them.

These symbols, which Professor Dewey regards as substitutes for arbitrary power, are themselves not certainties, but depend of course upon the particular experience of the person who is to act upon them and upon the associations which such symbols bring forth—to the expectations and biases of user and auditor of the symbol. To Joseph H. Choate, speaking about 1895, the income tax was a "Communistic March." Harvey Cushing, operating for months in war hospitals under bombardment during World War I, could write: "Only 2 or 3 thousand casualties in the 5th Army area, I believe; only 11,000 in the 2nd Army—very good considering the importance of position taken. . . ." For two-and-a-half millennia philosophers and scientists have sought to know the nature of Truth and Right, but Dr. Goebbels said: "Important is not who is right, but who wins." And a professor of philosophy at Heidelberg, once famous for its philosophic and scientific faculties, announced in 1936: "We do not know of or recognize truth for truth's sake or science for science' sake."

Moreover, as James Madison pointed out in *The Federalist*, "The use of words is to express ideas," and to be understood not only must the ideas be distinctly formed (which in the political world is unusual), but they must also be expressed by words which are "distinctly and exclusively appropriate to them," (which is perhaps even rarer in politics). He adds that language is inadequate to deal with "every complex idea" and that it has not a supply of words and phrases "so correct as not to include many equivocally denoting different ideas."

It is the very lack of certainty in language that makes it

a powerful weapon of distortion; for the majority of people have not had experience so full and adequate as to enable them to have become personally conscious of political and economic facts; nor have they sufficient training to analyze their experiences. Consequently they are at the mercy of personal axe grinders and the dupes of salesmen of cheap millennia which leave business going on as usual at the old stand.

In different ages, each ruling group, whether military caste, clerical, feudal, commercial, capitalistic, or communistic, has impressed a formalism of phrase and symbol on the political, economic, and intellectual life of its time. Succeeding rulers have attempted to liquidate such of these forms and phrases as seem inconsistent. The tendency of modern times has been to destroy that formalism which made pomp and ritual of so many common events in life, in politics, in religion, and in business. Simplification to save effort was necessary to the development of the commercial and industrial system. The mummery of the Middle Ages, which repeated acts and words that had long lost their original significance, could not continue in a civilization based upon credit and the transfer of rights through the medium of paper, although even today we have not entirely escaped from medieval formalism, as is illustrated by the law respecting sealed instruments and the administering of oaths. It would be error to believe that all formalism has gone; that the passing of the old ceremonies has meant the death of symbolism. New formalities have arisen to make transactions rapid and sure, through new technical words, new words of precision which make for economy of time, new labels for old merchandise, new signs which fix identity as telephone numbers or stock market symbols do. These modern symbols alone make possible transactions in volume in the world of finance and commerce and in the courts. Cybernetics has provided the means for great concentration of information (in the form of symbolic numbers) about individuals and gives the State a great new power to control them.

In medieval times, when property was chiefly in land, the passing of title, whether by seizin or by some other means, was a formal matter, certain rituals had to be observed. But the rights of the property holder were seriously limited by conditions as impressive and formal as the passing of title itself. Failure to perform the conditions meant forfeiture to the overlord. Even in the market where movable property was disposed of, a man could not sell in any manner that he pleased at the buyer's risk. *Caveat emptor* is a gift of the commercial system. For the distance between purchaser and consumer in the Middle Ages might be the width of a house wall; it was not so impenetrable as it is today. All this is to explain that while the mysteries of medieval formalism have been dissipated, and medieval restraints have disappeared, their magic has been transferred to new "rights" and powers and is just as effective today. Modern rights are acquired simply and modern restrictions are imposed without abracadabra, but the new symbols—bills of lading, deeds, stock certificates, and warehouse receipts—are as much formalism as the old.

Nor has the elimination of pomposity from political life been accompanied by the disappearance of old symbols, of phrases and slogans which have descended from past eras, where they were detonated in throne rooms of bishops, kings, and emperors or were roared from the throats of rebellious subjects who became respected rulers in their own right. No political weapons are as tenacious and ambivalent as the fangs of slogans. *For slogans, which are the test tubes in which new social life and economic cultures are developed, become in time the symbols through which old socioeconomic institutions are maintained.*

The development of the emphasis of symbols from acts to words, from the delivery of a piece of sod to the transfer of a piece of paper, from bowing before a monarch to the singing of a national anthem, has been facilitated by the advance in the technique of communication. This technical development has in great measure corresponded with the changes in power groups. The printing press, whose services were first devoted to Church and monarch, became a democratizing force because it was a weapon available to the opposition. Broadsides could be readily printed in cellars. Freedom of press, as we shall see, became a slogan closely associated with freedom of contract. Both were necessary to the expansion of the power of the merchant classes in their fight against Church and monarchy.

Cables, radios, and television, however, while infinitely facilitating the use of word symbols, have at the same time concentrated the propaganda power in the hands of the sovereign group (as also to a more limited extent has the development of the great rotary press). In almost every country of the world, radio broadcasting and television are governmentally operated; in all countries they are governmentally controlled. In moments of crisis cables and telegraph are dependent upon government force for their maintenance. Considerable capital is required to build and maintain electronic equipment for propaganda. Government censorship is simple. As has been pointed out, the words "passed by the censor" were no guaranty of truth but merely meant, during wartime, that the statements were not harmful to the interests of the censoring country or beneficial to its enemies. News transmitted through the censor might incidentally be the truth, but it bore the slant of propaganda. It did not tell the whole truth; it did not, for instance, tell what Harvey Cushing learned on the streets of London and what I heard in an Army Rest Camp at Southampton during World War I: "People very tired of the war. They universally voice the feeling that all would shortly have been over if America had not come in when she did." In this failure of candor, war news does not differ from publicity releases generally. Men in public office, political parties, financiers, industrialists, churches, farmers, and labor organizations fix the news. It is a credit to American and to some extent British journalism that the truth behind the handout is so frequently discovered and published.

The value of cable control is well set forth by O. W. Riegel in *Mobilizing for Chaos*:

British supremacy in world affairs until the World War was a striking object lesson in the value of communication control to the nationalistic state. London became the cable center of the world. This meant commercial supremacy, for she exercised a virtual monopoly on the transmission of quotations of market and currency prices. London became the hub and center of world mercantilism. In addition, she became the news center of the world, and was, therefore, unusually sensitive to change everywhere. This gave her merchants and bankers an advantage over the merchants and bankers of other countries, and helped to reinforce her position as the economic and political capital of the world. In the sphere of political influence, England was able to develop effective contact with her outlying possessions as well as to spread English political and commercial ideas in foreign lands served by British cables.

Dictatorial governments have used to great effect radio and television, from which they have studiously kept the voices of all opposition. Even in England during an election in the 1930s, the Labour Party had to make use of a Dutch radio station to obtain adequate radio facilities during the campaign. President de Gaulle has gone on radio in various crises to appeal to the French people for support. President Franklin D. Roosevelt sold to this country much of his program through the use of the radio, and succeeding presidents have done the same. A dramatic instance was President Kennedy's use of television to explain the Cuban missile crisis to the world, by showing and interpreting aerial photos of the installations. But whether in those nations where governments operate broadcasting stations, or in the United States, where private operators have no property rights in wavelengths or in permits to operate at a given power or at stated times of the day, programs offensive to the ruling groups can be cut off the air or denied air altogether. In the United States the Federal Communications Commission can refuse to renew a license or at least renew it only on disadvantageous terms so that even liberal stations (but not the great networks), have at times been scared of their own voices.

The power of this weapon of propaganda was well illustrated when in 1931 J. M. Keynes made a radio speech which was construed by many people as advice to spend all and save nothing, whereupon the sale of National Savings Certificates fell off from 250,000 to 170,000 a day. Thereupon Sir Josiah Stamp took to the microphone and pointed out that investment in those certificates was one of the few methods of saving which did not create unemployment. A few days later the sale of certificates went up to 450,000 and then to 500,000.

There is generally greater prestige to the word of the sovereign than there is to that of critics. With truth Richard II could say in Shakespeare's play, "Is not the king's name forty thousand names?" Modern techniques have combined to increase the propaganda power of symbols and to concentrate their use in the hands of the sovereign.

EDUCATION AS AN INSTRUMENT OF SOVEREIGNTY

Only in the twentieth century has public education become a direct and forceful propagandist weapon; but indirectly education has always been a medium for the continuation of the culture of dominant groups. Education has tended toward the classical; it has looked backward, not forward. Only within the last generations (if one omits such sports as the Socratic dialogue) has an objective approach been seriously attempted. This has been largely due to the introduction of science into the curriculum and to the effect of scientific method on other parts of the curriculum. Until the nineteenth century, such schools as existed have been largely conducted by the clergy—the propagandist arm of status quo—or "gentlemen's" schools such as the "public" schools of England wherein young squires and the sons of the industrialists who made good were trained in the traditions that "made England great."

When public education became a function of government, it was attuned to the prevailing chorus; it was utilitarian without being useful; it was democratic without being equalitarian; it was free but still authoritarian. Public education became utilitarian in that in consonance with the current of political and economic thought it sought to achieve a hypothetical "greatest good" for an uncounted "greatest number." It was not useful because its classical cast was unfitted for the majority of possible pupils. It was democratic in that rich and poor might attend public school (if they had the means of transportation and were not compelled to engage in child labor); but it accepted inequality of opportunity and power and was therefore not equalitarian. It was free in the sense that the State made no charge, but it was authoritarian in that the common technique was for the teacher to speak words of final truth rather than to stimulate free thought. The power structures of the nation and communities discouraged controversy.

This was inevitable because, with few exceptions, teachers have represented a cross section of their community, which has accepted the prevailing ideology; because teachers were, and in many places are today, dependent upon political acceptance for appointment; and because schools were, as they are today, dependent upon public opinion for financial support. One illustration will suffice. Horace Mann, whose yeoman work in Massachusetts did much to develop public education in the United States, was an uncompromising opponent of slavery. But when he learned that Samuel J. May, whom he had appointed as head of a normal school, proposed to speak in favor of abolition, Mann wrote to him: "I have further plans for obtaining more aid (for the schools) . . . but, the moment it is known or supposed that the cause is to be perverted to, or connected with, any of the exciting party questions of the day, I shall never get another cent." And as for the limitations upon teachers, varying from prohibition against indoctrination to disapproval of strolling with a boyfriend on a fine spring evening, see Howard K. Beale's excellent book, *Are American Teachers Free?*

Academic freedom is not respected by sovereign power in Communist States or in States in which an established church is part of the sovereign power. Although academic freedom is generally accepted in most American institutions of higher learning, there are exceptions. Legislatures and university trustees frequently condemn, and sometimes interfere with the uses of academic freedom. This is particularly so when war, economic depression, or social unrest threaten the nation's or community's sense of security. While the condition of teachers in elementary and secondary schools have improved since Beale wrote, the teacher who challenges the prevailing, acceptable pedagogical rituals and values is likely to be in trouble with the school authorities. Kozol and Kaufman give examples of how the bureaucracy of school systems tends to impinge on the teacher's freedom to make innovations and adopt an individual style of instruction, and how the teacher's colleagues bring pressures to enforce their informal code of professional behavior.

"Every system of education takes its color primarily from the culture of which it is a part. These cultural influences operate subtly, though powerful forces often openly oppose teaching that brings traditional mores and attitudes into question," Jesse Newlon writes in *Educational Administration as Social Policy*. Except in Communist nations, Communist theories could not be taught in the schools; for a time they could not even be mentioned in Washington, D.C.; in lands ruled by dictators, the ideals of democracy may not be taught; in Nazi Germany, facts or theories showing racial equality were taboo; the theory of evolution was (and in some places still is) barred from the schoolroom.

Groups with special interests have done direct propaganda in the schools. For example, at one time the National Association of Manufacturers, which was fighting to maintain the open shop, distributed literature to children in the public schools. Public utilities kept teachers on retainer, and arranged for them to give lectures and prepare textbooks favorable to the utilities. But it is in the undemocratic countries where straight-from-the-shoulder indoctrination in classrooms is the rule of the day. In Russia religion is treated with scorn and irony in the schools (so too in Mexico for a long period). In Germany, which has an honorable tradition in the development of theoretical and applied science, the Nazi Minister of Education, at the celebration of the five hundred and fiftieth anniversary of the University of Heidelberg, advised scholars to be emancipated from "the false idea of objectivity" because "the old idea of science based on the sovereign right of abstract intellectual activity has gone forever." Of course, objectivity and abstract thinking would be dangerous to a totalitarian state, for they would involve the raising of questions and the testing of hypotheses which necessarily are counter to the ideology of duty and obedience upon which the sovereignty of a dictator is founded.

It is important to recognize that free intellect is a threat to tyranny, and without the complete destruction of the practices of science and the research habit of mind, dictatorship is not safe, for there is always present a reservoir of intellectual energy which can destroy present tyrannies, as in its infancy Rationalism of the seventeenth and eighteenth centuries destroyed the tyrannies that had grown out of the feudal system. Castellio, in his work *De haereticis*, in which he attacked the burning of Servetus by Calvin, wrote, "To burn a man alive does not defend a doctrine, but slays a man." Men, being mortal, can be crushed by tyranny; but ideas are persistent and evade the police and the executioner. Men may be used to dramatize ideas, but it is not men but their ideologies and theories that, when they have proven their validity, are triumphant.

Public education, like printing, though primarily devoted to prevailing climates of thought and ideals, though generally engaged in doing homage to the dominant persons and economy, also affords an entry for ideas which challenge the prevailing ideology and economy, and eventually the sovereigns themselves. This is particularly true where education has trained students in the objective approach. And it should be remembered that education can no longer avoid facing the future by devoting itself to the classical past, for the ghosts of scientific achievements must eventually arise from that past. Just as Humanism absorbed the science of Aristotle and Lucretius to lay the groundwork for Rationalism, so nineteenth- and twentieth-century science will, if smothered by reaction, rise up again.

The technologically founded industrial systems of our time depend on basic scientific research which cannot succeed except as it is free. Stalin's paradox was that he believed he could compete in agriculture and industry with the Western world while dictating to scientists, and up to a point he could. But his successors knew that this could not continue and that greater freedom had to be given to scientists and technologists. Freedom of thought, however, cannot be compartmentalized for long. It is spreading in the universities and among the writers in the Communist countries. Freedom of thought and expression there, while not aimed at abolition of the Communist system, is in the course of becoming an instrument of resistance to autocracy. This is the meaning of the Soviet physicist Sakharov's essay "Thoughts on Progress, Peaceful Coexistence and Intellectual Freedom."

In *The Communist Manifesto*, it is said, "The ruling ideas of each age have ever been the ideas of its ruling class." More than two thousand years before, Aristotle had said the same thing when he stated that "the supremacy is everywhere in the governing class of the *polis* and the governing class is the *polity*," by which he signified the whole life of the people, secular, religious, and political insofar as it affected their city-state. It should not surprise us that education is primarily a weapon for those in power. It represents the resultant of cultural forces in which necessarily the pull of the prevailing forces is the strongest. In the orchestra of conflicting interests the harmony of the status quo sounds out loudest. But there remains the inevitable cycle: Even a dictatorial State today must depend upon a highly industrialized economy if it is to survive; a highly industrialized economy depends upon scientific method and experience; and scientific method and experience must eventually challenge the ideology and practices of a dictatorial state. Inevitably the ruling ideas are diluted; they are little by little doubted and then challenged and at last cracked by that group which succeeds in dominance; and the old ideas are absorbed into a new ideology expressed in new slogans and symbols. This occurs whether the sovereign power is overthrown by revolutionaries or absorbs or bends to opposing power factions.

In spite of Communist commitment to dialectical materialism, Soviet leaders from Lenin to the present have regarded *ideas* to be political realities because they affect people's lives. Ideas are consolers and threateners; they are the last straws to grasp from the past as well as straws in the winds that breathe of the future.

No study of sovereignty can be complete without an examination of some of these symbols—such as Liberty, Equality, Rights, Unity, Law, Popular Sovereignty, the Withering State, Divine Right, Authority—by which millions of men have been inspired, for which millions of them have died. Whatever these concepts may be in other fields, such as religion and ethics, they are tools to those engaged in politics. Some are stimulants to the sovereign, some are truly opiates for the people, and others dull the tyrant's sword or alienate groups upon whom the rulers have relied for power.

LAW

IN THE field of political action there is nothing sacrosanct about the law except as propaganda makes it so. Rather, it is a series of pronouncements with one hand on a club or accompanied by the rattle of the jail keys; for the law of the sovereign is positive law. It is not divine law or household law or ethics or even custom, all of which, as we shall see, have a place in the political process and can at times evoke physical force in their support on the part of opposition as well as of the sovereign. But it is positive law alone which is sustained by the power of the sovereign. "Positive [laws]," says Hobbes, "are those which have not been from eternity; but have been made Laws by the Will of those that have had the Sovereign Power over others." Law in the sense here employed is, in the language of Holland in his *Jurisprudence*, "enforced by a sovereign political authority. It is thus distinguished not only from all rules which, like the principles of morality and the so-called laws of honor and of fashion, are enforced by an indeterminate authority, but also from all rules enforced by an indeterminate authority, which is either on the one hand superhuman, or, on the other hand, politically subordinate."

Law, then, is dependent upon government whether it be the law of Pericles or Justinian, of Henry Plantagenet or Napoleon, whether it be oral or written, statutory or constitutional. It is more than coincidence that the Romans called the seat upon which their higher magistrates sat (consuls, praetors, etc.) the *sella curulis*, the "chariot seat," which was probably modeled after Etruscan chairs originally used on the chariot, that powerful instrument of war. The charioteer was, of course, a man of power who could enforce his judgment with his javelin. There was in early Roman times no great distinction between the administrative and judicial functions of government, just as in the husting there were merged judicial, lawmaking, and administrative power. Even today we are reminded of the tenuous line between judicial and administrative functions in Russia, where judgments in political causes are dictated from the Kremlin. And in the Vatican, jurisdiction of a contentious matter may go before a tribunal (the Rota) and jurisdiction of other matters to a Congregation of the Holy Office (or some other relevant Congregation) although the identical question may be involved. Similar, too, is the American practice in immigration cases, and in matters dealt with by numerous statutory boards and commissions which have legislative, administrative, and judicial powers.

Certainly in common law countries, by filling in gaps of the law left by legislative bodies, courts have legislated (and there is now some such tendency in some countries whose law is based on codes). Berle in his *The Three Faces of Power* has illustrated how the Supreme Court has done just this. But unless administrative power supports such decisions—or any legislation—with the strong arm of force, they are only expressive of norms. Thus violations of the rule of *Brown v. Board of Education of Topeka* requiring desegregation of public schools and disregard in the Southern states of the "due process" and "equal protection" clauses of the Fourteenth Amendment have in most instances run ahead of the power to restrain them, especially where contrary community values cause juries not to convict offenders. Although the police have and will continue to disregard the Supreme Court's limitations of their conduct, they must come before the courts to obtain and sustain convictions, and here the courts have power to enforce their judicio-legislative actions.

There are times when it is difficult to determine what rules or customs find sovereign support and which are merely observed as the result of habit, religious faith, and social pressure, such as the ritual observances which occupied the daily life of the devout medieval Jews. Before the destruction of the Jewish nation in 70 A.D., the law was enforced by judges, priests, and kings. Later the rabbis and community institutions could bring the power of great economic and psychological pressures upon those who failed in observance.

Maine believed that the definition of positive law, which is Austin's, could not be applied to the great tax-gathering empires where village custom supplied what law there was; or where, as in the Punjab during the time of Renjeet Singh, the people were governed principally by religious or semi-religious rules which were enforced without the intervention of the reigning monarch. Markby counters with the suggestion that in every state there are rules which regulate life and sometimes even enter into the decisions of the courts; yet they do not belong to positive law. But there is another answer, which is that at times the titular or legal sovereign is not the actual sovereign, or is at best a feeble sovereign, and at times customs or local prejudices may be enforced by persons who are less than sovereigns, as is frequently the case in lynchings and in the procedure of the *posse comitatis*. Holland suggests that actually disobedience of village custom is either repressed with force or acquiesced in by the local authority, and that if it be habitually repressed the local force must in the last resort be supported by the whole strength of the empire "if only for the preservation of peace."

An interesting illustration is the case of the Soviet attempt to change the traditional society of Muslim ethnic groups in Central Asia. Illiteracy was almost one hundred per cent. Traditional occupations were agriculture, some commerce, artisan trades, nomadic pasturalism, stock trading, and the caravan trade. Rule was by Muslim religious personages. In the late 1920s the Soviet government attempted to introduce into the region new legal rules and institutions relating especially to personal status and family relations and in this context to establish sexual equality involving the unveiling of women. The reactions were circumlocution by the local authorities, deviance from the new laws, and sabotage of the "cultural revolution" and "female emancipation." "The greater were the pressures to enforce the new code among the native Soviet cadres, the greater was the tendency among them toward mutual protective associations—often in alliance with surviving local traditional elites," says Gregory J. Massell in describing this cultural revolution. The new law "was felt to be forced upon traditional communities by men who were ethnically or ideologically outsiders . . . it not only posed a threat to traditional unities and values, but impinged directly upon the most intimate and sacred realms of local life-styles. . . ." In fact, the realization of the new norms "tended to be inversely related to the degree of forceable attempts to apply it [the new norms] in reality." For example, to a traditional Muslim "a woman who uncovers her face in the presence of strange men is a harlot," and men reacted to unveiled women accordingly. A Communist woman of the region described this attitude as a "[peculiar] psychological aberration." After two and a half years the Soviet authorities reduced the pressures and commenced a process of "long-term social rebuilding."

It is again relevant to refer to Machiavelli's comment that even a sovereign of "average powers" can "maintain himself in his state" if he respects custom and deals "prudently with circumstances as they arise."

Undoubtedly the motor faculties of the State are often slow to react to the sensation of disobedience; the sovereign is rarely single-minded, for conflicting interests and personalities intervene. The strength of the sovereign can well be measured by the correlation of action to disobedience. "Law is no more efficient than the state whose will it utters," Woodrow Wilson said. There are times when there is little of that obedience which Burke said is what makes government. ("Obedience is what makes government, and not the names by which it is called; not the name Governor, as formerly, or Committee, as at present.") If no sanctions are applied to the disobedient, then there is no sovereign and consequently no law. This does not mean that people have not on those occasions continued for the most part to carry out their customs—their day-to-day practices; it does not mean that loyalty and fear of reprisals will not keep them orderly in the main. But when no sovereign is obeyed and no sovereign enforces obedience there can be no law.

Law is of value to the sovereign because it serves notice on the subjects upon what occasions and in what circumstances the sovereign will use force. An utterly arbitrary use of force at the whim of the ruler would breed ill will; a failure to support the sovereign's mandates with force could only result in contempt for the sovereign. At the same time sovereignty, being never *de facto* complete and supreme, can be defined and limited by law. Thus the sovereign power can say by the medium of statutes and decisions when it will and when it will not use force, what interests of the sovereign power and its component groups, of its favored retainers, courtiers, and concubines it will defend with the sword and what interests it will not.

Examples are readily apparent. The criminal law describes those situations in which the police will apprehend the violator and the courts direct the seizure of his property or the imprisonment of his person. Tax laws and laws relating to eminent domain describe situations in which a government will seize property within its power for government purposes. Commercial law and property law announce situations in which the individual can appeal to governmental force for assistance. It is true that statutes are not fully descriptive of those occasions on which a government will utilize force. Legislators may be flamboyant and issue mandates going so much against the grain of public sentiment or so minutely into private lives that the mandates are unenforcible without the creation of a police force which would eat up the national economy. Administrators seeking results through short cuts may ignore the law, or as in many labor struggles accommodate themselves to the will of those who have the greater economic rewards at their disposal regardless of laws dealing with civil liberties. Crises such as rebellions and wars defy all common denominators of sovereign power and its application.

More accurately than legislation, the courts through their processes of determining facts, interpreting legislation, and applying it to the facts, determine when force shall be used. It is the courts generally that say through their judgments when sheriffs and bailiffs and police shall or shall not seize persons or property; when litigants shall or shall not act or desist on pain of being punished in their persons or purses. This descriptive process of the courts occurs not only in the exercise of affirmative judgments, but also in the very selection of the instances in which they exercise jurisdiction. Most courts will not assume jurisdiction of a cause where there is neither person nor property against which it can employ force in fulfillment of its judgment. Most courts are hesitant to take jurisdiction of matters under the jurisdiction of foreign courts; they will enforce conflicting foreign laws only where they can consistently read them as part of the law of the forum or as having been made the law of the forum through the consent of the parties to the litigation, as in an agreement which states that the law of a foreign jurisdiction is to control. Courts are generally chary of dealing with what they term "political issues." This does not mean that the courts avoid passing upon cases involving political questions. Every time an American court passes on the constitutionality of a statute or executive action, a political question is involved; but the judgment can be enforced by the ordinary officers of the court, if the mere declaration of judgment is not sufficient to bring about acquiescence. But, as was mentioned earlier, the Supreme Court has recently stepped in to fill the vacuum where legislatures have failed to afford people the equal protection of the laws (for example in *Brown v. Board of Education of Topeka* and *Baker v. Carr*) even though its officers have not power to enforce the decisions and some local authorities defy them.

However, there are certain questions that the Supreme Court of the United States will not even consider, except incidentally to decisions on other issues, such as the authority of foreign ambassadors, the existence of a state of war, the extent of the jurisdiction of a foreign power, jurisdiction over islands in the high seas, the rights of Indians to recognition as a tribe, which of two *de facto* legislatures is *de jure*. The subject is summed up by Charles Gordon Post in *The Supreme Court and Political Questions*: "If the Court was fully conscious that its mandate could not, or would not, be enforced in the particular case, obviously it was more expedient to leave the matter to the political departments exclusively. In general, judicial review or not, the Court has found it more expedient to leave the decision of certain questions to governmental bodies more appropriately adapted to decide them."

No sovereign can afford to use force on every occasion. The King of the Wood was not called upon to fight all comers but only runaway slaves who had plucked the golden bough. The definition of occasion which will call forth action, and occasion which will mean only a cold shoulder, is essential, but so too is the elimination of actual combat on those occasions which have been defined as circumstances which will call forth sovereign force. Most men will not fight if they know that a superior force is prepared to meet them. Rousseau has told us that punishment is evidence of the weakness of the government. The sovereign is not often defeated if his strength is respected. Where the police are not corrupted, holdups are not staged on the steps of a police station; nor does the average man wait for the sheriff to seize his home before paying a judgment that he has the means of paying.

The reason for this is that law has become the symbol for the underlying physical force. It is in itself a continual threat of physical force—"a warning that if it be unheeded something unpleasant will happen." The more highly civilized men are, the more willingly do they accept the symbol, the less necessary does the actual application of force become. Maine, in his *Early Law and Custom*, says:

> The law has so formed our habits and ideas that Courts of Justice are rarely needed to compel obedience to it, and thus they have apparently fallen into the background. It is only when the law happens to be uncertain, or when facts with which we are concerned happen to get unusually entangled, that most of us, who are not lawyers, ever come into contact with the administration of the law. No doubt the force which arms the law is still there; but it lies in reserve, in (so to speak) a compact and concentrated form, which enables it to keep out of sight.

It is no more possible to enforce all law, if it is continually or generally violated, than it would be possible to redeem all paper currency out of metallic reserves or for a bank to pay off all its depositors within the same hour. A run on the courts like a run on a bank spells failure. In the field of government this means rebellion if not revolution.

A stable culture, whether primitive or highly developed,

leads men to accept the symbol rather than to insist upon the use of force on every occasion because resistance is generally against their interests; for the complex economic structure on which man depends for a living in modern society and the inflexible social relationships in primitive society cannot endure the strain of continual rebellion and coercion.

Just as force may not be evident in the judgment of the court but is ready in the wings, so too it may not appear to be the motivation for observance of legislation or the sovereign's decree. The individual may not be consciously aware of legal penalties when he makes the choice to do what the law directs. He may be influenced by a feeling that he *ought* to act or refrain from acting. He may believe that the particular law or all laws *ought* to be respected. But Sherif and Asch have shown how people tend to adapt their perceptions to social norms; and the superego works in the unconscious to relieve the sovereign from the necessity to enforce a rule of law.

It is generally the judiciary, that is, the sovereign sitting as magistrate, which determines when force shall be applied. The early tribunals were without power to determine controversies; they could not call upon the executive branch of the sovereign power to enforce their edicts. The judges in their scarlet robes followed by the serjeants-at-law might attend on the day and at the place of combat and preside over the battle (as late as 1819 the British courts determined that the right to wager by battle existed), but they did not determine the justice of the cause. The courts long showed a "tenderness to immemorial barbarism" by a partial recognition of the remedy of distraint and "self-help" and private reprisals. The sovereign would have been as unable to enforce court decisions that were contrary to such popular customs as the American government has been to enforce sumptuary laws. The best that the courts could do was to refuse such protection as they were capable of affording to anyone who disobeyed their orders —after such disobedience "he carried his life in his hands." They put no mark of Cain upon the deviant, "lest any finding him should kill him."

Austin has pointed out that this power of judicial regulation or rule making is a power to make law. It is a power of definition and limitation inherently the same as any other judicial power, but out of it arises the power to determine to which customs the sovereign will give the *force of law*. In other words, courts do not only decide that certain contracts will be enforced and certain contracts will be disregarded, but they say in effect that as to contracts which they declare to be enforcible, the sovereign power will extend its mailed fist if need be for their enforcement, while the sovereign power will do nothing to effectuate agreements declared by the courts to be without protection of the law. The judiciary, then, exercise a selective process, choosing the customs and ethical principles over which the sovereign power will be extended and the instances in which that power will be applied.

At times the field of action selected by the sovereign power may be completely arbitrary. This arbitrariness may be just as great when uttered by the courts as when it arises from the stubbornness of an administrative bureaucracy. Judicial arbitrariness is usually accepted with better grace. This is so because the judiciary can point to written law as its excuse and thereby direct objection to other branches of the government, or because the judiciary has already laid a trail of pronouncements through previous decisions which lead to the decision of a given case; but it is principally because centuries of propaganda have invested the courts with a sacrosanct coating which people interpret as meaning "the court would if it could." And usually that conclusion is correct; a court will not step in where it cannot find a way to enforce its decrees. So, it will not ordinarily deal with the title of real property in another jurisdiction, nor will it enjoin someone over whom it cannot obtain physical jurisdiction.

However arbitrary may be the limits of legal jurisdiction, law is in general not arbitrary within these limits. It is generally consistent. Nor is it static within these limits; its process is the continual adaptation of old norms to new concepts. When the common law failed to meet the need of Englishmen, the King's court created new writs and thus new rights, and courts of equity offered remedies which courts of law denied. A legal system is like a farmer who tills his fields within the borders of his land, which he gradually fences; he cuts his wood lot and grazes his cattle there; he plants the old meadow, cultivates his farm as intensively as he can, refines his acres until at last the land is exhausted, and he moves on to more fertile fields. Just so, a legal system in a society which is becoming exhausted and which is crowded with conflicting interests, refines and rarefies its principles to meet such a multiplicity of circumstances that the ideology which in the first instance gave impetus, strength, and direction to the system is exhausted and infertile as an old farm. This progress from fallow to infertility in the legal systems of each socio-economic system is not contradicted by the fact that similar needs may be treated in a similar manner by various systems of law. The law of Rome, the law merchant, the New York statutes may deal in the same way with purchase and sale; theft was a crime in Mosaic law, in Athenian law, in medieval law; and it is a crime today in the common law and in the law of Soviet Russia. But the ideologies that impelled and guided the development of those several legal systems were quite different. Some flowered and died, others are still flourishing and will die, and law which is a part of the ideology inherent in a socio-economic system, an arm of it, passes with that system.

Law serves the purpose of building and defending the sovereign—which means building and defending the economic interests and ideologies of those political forces upon which the sovereign relies or which, through the sheer physical force and economic power that they can muster, comprise in themselves the sovereign power. Thus law today is mostly middle-class law, that is, it supports the values of the middle class. Even in Communist countries, though the law as in other lands supports the power of the State, it simultaneously supports the new bourgeoisie who are the officialdom, the Communist Party hierarchy, the sovereign power. In other ages it was the emperor or monarch and the imperial supporters or feudal lords (including priests and churches) in whose interests the law spoke. Only as the money power of the burghers and rural squires, and more latterly the lower middle class with their great purchasing power and their votes, brought pressure did law take recognition of their interests. The people of the slums have rarely been seen by sovereigns or benefited by their laws, except briefly in revolutionary periods as the result of the exercise of force, or to purchase quiet.

Law cannot in general be irresponsible because if it is to be a serviceable weapon of sovereignty it must be aimed at achieving unity, viz., an absence of those disintegrating conditions in which a competitor might find support. Therefore, legal systems tend to what Laski calls "the beatification of order."

It is inevitable moreover for governments in ordinary times to resist change. Ihering has shown that the end of law in enforcing contracts is to serve the original purpose of the contracting parties "against the prejudicial influence of a later shift of interest or a change of judgment touching his interest on the part of one of the parties. In other words, it means that *a change of interest has juristically no force*." This basic jural principle (which is imperative in an economy which depends for its functioning largely on credit) is in complete harmony with the necessities of sovereignty, that is, resistance to changes which may affect political balance.

The sovereign can sustain its power by the psychological influence of law with less wear and tear than by the constant application of physical and economic power. Recent findings indicate that law, as an expression of the sovereign will, can cause people to make a firm commitment to an unpleasant mode of behavior while still allowing them to feel a certain degree of freedom of choice. Under these conditions, which may be said to exist when an interracial policy against discrimination is enforced in public housing or in employment, the process of resolving cognitive dissonance gradually brings about an internalization of legal norms. To the extent that people's attitudes become harmonious with the policy of the law, the use of coercive enforcement becomes unnecessary. Such a resolution is more likely when the penalties for disobedience are mild rather than severe.

By rationalization, which forms so large a part of judicial law (a reason can be given for every decision or as Benjamin Franklin said, man can find a reason for anything he has in mind to do), the sovereign can also obtain psychological by-products which will ward off the animus that more drastic action would incur. The use of Cossacks may breed fear, but it also incubates hatred. A defendant or a litigant feels better for his day in court, though in defeat he may damn the jury and accuse the judge of corruption. A formal legal system, even with that degree of uncertainty which is inevitable in an institution applied by men to the situations of man, serves a valuable governmental purpose, for though right or wrong, legal systems have a degree of definiteness and authority which interests competing in their own names rather than in the name of sovereignty necessarily lack.

For the sovereign power to be effective, it cannot concede that it has a superior or that it is mortal. "Perpetuity is implied, if not expressed, in the fundamental law of all national governments," Lincoln argued in his First Inaugural Address. "It is safe to assert that no government proper ever had a provision in its organic law for its own termination." The sovereign ego must be self-confident, for the sovereign who hesitates is indeed lost. It is in expression of this essential egotism that the legal doctrine of sovereign supremacy has been fostered. Although in the first flush of conquest such a principle may not be needed for rulers whose reliance is principally on physical force, it is necessary for epigones and essential for rulers whose title is questioned.

Analogous to the doctrine that legally the sovereign is supreme is the principle that it is infallible in its exercise of power; that it possesses the legal right to the powers it exercises. This is illustrated in the opinion of Chief Justice Hughes in the Minnesota Moratorium Case, involving a state statute establishing a moratorium on mortgage foreclosures:

While emergency does not create power, emergency may furnish the occasion for the exercise of power. "Although an emergency may not call into life a power which has never lived, nevertheless emergency may afford a reason for the exertion of a living power already enjoyed. . . ." The constitutional question presented in the light of an emergency is whether the power possessed embraces the particular exercise of it in response to particular conditions.

The sovereign, the sovereign group, must by law, therefore, provide for its own continuance and for the annihilation of serious opposition. How far it can realize these aims depends upon the force of the opposition, as we shall hereafter see. Although the law, through the precise application of some solution, will settle conflict in respect to the sovereign power itself, just as with litigation among subjects, it cannot do so definitively but only temporarily in the political field. For it can never so consolidate everything that nothing of any force which will finally wear away, stretch, or tear down the system will be left outside it. Whatever its propagandist claims may be, the State in practice admits that it is vulnerable when it takes drastic action to suppress the opposition of groups which endanger it. An example of this is to be found in the decision of the United States Supreme Court in *Gitlow v. New York* and similar cases involving local statutes against "criminal syndicalism."

The opposition, those persons or groups whose interests are consistently or acutely impinged upon or disregarded by the rulers, can also appeal to law as a weapon (Bills of Rights are laws of this character). Fear that their clamor may prove contagious and arouse others may compel the sovereign to grant new rights or enforce slumbering remedies. (A good example of the latter was the enforcement against a Negro by the State of Georgia in the 1930s of a long-dormant statute, adopted as a Reconstruction measure after the Civil War.) Appeal may be made to legal precepts which declare limits to the authority of the sovereign, as in the case of Caius' statement that the "Emperor receives his *imperium* by a *lex*," which though a fiction in the days of the great emperors was repeated throughout the Middle Ages to plague rulers of all kinds. Legal restrictions may be imposed on a sovereign which he dare not fail to observe if the weapons in the hands of the opposition be sufficient to compel observance or a fight. This was the case in the struggle between the barons and King John, and again in that between the burghers and the Stuarts. The American Colonies in the years before Bunker Hill appealed to George III and Parliament in the terms of British liberties. But the shoe was then on the other foot and the sovereigns had no use for those legal concepts which had grown out of the Puritan Revolution in England. Thus Burke cried out, "To prove that the Americans ought not to be free, we are obliged to depreciate the value of freedom itself; and we shall never seem to gain a paltry advantage over them in debate, without attacking some of those principles, or deriding some of those feelings, for which our ancestors shed their blood.[1]

Respect for law, which arises in the first instance because

[1] *Conciliation with the American Colonies*. Compare Burke's own attitude toward the French Revolution; and the prevailing American opinion toward the Russian Revolution. And see the dissenting opinion of Mr. Justice Holmes in the espionage case, *Abrams v. United States*, 250 U.S. 616; see also *Schenck v. United States*, 249 U.S. 47.

there is some power which can and will enforce it, has curious throwbacks, and we find that sometimes the perpetrators of the most lawless acts attempt to sugarcoat their deeds with the verisimilitude of legal authority (the devil citing scripture). The ward politician throws out as defective those ballots which are marked in a way prohibited by law—ballots which he himself has made defective after they have been cast, so that in accordance with law he may discard them as improperly marked. He may not be acting in this manner out of respect for the law, but it provides a pretty label for an act which otherwise would bear a horrid name. "The attempt to disguise its first rebel steps with legality, both sacred and secular, has from time immemorial characterized the struggle of every revolutionary class, before it has gathered sufficient strength and confidence to break the umbilical cord which bound it to the old society," says Trotsky. He describes the first tentative seizures of the land by the Russian peasants in 1917. " 'We do not want to rob them,' they recite, 'we want to do everything nicely.' They are not appropriating the meadow, but only cutting the hay. They are only compelling the landlord to rent them the land, but are themselves establishing the price. Or with a similar compulsion they are 'buying' the land—but at a price designated by themselves." In bare fact there is little difference between the peasant cloaking his forceful seizure with legal phrases and governmental expropriation under the catchall formula of "due process of law." To the man whose property is expropriated it is the same, for due process of law does not necessitate reimbursement when the price is too great to pay. No one made the brewers and distillers whole when the Eighteenth Amendment to the American Constitution was adopted. As Karl Gareis tells us:

It is no longer a matter of doubt that the governing social entity cannot be prevented by anything or any person from invading spheres of private right and drawing therefrom the proprietary materials necessary to the attainment of its ends. It is, however, equally agreed, that in a legally ordered state, the invasion of private right must proceed in a legal manner.

Thus the symbolism of justice implicit in law affords a propagandist weapon which makes possible the peaceable reassembling of economic power.

Legal rights in private law, then, are only declarations of those circumstances in which the sovereign power will be applied in private controversies for the general peace of the land. That is, in order to avoid a situation in which physical power must be applied by the sovereign to pacify private disputes which might endanger the State, it posits certain conditions in which it asserts that it will use its full power if need be to support one of the contestants. Thus the sovereign makes an ally not only of a single party to a given conflict, but of all other potential parties with the same interest in possible similar controversies. This is the essence of magistracy. It is the most frequent and powerful application of propagandist or psychological force by the sovereign.

In public law the rights of the sovereign are coextensive with its powers and are only limited internally by powers of those it governs and externally by the powers of neighboring sovereigns. Public law is the definition of those powers which the sovereign thinks it can defend and is not afraid to admit that it possesses. "Law," said Schopenhauer, "is only the measure of power."

Because the sovereign had been deemed to be above law, i.e., had such weapons of sovereignty that law could not be enforced against him, claims against the sovereign until recent times have been granted if at all as a matter of grace, of good will, of noblesse oblige, not as a right. For there could be no legal right without a legal remedy and who, except by rebellion or revolution, could enforce his claims against a government? Now courts of claims have been set up to hear and adjudge claims against the State; but the legislative branch of government can still refuse to appropriate funds to pay a judgment of such a court or the administrative branch can fail to observe a court's writ of injunction or mandamus. However, this can only be done at a price, at the cost of disaffection. For an expectation aroused and then frustrated by a greater power will appear arbitrary.

It is to the advantage of a sovereign power to avoid such an appearance, for disaffection holds the threat of retaliation. This may be violent or by defeat of the government at the polls. But even an electoral victory might not give security to the sovereign power group; for people have repeatedly resorted to force when their votes failed them, failed to achieve satisfaction, and the election system became no longer acceptable as a symbol of force. It is not always advisable, therefore, for a sovereign power to win and cause its citizens to lose, though it has the power to do so. Furthermore, the decision of a court can be a protection to government. "The judicial process may enable the government to lose an argument gracefully and according to principle," as Roger Fisher said. "Responsibility for an unpopular but necessary action can often be passed to the courts and immunized from partisan attack."

6

CUSTOM

LAW GROWS most readily from below. It is most securely established when it arises out of custom and is then accepted or promulgated by the sovereign. This is by reason of the fact that through usage the subjects are familiar with the legislation and in the habit of observing it even before it is articulated as law. Custom is already *de facto*. Men followed the law merchant, they respected adverse possession and it was simple for the State to accept the status quo. This simplified the problem of enforcement. In common law countries it is especially through the courts that custom becomes a part of the law, for they are apt to have a closer contact with the problems of the law relating to customs of people than have other branches of government. Codes too can be derived from customs; and the uniform laws and model codes such as those drafted by the American Law Institute may be considered as developed from the customs of judicial action.

Law shapes customs sometimes, as for example bookkeeping and accounting practices required by income tax laws and bodies supervising the issue of corporate securities. The eligibility requirements for receipt of social security have sometimes developed the custom of voluntary unemployment. And fair employment practice laws have, where they have teeth for enforcement, changed prejudicial patterns of employment.

After the "barbarian invasion," with its conglomeration of peoples, it became especially vital for the Empire to take cognizance of tribal laws and customs. In 319 A.D. Constantine declared that the authority of custom and ancient usage was not to be ignored unless it was contrary to reason or to *lex*. Racial groups within the State were permitted to employ their own customary rules and "it often happened that five men were present or sitting together, and not one of them had a law the same as another." By the twelfth century the influence of the Roman law had diminished and that of custom had increased, so that in the *Libri Feudorum* it was said that the authority of Roman law is not to be disregarded except as it was contrary to *usum aut mores*. This reversal of the roles of *lex* and *usum* evidenced a weakening of the sovereign power which during the period had to counter the strong influence of the Germanic principle that law is primarily immemorial custom, not a legislative enactment by some superior authority; for it was the husting that had declared, enforced and set the model for Teutonic law.

The kingly authority in the early Middle Ages grew not from the legal basis of kinship, but because the elected warlords and their successors raised themselves to power by their ability in war. Like Pippin and Charles Martel, William the Conqueror and William Rufus, the sovereigns who established the new dynasties accomplished their work by the sword. In spite of the undoubted superiority of their physical force, these warrior kings were limited by custom and tradition. The "law" as established by the king could not be his mere whim; it had to be (at least in words) a promulgation of ancient tribal custom reaffirmed in the name of the monarch and binding upon him and the people alike. An example of this method of establishing law out of custom is to be found in biblical times. In the name of tradition a revolution was accomplished in Judah during the reign of Josiah when Deuteronomy was said to have been "discovered" in the Temple. Its effect was to concentrate worship in the Temple at Jerusalem and make possible the destruction of the village shrines to heathen gods. At the same time it gave greater prestige and power to the priesthood officiating at the Temple.

It is true that until modern times there have rarely been sanctions other than rebellion to compel obedience by the king; but the vested interests of the barons in their land, their dominion over men, their manorial courts, wardship, benefices, and everything that comprised feudalism[1] and went to make for baronial power, made rebellion an effective and permanent sanction. The whole theory of feudal tenure, the idea that all property, land, offices, dignities, chattels, immunities, franchises, and even money had been granted at some time by some grantor, generally on a condition, gave rise to reciprocal claims which the monarch as well as the feudal lords had to respect. Nor must it be overlooked that the king was not only a sovereign but also a

[1] "'Feudalism' is the word we use to characterize the sum of the conditions, social, political, and economic, which prevailed in western Europe in the period, varying from place to place, between the stabilizing geographically of the Germanic tribes in their conquered territory and the emergence among them of centralized administrative systems 'national' in scope, character, and extent." McIlwain, *The Growth of Political Thought in the West*, p. 180.

feudal lord in his own right, a landed proprietor with all that it implied, and in theory at least subject to *diffidatio* just as any other feudal lord.[2]

The devotion of people of all classes to custom has therefore afforded the sovereign strong support when he stood ready to implement custom and thereby convert it into law. On the other hand the stubborn adherence to custom has been a thorn in the side of sovereigns attempting to extend their power, for out of usage have grown habits not merely of action and speech but of thought and principle—symbols for which men have at all times been prepared to fight.

[2] It was undoubtedly this fusion of sovereign powers with those of landed proprietor in the same person that led to the failure to distinguish, as the Romans did, between public and private law. See McIlwain, p. 177. This combination of powers in the person of the ruler has also led to the theory that feudal lords were sovereign. Cf. M. R. Cohen, *Property and Sovereignty,* Cornell Quarterly, XIII (1927), 8.

7

POPULAR SOVEREIGNTY, THE SOCIAL COMPACT, AND THE WITHERING STATE

IN THE political process, in the struggle between those forces which control the machinery of government and those which seek recognition of their claims, one of the principal weapons is that of propaganda. Propaganda depends largely upon language to convey the ideas it seeks to establish. Language itself is symbolic of the realities behind particular words. In the political field particularly, key words, catch phrases, shibboleths are used—language that frequently has little or no reality behind it. Among the potent shibboleths of politics are such phrases as popular sovereignty, the social compact, and the withering State.

Except in early tribal organizations such as those of the Teutonic tribes, and in the first years of the New England villages, there has never been "popular sovereignty." Among the German tribes, we are told by Tacitus, decisive questions of tribal policy were not entrusted to the kings but were left to the assembly of warriors. The kings could not make war or peace; they could not make alliances or try offenders or execute judicial sentences—these were in the province of the husting. In time of war a man of greater vigor and influence than the king was chosen by the warriors as *dux*, as the mighty leader. Even in the Greek cities which nurtured many democratic institutions, Aristotle says that in oligarchies the "supreme power" is in the hands of a majority of the rich and in democracies it is in the hands of a majority of the freemen. Slavery for those who performed the manual labor was assumed by him to be a matter of course. This large section of the city's population was excluded from the "supreme power."

Whether a government is free or despotic does not depend upon sovereignty residing in the whole people. It depends rather on the distribution of the weapons of sovereignty and also on the proximity of the interests of the several groups in the community. Jeremy Bentham has well said that the difference between free and despotic governments depends "on the manner in which the whole mass of power, which taken together is supreme, is in a free state distributed among the several ranks of persons that are sharers in it; on the source from whence their titles to it are successively derived; on the frequent and easy changes of condition between governors and governed, whereby the interests of one class are more or less indistinguishably blended with those of the other; on the responsibility of the governors; *on the right which the subject has of having the reasons publicly assigned and canvassed of every act of power that is exerted over him.*" (Italics mine. —J.M.)

It is this power of the people to demand an accounting from their government and their power to vote—that sublimation of their power to use physical force—which has misled students of government to assert that the people as a whole possess sovereignty. At best they share some of its weapons with the ruling group.

The tenacity of the theory is due to the fact that in the struggle against tyranny, "popular sovereignty" has proved a useful fiction. Although it has no legal significance, it has political weight, when enunciated by a popular champion, as a symbol of resistance to absolutist tendencies; and it has a quieting effect when spoken as an earnest of good-will by the sovereign (directly, or through his law courts, or other officials), who may deem it politic to deprecate his true power.

The people as a whole have the ultimate power only in the same sense that groups of the people have, such as that possessed by bankers, farmers, soldiers, shopkeepers, trade unions, and religious sects. On most occasions they wield their powers only in a negative manner, for they permit sovereignty to remain with the governors so long as they receive some minimum of what they require, even though they may have the power of effectual resistance. It is the business of the sovereigns to meet popular demands, just as they must meet the demands of any other effective group (except to the extent of abdicating superior political power) to keep the people satisfied to a degree which will avoid overthrow of the sovereign group.

With the impetus given to reason by Descartes, and its application in fields of science and law in the seventeenth and eighteenth centuries, a new weapon of power was developed against autocracy. The political writers of the seventeenth and eighteenth centuries in England and France and the American Colonies exalted Reason with an adolescent exuberance. They had rediscovered the power of mind over matter, or at least a form of this power, quite different from that advocated by the Church—and they concluded that since men could think, therefore they were free agents and were ruled by their monarchs only as the result of their free consent. Governments and society were contractual relations bearing rights and duties similar to those incidental to commercial contracts. The reactions of the eighteenth-century political writers were like those of adolescents who have suddenly discovered, at least subconsciously, their own powers and who refuse any longer to submit to parental rule. They must know what they are doing; they must be privileged to decide for themselves on their own course of action. It is only with maturity that people realize the limits of their powers and accept defeats objectively, as the result of opposing forces rather than as personal to themselves. But what a power for growth this adolescent self-confidence is! Just so, this eighteenth-century sanctification of Reason and insistence on freedom of contract gave immense impetus to the self-confidence of the flowering bourgeoisie.

The academic doctrine of freedom of contract is well set forth in the majority opinion in the first minimum wage law case in these words: "In making contracts, generally speaking, the parties have an equal right to obtain from each other the best terms they can as the result of private bargain." The slogans "Reason" and "Freedom" afforded powerful support to the "protest against the desolating theory of divine right"; they have continued and will continue to be effective weapons against tyranny; but real freedom of contract is impossible except between power equals, as the battle over "yellow dog contracts" has shown; as recent decisions have asserted regarding warranties by large corporations manufacturing dangerous instrumentalities (automobiles) to purchasers with little freedom of choice; and as the equitable theory of fiduciaries and the law as to minors and incompetents have admitted. (Thus a court of equity will scrutinize transactions between a trustee and the beneficiary of a trust and between a guardian and a ward, to see that trustee and guardian have not overreached; and minors and incompetents generally are deemed to lack the legal capacity to contract.) Nor has the social compact —the organization of society through common consent, a sort of meeting of the minds in mass—ever existed except in the case of sports such as the Mayflower Pact, because the sovereign power, with its control of physical force and the means of subsistence, has weapons of compulsion which the masses must respect. Silence in the presence of superior force cannot be accepted as the equivalent of consent.

In a negative sense, subjects do consent to their rulers in general: but such consent is like the consent of the well-trained dog of Ihering, who will not drink when forbidden by his master, "because over against the idea of water which he knows can quench his thirst, there presents to him the idea of the beating which he receives when he drinks against his master's orders." Thus the party of the second part to the social contract, except in times of desperation, measures forces and acquiesces. After World War I, intellectuals and political leaders came more and more to accept (often unconsciously) the Marxian doctrine that it is not in the power of majorities, sheer force of numbers, but in the power of finance capital to direct and control the economic destinies of nations. Whether or not this is so, power groups set the norms and values prevailing in each society. The people as a whole have not been consulted as to the acceptability of this clause or many others of the social compact. And currently in many parts of the world young people are protesting through various forms of civil disobedience the assumption that they have or must accept controls to which they have not affirmatively given consent.

The feudal edifice of *status* had to be destroyed to make way for the free market of nineteenth-century capitalism. This could only be done by exalting the individual over the existing institutions of church and state and simultaneously ignoring his power status relative to and in competition with others. To have paused to face the problem that individuals were too unequal to meet in a fair fight would have involved the loss of those allies who supplied the chief energy for the overthrow of the existing institutions, the merchant class. The merchant class was imbued with the ideology of profit making, and the logic of profit making forbade building up your competitor. That the social compact contained an unwritten clause, among others, which guaranteed the rights of private property even to the extent of placing restraint upon government itself, is illustrated by the argument of Daniel Webster before the Supreme Court of the United States in 1829: "Though there be no prohibition in the Constitution, the legislature is restrained from acts subverting the great principles of republican liberty and of the social compact." To which William Wirt replied: "Who is the sovereign? Is it not the legislature of the state and are not its acts effectual, unless they come in contact with the great principles of the social compact?"

The fictions of the social compact and popular sovereignty were necessarily preparatory to the laissez-faire philosophy which was essential to the flowering of the dominant class of the ninteenth century. They were fictions not in any invidious sense, not as conscious deceptions, but as a sleight of mind to bridge the gap between the ideal of unity which obsessed the medieval mind and the ideal of freedom which has dominated the thought of the last century and a half in Western Europe and America.

Another political fiction is that of the withering State. In Marxian doctrine the armed workers must "put an end" to the bourgeois State. Then follows a sort of purgatory—the dictatorship of the proletariat—during which the proletarian State must wipe out all vestigial remains of capitalist practices and attitudes and create, through the achievement of an economy of plenty, a society in which all will labor according to their respective abilities and all will receive according to their respective needs. When this "higher phase" of Communist society is attained, then, according to Engels and Lenin, the State will "wither away." It must wither away because the State—which is "an organ of class *domination*, an organ of *oppression* of one class by another"—will be rendered unnecessary by Communism, "for there is *no one* to be suppressed—'no one' in the sense of a class, in the sense of a systematic struggle with a definite section of the population."

Of course if you change the definition of symbols, the equation will have a different result. You get a different arithmetical universe through a geometry in which two parallel lines meet from that which you do with a geometry in which they do not meet. But you do not change the universe. Similarly, different results are obtained when the definition of nouns is changed. Altering the definition of a noun may prove an economy of adjectives but it also removes the argument to a different frame of reference and makes comparative analysis confusing, if not impossible. The similarity between Bentham's State and Lenin's State is one of assonance. But that does not detract from Lenin's redefinition of "State" and "class" and "revolution" as instruments of propaganda—old words with old associations but a new innuendo. It is a familiar practice in the everyday advertising of merchandise. "Without a special rhetoric it is not possible to make a revolution," said Michele Bianchi, one-time Secretary-General of the Fascist Party.

If, then, capitalists who exercise control directly or indirectly over physical, economic, and propagandist forces are to be deemed a *class* in society, although bureaucrats who control the same forces in a dictatorship of the proletariat are not to be considered a *class*, the result would follow that, with the liquidation of capitalism, there would be an end of classes and *ipso facto* of class struggle. And if the State can only be an instrument of suppression used by a class in the class struggle, then, if the bureaucracy itself does not constitute a class employing the instrument of the State for the purpose of suppression, the bureaucratic machinery could not be a State. By arguing on this plane, of course, one begs the question, for one ignores the existence of pressures which are exerted by and against the bureaucracy even under a proletarian dictatorship and which will continue as long as physical, economic, and propagandist forces exist in the hands of the bureaucracy and, in some degree, in the hands of those with whom the bureaucracy interferes. Marx recognized that a bureaucracy tended to create itself into something apart. This fact in time must give rise to a "systematic struggle with a definite section of the population." Whether one calls this a class struggle or not is of no importance if one stops there; but when, upon this definition, one builds the proposition that because there is no "class" there is need for no "State" and that therefore the State will "wither away," Q.E.D.—one must pause. Then the solid reality of a bureaucracy exerting sovereign powers, wielding and yielding those powers in accordance with the customary action of the political processes and the inevitable interaction of political forces, must warn one against the postulated definitions of "class" and "State."

Furthermore, the proposition that the economic class struggle alone gives rise to a need for organized police power, call it State or what you will, could not well be sustained. Men will continue to fall in love with the same woman and sometimes to quarrel over her; sensitivity, pride, jealousy, and misunderstanding will still set people against one another; honest differences of opinion as to techniques of production, as to who shall lead or supervise, as to what each man's ability to perform may be, and how much he requires to live on will all at times call for some mechanism for settlement and for some machinery to enforce the settlement.

But Lenin admits that he is not a utopian and so he does not deny "the possibility and inevitability of excesses on the part of *individual persons*, nor the need to suppress *such* excesses." For this suppression no special machinery or apparatus is necessary, he believes, for "this will be done by the armed people itself, as simply and as readily as any crowd of civilized people, even in modern society, parts a pair of combatants or does not allow a woman to be outraged." Assuming that the evidence of such "excesses" by "individual persons" will be readily perceptible to "the armed people itself," might not the emotional state of these people rather than the offense determine the method and extent of suppression? If the evidence were not apparent might not the offender escape entirely? And does not this manner of suppressing excesses smack of lynch law rather than of "civilized people"? This truth is driven home by comparing another passage in Chapter V of *The State and Revolution*, wherein Lenin says that when all have learned to manage by themselves social control, escape from such control will be rare and "will probably be accompanied by such swift and severe punishment (for the armed workers are men of practical life, not sentimental intellectuals, and will scarcely allow anyone to trifle with them)" that observance of "the simple fundamental rules of every-day social life in common will have become a *habit*." Lynch law? No indeed. The term is too mild. For here we have no sudden emotion sweeping away a mob, but a deliberate ideology which abandons fact finding, reason, and judgment and, in the manner of primitive peoples, revives the method of achieving social solidarity and uniformity through cracking down on deviations, no matter how sound and reasonable. There is a further difficulty presented by the passage under discussion, in that all people will not acquire the identical habits. Even children of the same parents brought up under apparently similar conditions will have different habits, different needs and capacities and satisfactions, and out of these differences there will arise emotional strains and difficulties and the need for the strong arm or conciliating words of parents.

When Lenin writes in Chapter I of *The State and Revolution* that as compared with the bourgeois State which can only be replaced by "violent revolution," "the abolition of the proletarian State, i.e., of all States, is only possible through 'withering away,'" he imprinted upon the political theory of Communism a symbolism with which to fight "violent revolution" against the proletarian State. No State is free, Lenin says. It would follow that "violent revolution" is of no value under Communism, because, its function being accomplished, the State will somehow automatically wither and concurrently freedom will be achieved. As an instrument of sovereign self-defense, this symbolism is comparable to the doctrine of sovereign supremacy and immortality expressed by the bourgeois State. In one instance you have the juridical swagger of supremacy to conceal the limits of power (a sort of bristling mustachio to deceive the onlooker) and in the other the seductive narcotic that there is no reason to cry out against the domination of the bureaucracy because the poor old State is not going to survive anyway; like many another unpleasant insect it will perform its task for posterity and die.

When the "special repressive force" of the proletarian State, the dictatorship of the proletariat, supersedes the "special repressive force" of the bourgeois State, the State will not yet have "withered away." This process, Lenin tells us, will only commence, and then "inevitably," when exploitation of the masses, with the resulting want and poverty of the masses, has been removed; for the fundamental social cause of those "excesses" which might require machinery for their suppression will have been removed. To discover how this withering process is to be brought about we must descend to mysticism. Marx was silent as to withering. Engels says only that "the State is not 'abolished,' it *withers away*." Lenin himself has no clear conception as to how Engels thought this was to happen.

"With the removal of this chief cause [i.e., exploitation of the masses], excesses will begin to '*wither away*,'" Lenin tells us in discussing Engels' proposition: "We do not know how quickly and in what succession, but we know that they will wither away. With their withering away, the State will also *wither away*." Is the wish father to the thought?

In another passage, in speaking of the "higher phase" of Communism when each shall render according to his ability and each receive according to his needs, Lenin says: "Consequently, we have a right to speak solely of the inevitable withering away of the State, emphasizing the protracted nature of this process and its dependence upon the rapidity of development of the *higher phase* of Communism; leaving quite open the question of lengths of time, or the concrete form of withering away, since material for the solution of such questions is *not available*." Again he says, "it has never entered the head of any Socialist to 'promise' that the highest phase of Communism will arrive." In other words, the intermediate period of proletarian dictatorship (which is in the hands of the bureaucracy) will terminate when, as, and if the "higher phase" of Communism is achieved. But no promises, mind you—nothing is promised. Meanwhile, the proletarian state will enforce that solidarity and suppress those deviations which the "armed workers" (temporarily disarmed) will eventually suppress; that is, if the higher phase arrives.

Here we have no promise of the millennium, no certain course of faith and conduct through which to achieve the City of God, but there is at least the hope of a millennium when the world will be free of repressive States. And the hope of a millennium has long proved a diversion from too intensive thought concerning earthly purgatories. There is no reason to question the good faith of Lenin and Engels in advancing this doctrine of the withering State any more than to doubt the good faith of Rousseau or St. Augustine. The essential fact is that each in his own vocabulary and according to his own rationale has forged a symbol which has proven itself to be a good weapon in struggle for sovereignty, in the political process.

8

LIBERTY AND FREEDOM

ANOTHER SET of symbolic weapons is Liberty and Freedom. These are arms of the opposition generally and not of the sovereign, except when the latter desires to describe its foes as threatening to violate liberty and freedom. There is no constant conception of either liberty or freedom, the terms being defined to fit the philosophy of protagonists seeking to measure some concrete application of their particular ideology. As John Dewey has pointed out in his *Liberalism and Social Action*:

> If we employ the conception of historic relativity, nothing is clearer than that the conception of liberty is always relative to forces that at a given time and place are increasingly felt to be oppressive. Liberty in the concrete signifies release from the impact of *particular* oppressive forces; emancipation from something once taken as a normal part of human life but now experienced as bondage. . . . Should a classless society ever come into being the formal *concept* of liberty would lose its significance, because the *fact* for which it stands would have become an integral part of the established relations of human beings to one another.

If we are correct in considering political action as a continuing struggle by competing interests for power, there could be no normative, no absolute liberty and freedom unless power somehow became absolute and then at once frozen. For in such hypothetical circumstances, struggle would cease because the sovereign power would be adequate to satisfy all interests in the community; no one would seek freedom from oppression because there would be no oppression; no one would resist because there would be no counterresistance. But such metaphysical liberty does not concern us, except as it forms the core of the Hegelian concept of the State and its function, that "perfect" Prussian State which is the ideological ancestor of those cold-blooded twins, the Fascist and Communist dictatorships. Empirically, the concept of liberty involves potential release, even though that release be postponed. For if no release from oppressive forces were even possible, liberty would be meaningless.

Objectively, that is from the point of view of the sovereign, liberty, in the words of René Demogue, is "nothing but a doctrine of despair; powerless to do better, the state allows everyone to accomplish within a certain sphere what he thinks best for himself and others." For coercion, whether by force or persuasion, though indispensable, is insufficient to achieve its purpose completely by obtaining complete submission to the State.

Subjectively, that is from the point of view of the subject, liberty, says Demogue again, "is a necessarily insufficient tolerance" because the complete satisfaction of one man's interests must frequently, if not inevitably, conflict with the interests of some other man. The art of government is to meet these interests and the demands which they actuate with something less than complete satisfaction, with something less than and different from freedom.

Since the later Middle Ages political opinion has been in open conflict as to whether there can be a "free" government that is not self-government. Those who favored monarchy and absolutism in government have found these forms compatible with freedom. Thus St. Thomas and Bodin found in an absolute king the best sovereign to assure freedom. St. Thomas found it most in accord with the divine plan. In theory it was the plan of the Church. Marsiglio of Padua, Nicholas of Cusa, Tholommeo of Lucca, and others believed in popular government. They followed more or less the Aristotelian principles that a monarchy was not a true "political" government because it has no true "citizens." "There is nothing by which a citizen in the absolute sense is so well marked off as participation in judicial power and public office," Aristotle had said. He recognized that it was the ruling class which determined the nature of the State and its constitution; that "the supremacy is everywhere in the governing class of the *polis*, and the governing class is the polity," i.e., the "constitution." It is true that the "constitution" meant more to Aristotle than it does to us today, that to him it signified the whole life of the people—secular, religious, and political—all bound up in their city. But for us the important thing is that his state was the picture of its ruling class and that he opposed a supreme monarch, preferring supremacy neither in the very rich nor in the very poor. Virtue in politics as in life was in the mean. Aristotle advises us, however, that virtue is not enough for government: It must be accompanied by the ability to put it in practice. He approves of ostracism for individuals of special merit, who are "themselves a law," who would interfere with putting into practice that virtue which is the mean, the supremacy of the neither very rich nor the very poor.

Ideas of freedom (even as understood by Aristotle, to whom freedom was not essential to a good polity) and ideas of liberty (that child of Reason out of Free Will, as we know liberty) are obnoxious to anyone seeking absolutism. As Machiavelli put it, citing the instance of Pisa after one hundred years of bondage to the Florentines: "He who becomes master of a city accustomed to freedom and does not destroy it, may expect to be destroyed by it, for in rebellion it has always the watchword of liberty and its ancient privileges as a rallying point, which neither time nor benefits will ever cause it to forget."

Unfortunately for monarchs, they had to broaden the bases of their power against the barons and at the same time add to their sources of revenue which the diminishing wealth of land economy could no longer supply in adequate volume. They had to give support to the middle classes—the neither very rich nor very poor—which gave rise to Parliament in the thirteenth century and the Estates-General in the fourteenth century. It is true that these bodies had little power and offered at first only a theoretical vehicle for political expression by the rising middle class—the guild merchants and artisans, the ship owners and professional men. But the impetus toward the "liberty" of Montesquieu, Adam Smith, and John Stuart Mill which was contained in the instrumentality of the very idea of representative government must have been immense.

Laski says that the modern State could not emerge until the universal interest of the community had obtained at least in theory an organ for the protection of its demands against the innumerable and various liberties and franchises which competed against its will. Parliament provided this organ; it provided finally administrative safeguards essential to secure a broader base for "popular rights." The Puritan Revolution was really the implementing of this theory of representative government by the middle class. It was the transfer of power to the middle class from the nobility, of whom the king was chief. Under the Tudors, the nobility had, in their time, in the Wars of the Roses finally reduced the power of the barons and concentrated it in the monarch. True, as Trotsky pointed out, the Puritans put in biblical phrases the symbols of the liberties they were seeking. This was incidental to the adjacence of the Puritan Revolution to the whole Protestant Reformation and resulted from the accident that the Stuarts as high churchmen, sympathizing with—where they did not actually espouse—Roman Catholicism, symbolized not merely monarchical absolutism but also counterreformation. Whether or not one agrees with Ernest Barker that "it was private *conscience*, rather than private property" which was at the root of the Puritan Revolution, it is clear that in the issues as framed it was liberty that was proclaimed most loudly. Thus, when Hampden was found guilty (1637) for refusing to pay the ship money tax levied by the king without the authority of Parliament, the decision was eventually set aside by the Long Parliament not merely because it was contrary to the "rights of property" but also because it was contrary to "the liberty of the subjects, and the Petition of Right." [1]

The American Revolution was a variation on this same theme. It was the extension of the transfer of power from

[1] It was during this struggle that John Milton wrote *Areopagitica*, his great defense of freedom of the press.

the king and his ministers, from the aristocracy to the commercial classes, this time from the holders of royal grants of patent and monopoly for colonial exploitation to local landlords and merchants. In this instance, however, the symbols varied: Liberty was no longer expressed in the King James version but in Locke and Montesquieu and Tom Paine. Liberty—liberty of social compact—liberty of contract; this was the natural sequence of their articulation; it was essential to the fulfillment of the economic development of the Industrial Revolution. The obligation of contract was protected in the body of the Constitution, as were national finance and currency. These were basic to a consummation of the Revolution. But American civil liberties, the Bill of Rights, only came in by amendment on the insistence of Jefferson, who foresaw that a strong Federal sovereign would ignore those principles if it were not committed to them in advance.

After the adoption of the Fourteenth Amendment in 1868, which forbade the states to deprive any person of life, liberty, or property without due process of law, the Supreme Court rulings made it clear that, under the Constitution, liberty meant the right to indulge in cutthroat competition with a bare minimum of government interference and the corollary right to take economic advantage of those seeking private employment. Although it has been customary in "liberal" circles to attack the Supreme Court for this position, the Court was only applying the Utilitarian political principle that that government is best which governs least—a principle which is the political counterpart of the competitive system—and later a current misconception of Darwinism that "survival of the fittest" meant jungle law. But note that sociality, which among men was part of the equipment of survival, also found its way into the decisions of the Supreme Court by recognition of the "police power" through which at times the states could correct the grosser abuses of industry. The Supreme Court cannot be condemned for accepting the fundamental theses of the competitive profit system. Its sin was that it had grown young too slowly, that it was insufficiently pliant, that its responses to new stimuli proved sluggish.

The Supreme Court headed by Chief Justice Earl Warren moved in a direction more harmonious with the needs and sentiments of the defenseless and those subject to discrimination, whether as voters, members of a minority or persons accused of crime. It has vastly widened the concepts of "equal protection of the laws" and "due process of law" in political, social, and economic areas. It has used its great sovereign weapons to protect the common man from oppression by local authorities, as the king's men and the clerical power did in fighting local princelings.

Again, in France, says Trotsky, the revolution "found its expression and justification for the tasks of the bourgeois society, not in texts from the Bible, but in the abstractions of democracy."

These same abstractions were carried over into the French Constitution of 1848, in which citizens were assured an absolute right to civil liberties except as restricted by the "equal rights of others and the public safety." The exceptions were important, for the "rights of others" always present a nice question where economic powers are unequally distributed; and "public safety" is inevitably in jeopardy whenever the holders of sovereign power are seriously threatened, or as in the case of Louis Napoleon, when the confusion of the ruling group gave opportunity to his ambition to seize power. "Each paragraph of the

Constitution," Karl Marx said in *The Eighteenth Brumaire of Louis Bonaparte*, "namely, contains in itself its own antithesis, its own Upper and Lower House, namely, liberty in the general phrase, suspension of liberty in the marginal note. So long, therefore, as the *name* of freedom was respected and only its actual realization prevented, of course in a legal way, the constitutional existence of liberty remained intact and inviolate, however mortal the blows dealt to its *everyday* existence." Of course the "public safety" became threatened, civil liberties were in abeyance—and Louis Napoleon became Emperor: then the Constitution of 1848 was no more.

In Utilitarianism, liberty, and especially the freedom of contract motif, found logical expression. Herbert Spencer even went so far as to say that all coercion of one human being by another is immoral; therefore immorality is inherent in government and is attached to all its functions. The calmer Utilitarians admit that complete freedom is undesirable, if not impossible. So Markby, quoting Spencer's "every man has freedom to do all that he wills provided that he impinges not the equal freedom of any other man," hastenes to say that Spencer meant "every man *ought to have*" such freedom. John Stuart Mill believed that because the State is fallible, the individual knows better than the State what is good for him or what his freedom is. And Bentham taught that since men were fundamentally selfish, each man could be trusted to keep an eye to his own interests; consequently individualism was the inevitable result of the nature of things.[2] Nevertheless, Bentham said that the

[2] See Walton H. Hamilton's study of the development of the doctrine of *caveat emptor, Yale Law Journal*, XL (June 1931), 1133. And see Ihering, *Law as a Means to an End*, p. 100, for the relation of egoism to contract and remuneration.

worst government ever known is infinitely better than no government at all. Freedom? Yes, indeed, but with government; for as Markby maintained, without government half the world would be robbing and murdering the other half. Of course, one might inquire of Sir William whether that is not just what half the world is doing. What other meaning in an ethical sense can there be to *caveat emptor*—let the consumer beware—and sweatshops and the toleration by the middle class (whether commercial, financial, industrial, professional, governmental, or labor union) of the degradation of slum cultures and the relegation of generation after generation to discrimination? Possibly this is a propagandist use of the symbols "murder" and "robbery"—as indeed is Markby's own use of those terms.

This need for police, Markby assures us, "and not the loyalty or affection which we owe to our rulers, is the really strong argument against revolution." This argument assumes that revolution results in no government, which is disproved by the history of Italy, Germany, and Russia since 1917, the American, French, and Chinese Revolutions, and so far as we know, by every other revolution.[3] What the Utilitarians actually feared was not so much the license of one half the world robbing and murdering the other half as a government which would control or limit the freedom of contract, freedom of the nineteenth-century middle-class sovereigns.

At any rate, Liberty as developed by the libertarians of the eighteenth century involved the acknowledgment by

[3] Although, according to a Marxian, the establishment of Fascist regimes in Germany and Italy was not "revolution" because they did not involve a change of "ruling class," the Fascist triumphs were certainly revolutionary in the sense that Markby and other democrats have used the word. Thus the term "revolution" too has its propagandist uses.

the sovereign of specific powers which armed the opposition with political weapons (used in the revolutions of the merchants, artisans, and small landowners in England, France, and America), such as freedom of speech and press, the right of assembly and petition, freedom from search and seizure except for cause shown, and other so-called "civil rights." The argument for such liberties is admirably stated by James Madison, one of the great revolutionary statesmen, in *The Federalist*:

> Liberty is to faction what air is to fire, an aliment without which it instantly expires. But it could not be less folly to abolish liberty, which is essential to political life, because it nourishes faction, than it would be to wish the annihilation of air, which is essential to animal life, because it imparts to fire its destructive agency.

But this liberty, which was the air upon which the middle class and the first phases of industrialism throve, is not conducive to concentrated sovereign power; and so dictators of every class and caste prefer to abolish "air" in exchange for steel and guns.

This does not mean that absolutism is without its theory of freedom to which its philosophers and propagandists do homage. No indeed. They too have ideals of freedom. The ideal of freedom under absolutist rule also found nineteenth-century advocacy, notably among the disrupted and humiliated German states which were searching for a formula to give them power, security, and cultural self-respect. To Hegel the sum of all individual wills was the General Will. This was a new personality, a god without either supernatural powers or halo, over and above the individual personalities—it was the personality of the State. "Nothing short of the state is the actualization of freedom," he said.

All of the rights which an individual may have he gets from the State; consequently he could have no rights in conflict with the State (again, of course, the theory of absolute sovereignty). Joad, in his *Modern Political Theory*, commenting on these ideas, has said:

> It is difficult to escape the conclusion that the attribution of a "real" will to the individual which is necessarily and always in accord with the general will in which it is merged, is only a device for giving an appearance of justice and democracy to what must otherwise appear the purely arbitrary and tyrannical acts of a sovereign state. The absolutist theory of the state is in fact inimical to individual freedom, because, whenever a conflict occurs between an individual and the state, it takes the view that the latter must inevitably be right.

In antithesis to the Hegelian conception of freedom and in contempt of Utilitarian Liberty is the doctrine of the Communists, that there can be no freedom while there are classes—that is, groups other than the mass of the entire people holding sovereignty through economic power. To them the State has no function in the preservation of freedom. On the contrary, in the words of Engels in his letter to Bebel:

> Since the state is only a temporary institution which is to be made use of in the revolution in order forcibly to suppress the opponents, it is perfectly absurd to talk about a free, popular state: so long as the proletariat needs the state, it needs it not in the interests of freedom, but in order to suppress its opponents; and when it becomes possible to speak of freedom, the state as such ceases to exist.

It will "wither away."

It is not for us to pass judgment now as to which if any

of these conceptions of freedom are sound or desirable or even possible. The point is that like other political concepts they are not absolute but are propagandist. Men have given of their strength and their substance in support of liberty and freedom as by them at the moment defined. They have found inspiration in these ideals to resist autocracy, one sovereign group succeeding another to a realization of its needs and demands to which the label of freedom has been pasted. In no other field of political struggle can it be more aptly said that one man's meat is another's poison.

9

EQUALITY

WE ARE all born equal in our inability to sustain our own lives. We are physically, mentally, and socially unequal to those who were born ahead of us. We depend upon far more powerful beings who nurture us, guide us, and protect us. We are dependent for physical care and are subordinated to our elders in the process of acculturation. Dependence and subordination are not equality.

We later seek equality, at least equality with those of our generation, though we are still dependent on our elders. We attempt to gain acceptance by those who have authority—power over rewards and punishments. We suffer from their rejection of us. We resent treatment which may make us appear less grown up than others. We regard it to be a form of rejection. On the other hand, we resist accepting others younger than our own peer group as our equals, and, indeed, because we have different experience and perceptions, we and they can never be equals.

At the same time we seek special treatment. It appears to us we are rejected when we are treated identically with our brothers and sisters or classmates or fellow workers. We want to be treated not just as equals but as something special. Though we may learn to accept identical or similar treatment, we want our particular attributes consciously recognized and respected, not to be an undifferentiated one of hundreds in a classroom, factory, or army. We each want other I's to pause and listen to our own personal I.

As children—and less frankly, frequently as adults too—what we ask of others is instant and complete attention to our expression of our own personalities and the satisfaction of our needs. As children we do not want equality with other children in the love of our parents and their ministrations to us; and as adults we do not want equality with other men in the love of our wives.

When our personality growth is retarded in such a way that we cannot accept our difference from others but regard it as failure and personal rejection ("I'm a failure"), we must submit to authority in the hope of picking up some satisfactory crumbs of acceptance; or we must gain power to bring others to us in search of our acceptance of them. This has been called the "authoritarian personality." This is not egalitarian behavior.

Even people who could not properly be classified as authoritarian personalities tend, when they have authority, to associate with others with authority, while those on a lower hierarchical level, or having less prestige, try to earn acceptance by those with greater authority or prestige. Low-status people who feel they have a chance for upward mobility tend to try to communicate more with people of higher status than with their peers or people of lower status. But low-status people with little expectation of upward mobility tend to feel hostile toward those with greater status and to communicate more with their peers. This also is not egalitarian conduct.

Sometimes we recognize that certain relationships of equality are necessary for satisfaction, for a more self-respecting and mutually respectful form of acceptance. This recognition of the value of equality may, however, be only intellectualized. It may have no emotional acceptance. It may not be translated into behavior. As an intellectual concept it is often expressed by the authoritarian—"We're all one big happy family" or "anyone can get to the top if he works hard."

The concept of equality is used as a power weapon in the political process and in economic struggle. It is a formula for leveling. But because in the name of equality we may strive to raise our own level or to level others down to ourselves, it does not follow that we are willing to raise others to our level. Rather the demand for equality is used as an attempt to gain reassurance by achieving power equal to (or even greater than) that of others. When utilized as an instrument of power there is a tacit acknowledgment that no equality exists, that is, one is either inferior to or superior to the adversary.

In every relationship there is a tendency for one or more members of a group to be a leader, to exercise or possess authority. This may occur on an institutional or an interpersonal basis. The mayor, the president of a corporation or labor union, a department store floorwalker, and a teacher have institutional authority. This is legitimized authority. Authority goes with the role and is so accepted by the authority himself and, with limitations, by those subject to it. Where it is not legitimate, as when someone seizes the authority role, there is resistance extending from noncooperation to counterrevolution. The informal organization of factory workers has its own leadership on an interpersonal basis. This may be considered legitimate authority of an ad hoc nature so far as those in the informal organization are concerned. The difference between institutional and informal leadership is in the nature of the power to create rewarding and punishing situations for subordinates, not in the degree of leadership or the method of the selection of the leader. Interpersonal, informal leaders have authority because other members of the group recognize in them special capacity to represent the group's experience, expectations, and goals. With such a leader they can identify, and by identifying with him can feel acceptance and security.

Situations may change authority roles and cause the subordinate to be accepted as the leader. It was found, for example, that when bomber crews were shot down it was not necessarily the commanding officer—the legitimized authority—who was accepted as leader but a subordinate who could better meet the needs of the situation.

Power is a barrier to relationships of equality. Where power exists, relationships tend to focus about the power situation. When you are a parent or teacher you may want to be like the children (and be liked by them); you may say "I act just like one of the children," but you don't and they know you don't. Age, experience, strength, and authority are blocks. Age difference itself is a barrier because difference of experience is implicit and because to the younger the older generation symbolizes strength, authority, and power. Nor can the boss be "like one of the men." He can still reward and punish, and although he may not do so the possibility that he might reward or punish action, or make a relationship rewarding or punishing, remains in the back of everyone's mind as a divisive fact. It is at least unconsciously an admission of inequality. The same is true of teacher and student, the disparity of authority being generally fortified by a disparity in age. Consciously there is an economic barrier. Generally a hierarchy of salary scale exists so that it is deemed improper for one with a lower salary to direct someone with a higher salary, or to be on an organizational level of equality.

Otto Kirchheimer reminds us that "During the course of the last decades, workers have learned that increasing material benefits and a much greater amount of social security were not accompanied by greater equality on the job." Nor for that matter do they attain equal acceptance socially by those with larger incomes or more education. This is as true in socialist as in capitalist societies.

Much of inequality is subjective, the psychological reaction to the threat of power applied. When one is anxious that someone with power to do so may withhold, reduce, or not increase remuneration, or when one is fearful that force may be applied to one's person or to someone one loves, then one feels unequal. One feels unequal although such threats may never materialize. The fact that they are imagined as possible of itself may cause one to feel subordinate.

The subtle nature of this quality of inequality is evidenced by the fact that people are anxious not only because rewards and punishments may be administered by those in authority, i.e., those who possess power to reward and punish. This anxiety also extends to rewarding and punishing situations arising out of interpersonal relations, although no member of the group may be seized with authority to reward or penalize. One's peers, for example, might withdraw their favor and reject one, thereby denying equality. Consequently we find people avoiding the dangers of taking positions or acting in such a way as may invoke ostracism or humiliation, imprisonment or death. Even high Soviet officials and old Communists dared not take positions disapproved by Stalin, nor did Nazi leaders (with few exceptions) risk questioning Hitler's orders. Often labor union members have been removed or threatened with removal from the roles of unions for opposing their leaders; school teachers cautiously avoid controversy; and ambitious young bankers imitate their officers' dress and manners. "Play it safe," "Don't stick your neck out," "When in Rome (or the organization) do as the Romans do."

So long as they can share experience, expectations, and goals, there is a kind of equality acceptable among peers. But at best it is a *quasi*, unstable equalizer. It is always vulnerable to anyone who steps out of line to seek advancement (inequality), or it may become unbalanced by one who wants to inquire into how things are working or explore or seek new means, new adjustments in an existing bureaucracy. New relationships upset the equilibrium and foster new feelings of inequality and equalitarian demands.

What we want and can to a great extent obtain is freedom from autocratic, arbitrary authority. What we want to do and to a great extent can do is to share with others our ideas and join with them in their efforts to achieve some end. We can share some experiences and expectations and participate jointly to achieve specific goals. These can be highly generalized, as when a nation wants to defeat the enemy in war, maintain a high standard of living, or protect a city against a flood. There may be equality in such shared experiences, expectations, and goals.

Such equality may, however, be largely verbal. The

achievement of a higher standard of living may mean to some their exploitation of others, monopolistic practices, and autocratic administration. The concept of equality itself may be shared as an experienced fact or goal only on a verbal basis. People who would resent as unpatriotic or even "Communistic" a slur on the Declaration of Independence or a denial of the perfection of American constitutional order might be unable to accept the equal rights of Negroes or of pacifists or other dissenters whose equality is declared in the one document and guaranteed by the other.

It is on a more personal or intimate basis that equality is generally found in shared experiences, expectations, and goals. In love relationships, in personal friendships, and in informal groups among fellow workers or students there may be equality because they already possess or develop among themselves similar experiences, expectations, and goals. Above all, in such cases, there are no threatening power differences.

In other relationships—such as relationships among strangers or competitors or with people on a lower power or economic level—there is little desire to be equated. Who wants it said that he equals someone else: Tom = Dick = Harry or Mary?

We all want to receive different treatment because each of us is a distinctive person. And the probability is that most of us need someone upon whom we can look down to compensate us for the indignities we suffer. It is recognized that the strength of the feeling that Negroes must be kept subordinate long issued from the need of the "poor whites" of the South to have scapegoats, and more recently from the need of the lower middle class to feel themselves better than the slum dwellers. The middle class fear that association by them or their children with the people or children of the slums will contaminate them by subjecting them to language and emotional behavior not acceptable to them, or which they have sloughed off as they rose in socio-economic and educational status. When people, Kirchheimer said, have "reached a certain plateau . . . their psychological investment in this position must be defended against the more unfortunate classes."

We say that in a democracy all people are equal before the law, must be treated without favoritism, and must have equal opportunities. These are some of those fine generalizations about equality that stand up well in the realms of rationalization and ethics. But would we not really like the judge to lean our way, and when we go to court have a judge who has already rendered opinions pointing in the direction we wish him to go? When people feel they have influence, is there any land in which they would not like to be favored over their competitors for appointment or promotion or admittance? Equal opportunities? Yes, but my son and daughter are so bright (and I was a classmate of the dean) that they ought to have *un*equal opportunity.

Not only do we usually not want equality, but we do not expect it. Constitutionally any American-born child can become President of the United States. Any youngster in the Soviet Union has presumably the right to rise in the Communist Party ranks to First Secretary. But not many adults believe they have a chance even if they were to perform all the essential rituals. Nor do we who do not hold high place in the hierarchy of the sovereign power expect to match the sovereign in the power of our weapons. The same limitation of expectation is true in industry and education and the civil service.

What we want is not to be hurt by inequality, by the

use of authority in an arbitrary manner, or be humiliated. So equality before the law, elimination of favoritism, and equal opportunity are slogans in the power struggle evoked by those who feel the need for protection because they cannot sway the judge, obtain a civil service appointment, or get their children into college except on their merits. *Thus equality emerges as a weapon with which people fight against the inequalities forced upon them when they dare not venture a society in which each member pushes for the inequality he longs to have.*

Equality is a yardstick by which society—that is, people in their many interrelationships—measures the strength of autocratic power. It is reassuring to most of us that to the extent that "everyone is somebody, then no one's anybody." Therefore, under such banners as "Liberty," "Fraternity," and "Equality" we place roadblocks to the progress of autocracy. This is to the good because it satisfies a need for defense against aggression. Some institutions, too, such as equality in the polling booth, afford a legitimized opportunity to express hostility toward authority, a sort of nose-tweaking by secret ballot, the safety-valve anonymous.

The safety valve functions of institutions are vital to a healthy society. They can canalize aggressions to useful ends or to backwaters of splinter parties and sects. Aggressions need to be handled in some such way to avoid their accumulation and discharge by scapegoating or other destructive action. That is why in some countries the atomization of political parties recurs. That is why—finances permitting—voluntary organizations exist in such large numbers to push for equality and other rights against the autocratic drives in government and the ready tyranny of majorities.

As a yardstick the concept of equality does not create equality, but it can measure deviations from normative equality. More than that, it is a measure of power relationships in and among groups, organizations, and nations.

Nor do safety-valve institutions establish equality between those in authority and those who are subordinate to their authority. People may even have put themselves in subordination to authority, as by election of officials to positions of power. Such safety-valve institutions do, however, tend to limit the arbitrary and overly aggressive, the violent, uses of power.

Even if "equality of opportunity" be an unlikely achievement, the opportunity to participate in planning *and appraisal* has been demonstrated to result in better production by bringing out more common experience, expectations, and goals among those in authority and their subordinates. These results come about because the gap of inequality is narrowed at least to the extent of participation—if it be real, not merely lip-service participation. This results in a greater sense of acceptance of management by workers, of subordinates by those with power. The reaction to feeling perceived and accepted is reduction of hostility, lowering that great bar to equality. Moreover, such a sharing of experience, expectation, and goals makes possible continued acceptance by one's peers at the same time that there is interpower-level acceptance. This reduces the anxiety barrier.

Interpersonal acceptance is after all a symbol of interpersonal love which can be a relationship of true equality and which we certainly tend to idealize as such. Those institutions and procedures, consequently, which tend toward a greater degree of mutual acceptance tend toward greater relative equality. But it would be a mistake to suppose that mutual acceptance in one situation could necessarily carry over the same degree of equality to a different situation. Men may share as equals in a work relationship and nevertheless regard themselves as unequals socially, intellectually, and in virtue. For we expect of ourselves and others different behavior in different roles.

Finally, to arouse unrealizable expectations of equality can upset the balance of power. When the Supreme Court in *Brown v. The Board of Education of Topeka* held that segregated education was not equal education and required desegregation "with all deliberate speed," it was stating a truth, a just principle, and a democratic goal. It was also arousing expectations which could not be satisfied "with all deliberate speed." It was building hopes which when not promptly realizable turned to disillusionment and anger—hopes, disillusionment, and anger which spread to other areas in which equality was denied, areas in which because of its very nature equality could not be realized. Nevertheless, without this weapon of expectation put in the hands of minorities by the Supreme Court, progress against discrimination and prejudice would have been slow, it would have occurred "with all deliberate" sluggishness.

Unrealizable as equality may be, psychologically and objectively, it is a battle flag with which to arouse the passions and loyalties of partisans against the arbitrary and self-aggrandizing uses of power, a creed which can force sovereigns to listen to and hear the voices of those whom they have not heard or seen. But the power rallying around a battle flag must create a new disequilibrium, or emphasize an old, and stress discrepancies between equalitarian norms and the realities of inequality.

10

THE POLITICAL PROCESS

IT IS well to keep in mind in discussing sovereignty that the State, which is an agency of sovereign power, the wielder of the thunderbolts of sovereignty, is never static and that the word "state" itself has the meaning of temporary condition. The State is like a scale that is never stationary and never in balance; and the political process is similar to the attempt of a man to balance such a moving scale. Put in another way, the sovereign must continually measure its powers against those of possible opponents, it must count the weapons in its armory, and judge the skill of its adherents against that of its rivals; it must trade and deceive and fight to retain its dominance. It can tolerate no near equal if it is to survive.

POWER

The maintenance of power is the grim theme of all sovereignty, not merely because there are rival interests ready to snatch the power, but because subjectively the sovereign is unable to yield except under compulsion unless he is prepared for complete surrender. For to one who is in a position of power the loss of that power is psychic death; any diminution of power may arouse fantasies of a failing manhood; and this symbolism accounts for the reluctance of sovereigns to accept modifications of the status quo which at times appear to others to be inevitable.

"Power is like the Medusa's head. Whoever has looked on her countenance, can no longer turn his face away, but remains for always under her spell. Whoever has once enjoyed the intoxication of holding sway over his fellows, can never thenceforward renounce it altogether." Stefan Zweig says in his *Joseph Fouché*. If the King of the Wood, for example, were to say "Let this one slave break off the golden bough; it will be time enough to fight him afterward," he would be yielding to a psychological softening on his own part and granting to the slave not only a legal warrant to fight for the priesthood in accordance with the rules of succession but also a distinct psychological advantage. A sovereign must have self-confidence even when the country as a whole has lost respect for and faith in its sovereign. He can continue to rule for a time if he has faith in himself, but no ruler can continue in power who does not believe in himself.

Although a sovereign may be no autocrat, although government officials may not be legally vested with bureaucratic powers, the mere possession of power over others, "the intoxication of holding sway over his fellows," tends to corrupt the possessor of that power. "This or that despicable minister might have been an excellent man, if power had not been given to him," Kropotkin said. "It is a commonplace of history that power is poisonous to those who exercise it. . . . The special vice of every historic system of government has been its inevitable tendency to identify its own private good with the public welfare," Laski wrote. And in the same vein Aristotle warns us that "even the best of men in authority are liable to be corrupted by anger."

THE CONFLICT OF INTERESTS

Consequently, even if all other interests in society were otherwise in equilibrium, even if there were no other conflicting interests—a felicitous condition unknown to history—*the very fact that one person had power over another*, as a straw boss or superintendent must necessarily have over a worker, *would cause pressure which would set in motion the political process and involve the use of political weapons in one or another form*. "The inference to which we are brought is, that the causes of faction cannot be removed," Madison said in *The Federalist*. On the one side will be the interests suppressed or offended seeking recognition, and on the other the suppressing or offending sovereign power resisting the pressure of the very forces which it may itself have raised.

It has been frequently pointed out that rulers breed the difficult situations which they often cannot solve and which eat into their vitals. Thus the problems of the serf have come to plague all states built upon feudal systems and the tradesmen have harried and clipped the monarchies which had built them into an army against the powerful landowners; and the industrial workers, the proletariat, are threatening the industrial system which created them, not often with overt rebellion but frequently with disinterest, ennui, irresponsibility.

But it is not only this psychological tendency of persons in power to swagger, to enrich themselves or to bully others (the arrogance of power, as Fulbright calls it), which creates pressure groups; it is not only the desire of the sovereign to amass the means of self-preservation which causes the sovereign to apply pressure. These activities result from the circumstances in which people are placed by unfulfilled needs and the possession of one or more weapons to fight for the satisfaction of those needs by those who possess the means for satisfying them. Thus Trotsky observes:

> Antagonistic classes exist in society everywhere, and a class deprived of power inevitably strives to some extent to swerve the governmental course in its favor.

This is the same conclusion reached by James Madison:

> From the protection of different and unequal faculties of acquiring property, the possession of different degrees and kinds of property immediately results; and from the influence of these on the sentiments and views of the respective proprietors, ensues a division of the society into different interests and parties. . . .
>
> But the most common and durable source of factions has been the various and unequal distribution of property. Those who hold and those who are without property have ever formed distinct interests in society. Those who are creditors, and those who are debtors, fall under a like discrimination. A landed interest, a manufacturing interest, a mercantile interest, a moneyed interest, with many lesser interests, grow up of necessity in civilized nations, and divide them into different classes, actuated by different sentiments and views. The regulation of these various and interfering interests forms the principal task of party and faction in the necessary and ordinary operations of the government.

In a prophetic passage, Daniel Webster described the political struggle between conflicting economic interests in this manner:

> The freest government, if it could exist, would not be long acceptable, if the tendency of the laws were to create a rapid accumulation of property in few hands and to render the great mass of the population dependent and penniless. In such a case, the popular power must break in upon the rights of property, or else the influence of property must limit and control the exercise of popular power. Universal suffrage, for example, could not long exist in a community where there was great inequality of property. The holders of estates would be obliged in such case either in some way to restrain the right of suffrage, or else such right of suffrage would ere long divide the property.

This is well illustrated by the patterns of land ownership, suffrage, and autocracy in Latin America, the Arab states, and Vietnam.

Certain political philosophers have argued that the evils of political power can be eliminated by the abolition of organized government. Thus it is stated in *The Communist Manifesto*: "Political Power, properly so called, is merely the organized power of one class for oppressing another." It is argued that "the public power will lose its political character" if class distinctions are abolished by placing the means of production in the hands of the whole people. In anarchist thought the abolition of the State is to be desired in order to avoid the compulsory associations which require force for their maintenance and which prevent such free associations into natural groups as will insure richer and more harmonious living. These theories cannot thoroughly be discussed here except to note that there are other inequalities in the world in addition to those of an economic nature and other forces than State violence, all of which is admitted in Marxian philosophy. If this be so it is difficult to see how either Communist or anarchist utopias can be achieved while any political weapons, propagandist as well as economic and physical, remain outstanding, that is, are not incorporated in an all-inclusive ruling group with unified interests. (See discussion of the withering state in Chapter 7.)

The use of power for the personal ends of the sovereign which brings political pressure is, then, not merely the conscious use of power, but is generally the unintentional resultant of those economic and social forces which the sovereign power releases. In other words, each action of the ruling group brings about some reaction among other parts of the population which in turn demands further compensating action from the rulers. As a consequence the pressure of changing conditions is not uniform and the disequilibrium is emphasized. "Not all parts of our organization are changing at the same speed or at the same time," says the report of the Research Committee on Social Trends in the United States: "Some are rapidly moving forward and others are lagging. *These unequal rates of change in economic life, in government, in education, in science and religion, make zones of danger and points of tension.* It is almost as if the various functions of the body or the parts of an automobile were operating at unsynchronized speeds. Our capacity to produce goods changes faster than our capacity to purchase; employment does not keep pace with improvement in the machinery of production; interoceanic communication changes more quickly than the reorganization of international relations; the factory takes occupations away from the home before the home can adjust itself to the new conditions. The automobile affects the railroads, the family, size of cities, types of crime, manners and morals." (Italics mine—J.M.) The resulting friction at the "points of tension" calls forth the political process, the struggle for power among the possessors of political weapons whose interests are brought into conflict.

The balance of sovereign power is continuously unsettled—often precariously. To maintain near equilibrium it is necessary for a sovereign to know the values, expectations, and perceptions that give urgency to opposition pressures. Serious confrontation is to be avoided, but without sensitivity to the nature of opposition it cannot be avoided. Once there has been confrontation either by violence or by freezing positions, then when either party increases pressure the other also tends to escalate. Lewin's Force Field Theory is relevant here. Under this theory escalation can be avoided and the forces of confrontation reduced either by diminishing or diverting an opposing force. Such a tactic is usually available to all factions. An example of diminishment is social security, now regarded as an instrument of democracy (or socialism) but instituted in the 1880s by Bismarck to reduce the growing strength of socialism against the Hohenzollern autocracy. An instance of diversion is involving opposition factions (or potential opposition) in hostility toward a foreign power or a minority group within the country. Anti-Semitism has provided such a diversion for two millennia.

POWER VACUUM

It is not uncommon for the exercise of power to be withheld. This may be because the sovereignty does not feel capable of dealing effectively with a problem. At various times in all lands from the Irrawaddy to the Mississippi, on the Russian steppes, in the Italian Renaissance cities and in Sherwood Forest, robber bands have flourished undeterred by sovereign states. In no modern country are the police capable of enforcing all the multitude of laws and ordinances. Power is then selectively withheld.

A problem may not be apparent or precise enough for the State to take action. Conflicting interests may not have demonstrated which is more profitably to be supported. Shall it be producer or consumer interests? Or possibly there is an indolence or hedonism, a conception that the momentum of life will not be interrupted by challenging forces. This was the prevailing attitude of the court of the Bourbons before 1789. For whatever cause the exercise of sovereign power is withheld, the vacuum will be filled. It is as though inaction were a grant of power to others. The doctrine of laissez faire was such a grant to entrepreneurs, finance capitalists, and industrial management in Europe and America. Today, when the doctrine of laissez faire is no longer an accepted principle of statesmanship, its chief beneficiaries still enjoy some of its rewards because the State had not seen fit or felt powerful enough to restrict them further. Berle has demonstrated that a number of corporate practices today, in effect, deny men the "equal protection of the laws." Job mobility may be restricted by the forfeiture of retirement rights provided by great corporations or by the arbitrary rules of labor organizations which tie men to the corporation or to the union. Negroes may be denied jobs or insurance. In fact the power of insurance companies to deny or cancel insurance policies may make it impossible for a man legally to drive a car and so deprive him of available jobs. "The computer can erect walls, unbreakable though invisible. It may block a man in any number of directions . . ." Here State inaction amounts to permissive law that denies equal protection, equal opportunity.

CONCILIATION AND COMPROMISE

In the initial stages of the power struggle, opposition to the dominant interests is by protest propaganda and by economic resistance, which may be accomplished by such things as failure to pay taxes or the institution of boycotts, or even unconsciously, as when underfed labor is unable to give maximum production. In these circumstances the sovereign power propitiates, it compromises, and in this process it too utilizes economic power and propaganda of its own. Physical power appears principally in its symbolic form as law. "It is well indeed," Dicey says in *Law and Opinion in England*, "to note that the public opinion which finds expression in legislation is a very complex phenomenon, and often takes the form of a compromise resulting from a conflict between the ideas of the government and the feelings or habits of the governed."

The phenomenon of compromise is described by René Demogue, the common-sense French legal philosopher, in a luminous passage in which he discusses Tarde's theory of opposition. André Tarde had said in his *L'Opposition Universelle*:

Whatever be the method employed to suppress the conflict between beliefs and interests and to establish an accord between them, it almost always happens . . . that the resulting harmony has created a new variety of antagonism.

Demogue expanded on this theme. Frequently he said, adversely affected interests are important, though they may not be equal to the protected interests; and these adverse interests persist. Because of this and because men more readily recognize the evils from which they suffer than the advantages which profit them, a need for change results. This develops slowly at first because of hostile interests, of the difficulty of disturbing routines and of the force of imitation, "but it is the beginning of an evolution which follows the line of least resistance." The result is often no better than what was; thus new movements come into being and "we notice sometimes a curious backward trend, though with improvements on the past" (or at least with modification of that past). Ideologies, "the movements of ideas," can rarely be driven to their extreme limits, because they are opposed by "irreconcilable" ideas which though not of equal value "cannot be reduced to nothing." The technique or art of the reconciliation of adverse interests is susceptible of prolonged development, through "measures better adapted to the end pursued," says Demogue. Evolution is not "recti-linear," he continues, but is "a series of unfortunate attempts, more or less successful, to make conceptions without doubt largely irreconcilable get along together."

Compromise has dual aspects. It is not only the act of the sovereign in temporizing with the opposition; it is not merely a purchase of peace by the dominant interest. For to the opposition, compromise may be a sapping of the strength of the ruling power, a chiseling away of that power. To both parties it is essentially a maneuver for strategic position without actual engagement in combat. The interest seeking relief nevertheless attempts to gain some particle of the substance of its demands and the sovereign tries to yield only the form. In general the sovereign is more successful, having the weight of political weapons on its side. Those rights or privileges which were conceded by medieval law to the small farmer and the serf were usually meaningless because there were not sanctions sufficient to enforce them. Nor have states in which powerful industries have preponderated enforced uniformly laws intended to protect laboring people. Minorities have been denied rights and privileges to which by law they had been entitled because the authorities have been supported in these denials by majorities or other, more powerful groups. Corruption and political influence have again and again prevented the enforcement of the tenement house laws and the building codes in cities like New York. The weapons of opposition must therefore have greater power to achieve actual enforcement of such laws by the sovereign and faithful compliance by interests adversely affected than is necessary to obtain the mere verbal approval of demands.

The occasions are rare in which interests are sufficiently powerful in the modern state to carry their program in one offensive against the resistance of other interests affected by that program. Moreover, the results of political struggles are always to some extent compensatory and the reward of a friendly interest here and the punishment of an inimical interest there will generally create a new antagonism to the dominant power or strengthen an old one. "Solutions satisfactory to one cannot help violating the desires of another, so we are forced to use empirical methods: to weaken opposition by creating a public spirit in various ways such as by watching publications or schools; the end is hidden, the proposed solutions are toned down; little by little they are carried. This is politics with its ruses and its methods that are so often called immoral," says Demogue.

THE DIALECTICS OF POWER

It is clear that as one problem is rectified another is produced, for the sovereign, in giving powers and privileges to one group, changes the balance of power, reduces those of another faction or must surrender them himself or in some other way disturb the existing equilibrium or interrupt the social rhythm. It is true that such action is commonly followed by a process of limitation of the grant or evasion of its terms, and by the use of all political weapons available to those interests which have been adversely affected by the sovereign's action, to restore that *status quo ante* which history shows can never be restored. Thus where courts of law exist, they have an important function to interpret and restrict legislative and administrative innovation in order to temper the severity; and as the judges must generally gauge and describe the new by accepted standards and by words of art their tendency is toward conservatism if not toward reaction.

These oscillations, this consistent rhythm of contradictions, this resistance, concession, and minimizing by the dominant power; and battle, achievement, and retrogression by the successful opposition (with the occasional overthrow of the sovereign and the reversal of roles) are the dialectics of power, the earnest political discourse without words. As Walther Rathenau pointed out: "A constant warfare has existed between the individuals wielding power, in whatever form, and the subjects of that power. Just as there is a continuous desire for power, so also there is a continuous desire to make that power the servant of the bulk of the individuals it affects." That is to say, those who are adversely affected by power attempt to limit that power or bend it in a direction favorable to them.

As we have already seen, compromise, which is the daily technique of sovereignty, can be of two varieties. For one or both parties to the power struggle it can mean the saving of face and the achievement of nothing but the evasion of a conflict; or it can mean that one combatant, regardless of the picture and conscious only of the realities, makes out of compromise a stride toward greater power. This was the sense in which Lenin approved of compromise. Obviously both parties cannot be triumphant in such a situation (except when avoidance of conflict may be deemed mutually advantageous); they cannot both attain fifty-one per cent of the battle for power (although each may calculate that it has); and it is in such a crisis, when neither will concede power to the other, that physical force is called upon in the political process. This is the situation when the State resists rebellion and also when it enforces its law against one who has violated the law or otherwise becomes subject to its sanctions. But consider the possibility that compromise need not have a win-lose result where one party triumphs and the other is vanquished. The result may be a win-win resolution which is creative of new positive relationships. (See further discussion, Chapter 14.) This will depend in large measure on the expectations of the parties to the conflict or the skill and initiative of a third-party mediator.

THE USES OF FORCE AND PRESTIGE

As exemplified in the case of law, the wise sovereign does not call upon its physical force except in extremity but rather prefers to rely upon its prestige, that is, its reputation for power. The prestige of one group as against another is of the greatest importance, because a consciousness of inadequate strength of one party or the belief that superior strength resides in the other is the focal point from which radiate those concessions which make physical conflict unnecessary. This does not mean that violence will not occur even where one contestant realizes the weakness of his position. Such an occasion was the seizure of Harper's Ferry by John Brown. There the success of the raid was less important than the dramatic possibility of stimulating an uprising of slaves. But the use of physical force by one recognizing the weakness of his position is then applied for propagandist purposes, for the creation of prestige or for concentrating attention upon the instigator of violence and his cause. However, force is necessary at times to preserve that reputation for power which makes the actual use of force generally unnecessary. Hawtrey, in his *Economic Aspects of Sovereignty*, has shown this paradox in the international zone, and it is equally true of domestic sovereignty. His text can be paraphrased in this manner: A decline of prestige is an injury to be dreaded. But in the last resort prestige means reputation for strength in physical conflict, and doubts on the subject can only be set at rest by physical conflict itself. A sovereign will fight, will use force, when it believes that its prestige in politics through the symbolism of law is not equivalent to its real strength. Trial by battle is an exceptional incident, but the conflict of political forces is continuous. That is inherent in the political process.

Prestige is gained not only through a reputation for the power to use force, but also for power to pay, to apply economic means in the form of rewards and penalties such as the granting or denial of privileges and opportunities. And there is, finally, the prestige which comes from a reputation for reliability and honesty, keeping one's word; performing agreements or treaties for which the law provides no sanctions; practicing what one preaches; giving full measure in trade and unselfish devotion in services; dealing fairly and rendering honest judgments. This latter form of prestige is the very essence of a stable society under any economy or social system, whether it applies between individuals dealing as equals or as unequals, between sovereigns and those who are ruled, between state and state. It is true that social organization and economic ideology will color the instant definition of reliability and honesty. Trade by bargaining is deemed honest in the Orient but less honorable where the one-price store is the prevailing method of trade. The absence of such prestige for reliability and honest dealing must result in an ambivalent organization of society, and frequent experience of unreliability or dishonesty inevitably gives rise to insecurity and disillusion which bring about antagonistic (sometimes antisocial) attitudes in the individual and, if widespread, create antagonism toward the sovereign group and distrust of the ideology on which it relies. Thus the practices of corporate financiers and the Stock Exchange weakened the faith of the American public in the bases of finance capitalism and made possible New Deal legislation. The failure of President Johnson to give the American people confidence in his statements about the war in Vietnam weakened his support and authority and forced him to seek peace actively instead of by speeches even at the price of foregoing the chance to be reelected president. And the disillusionment of the American Negro in his expectations that laws would assure him equal treatment has stimulated riots and other violence as ways of satisfying frustrated power needs. When the conserving forces of prestige are wasted the sovereignty must be maintained by the expenditure of economic substance or physical force.

Sovereigns evade the use of physical force wherever they conceive it possible to retain power without force, because violence is costly not only in the economic goods which the sovereigns must generally distribute to their adherents and consume on the enemy, but also in the resistance that is built up in adverse interests which cannot be completely destroyed. We have seen how compromise may displace one adversary for another or creates two where there existed one before. Force does the same thing, only with greater dynamics. Thus violent oppression will at times fester until it brings revolution. Revolution leads to counterrevolution. Counterrevolution results in rebellion until both sides are exhausted and defeated, as was the case in so many of the chaotic medieval conflicts for power, or until one interest can establish an acknowledged superiority and dominance. Eventually a new equilibrium is achieved. On the other hand, great political and economic organizations may be broken up into local units, as was the case with the Roman Empire, and intercourse between the units ceases. Thus the number of sovereignties would increase and in a world as industrially complex as Europe and the United States the economy would retrogress.

We have referred to those crises when the use of physical force becomes inevitable for the sovereign because his reputation for power is insufficient to compel compliance by the opposition and because he is unwilling to abandon his sovereignty or concede a diminution of power. In what phases of the political process, on what occasions, do these crises occur?

In the first place they occur when authority has been openly flouted by one or more persons using force or open resistance (including civil disobedience) to a command of the sovereign issued in the form of positive law. In such a case legal sanctions are invoked and the police or sheriff or troops are called upon to uphold the prestige of the sovereign. In this the sovereign power finds general support in the community, at least among those interests in whose benefit the law is phrased, the possessors of those political weapons upon which the sovereign relies. If the sovereign did not exercise power in these circumstances it would risk the displeasure of those interests and thus suffer more by the disorganization which would result from this failure to use such means of law enforcement as were at its disposal than by the exercise of force. Where the gang and the Camorra are not suppressed the sovereign's power is not respected: and in time the gang and the Camorra will be able to sell their power and compete with the sovereign. In American cities thousands of merchants pay tribute (protection money) to gangsters who in turn may be protected against the law by politicians. In recompense the gangster has often aided the politician on election day. A similar condition has existed in Sicily for generations. In such situations the symbolic nature of law as force is ineffectual. From the viewpoint of sustaining sovereign power, if sovereign prestige is to play an effective role in the maintenance of that power, a breach of the law justifies forceful repression in ordinary times.

In the second place crises occur in which the sovereign must use force, when there has been such a breakdown in the ability of the dominant group to give satisfaction to the minimal requirements of other groups that realignment of political forces is threatened. Then there is rioting or rebellion which the government must suppress in self-protection. Where representative government exists, this rebellion is not generally displayed by a resort to force but is usually sublimated in the ballot, as we have already noted, and through elections there may be a change in personnel or the displacement of one parliamentary party by another (virtually a palace revolution). Within limits there can be even a change in ideology, in the approach to political problems. This happened when the agrarian party of Jefferson succeeded the commercial party of Adams and Hamilton and when the bourgeois Liberal Party of Asquith and Lloyd George replaced the Conservative Party, which had been influenced largely by the great landowners of England. Another example is de Gaulle's assumption of the presidency of France on the condition that greater power be vested in the president and less in the faction-ridden Chamber of Deputies. But there is no basic change in ideas in such an exchange of governments, and the dominant interests in the community act through the new technicians of government who for the time being are absorbed into the sovereign group.

As was pointed out, the symbolism of the ballot emerges from the count of spears at the husting. The parliamentary system can be traced to former symbolic practices. An example of this is the medieval revolts of the barons against the king's "wicked advisers." They dared not destroy the anointed king who was sacrosanct; nor dared they destroy the kingship for their powers were derived from him. However, to attack "the wicked advisers was a ritualized form of rebellion and, therefore, a conservative one." This, Rosenthal explains, is because:

> Like most cliques working for their own interest, the barons were anxious to proclaim their innate conservatism, to assure both king and populace that only slight demands were sufficient to satisfy them, regardless of how deep their alienation really went. . . . A direct clash of ideologies was welcomed by neither party.

In constitutional monarchies today, it is not the monarch or chief of state (themselves symbolic officers) but his chief minister and cabinet officers who are attacked and removed, i.e., the "wicked politicians." In the United States it is different because the president has great political powers and every four years he can be deposed by vote of the people; but even here the tendency is to attack his cabinet or other officials.

THE HOLDERS OF THE WEAPONS

For it is true as Trotsky tells us that "in ordinary times . . . history is made by specialists in that line of business—kings, ministers, bureaucrats, parliamentarians, journalists," that is, the weapons of sovereignty are for the most part in the hands of professionals. But it would be an oversimplification of the problem to conclude that sovereignty is therefore vested in officialdom. Nor was it vested in the big landlords alone in feudal times; nor is it in the big bankers and industrialists today. Only a few government officials have the power; the bulk of officeholders, whether elected, appointed, or civil service, in general follow the instructions of their leaders; and these leaders are themselves a shifting group, the influence of each member of which rises, fluctuates, and wanes from issue to issue.[1] Nor is there unanimous agreement among the predominant economic group on current issues; the banker, the landlord, the industrialist, the importer, the railroad man, the shipper has each his day of weight. Nevertheless they are acting within the orbit of the same politico-economic ideology. The use of private property for profit and a governmental machinery which will guarantee such use are keystones of the system upon which all these interests rely, and although one of them may place emphasis on one word and another may underscore a different one they are joined under the same formulae, such as "seizin," "judgment of his peers," "due process of law," or "sanctity of contract." In Communist countries the formulae of the power centers are different in terminology, but they perform the same unifying function.

This amorphous group, official and unofficial, who control the army, police, means of sustenance, and the machinery of propaganda, whether capitalistic or Communistic in ideology, apply the slogans in which the philosophy of their power has been formulated just as long as those slogans can be vitalized. They breathe upon the dying bones

[1] However, it not infrequently happens that there is passive opposition in some parts of the governmental apparatus to decisions of policy made by those in authority with the support of other parts. Opposition results from different special interests and different clienteles of the various organs of large and complex governments.

of revolutionary slogans of the past to rekindle passions against old tyrants and to renew the hosannahs for their downfall. Time magnifies sufficiently the differences to make the new sovereigns appear in essence unlike the "tyrants" of old. "Symbols, when their significance has been great, outlive their first significance," Santayana says.

REVOLUTIONARY CRISES

But from time to time revolutionary periods occur. What is it that distinguishes them? Trotsky says that "a period of revolution, that leaping movement of ideas and passions which seems to the police mind a mere result of the activities of 'demagogues,'" is created by "the chronic lag of ideas and relations behind new objective conditions" to the moment when those conditions "crash over people in the form of a catastrophe." *The chronic lag of ideas on those occasions is due to such causes as 1) the failure to receive feedback or recognize it and react with timeliness to it, so that the behavior of the sovereign power is ineffectively related to new objective conditions; and 2) to the fact the sufficient modification to meet objective conditions would imply the surrender of sovereign weapons of such magnitude that the sovereignty itself would be endangered if not forfeited.* For in such crises reform equal to prevent revolution may need to be revolutionary. But under stress perception becomes distorted, we cannot realistically evaluate what is occurring, and our capacity to solve problems deteriorates. Thus relations too become distorted.

It is the lag of *relations* that is the most important; because it is when the disequilibrium between conflicting interests, that is, when the conflicting interests fail to neutralize each other, becomes so great that a surrender of something less than the dominant power can no longer bring about a balance, that the ideas which are the formulae of the sovereign group cease to function. In other words the ideas of a sovereign group become hopelessly laggard at the moment when their death is threatened, when their vitality must be husbanded for the struggle for life and can no longer be called upon to yield some of their vigor to redefinition and qualification. But in spite of severe deflation of values and the fall in volume of business and employment, the principle of private property remained vigorous in America during the great depression of the 1930s. For new elements entered the sovereign group, labor and the intellectuals, who gave their support to legislation which though it limited free enterprise did not require critical reduction of the power of private finance—capital and industry. After World War II American investment in Western Europe through the Marshall Plan made possible the survival of private enterprise there; the international elasticity of the economic power deflected the trend toward Communism. But on July 4, 1776, the principle of rule by the British Crown could no longer be stretched or split to meet the objective conditions existing in the American Colonies. The satisfaction of each protest of the colonists led to new demands. The substitution of new duties for taxes previously levied and opposed only resulted in the denunciation of all taxes levied by Parliament. Events had moved to that point at which force alone could determine whether the principle was to survive.

A further example is to be found in the events on the threshold of the Civil War. To pacify the slaveowning states, the Republican platform of 1860 assured the nation that slavery would not be disturbed in the states in which it then existed. Lincoln in his inaugural address reiterated this pledge. Thereafter Congress passed a constitutional amendment against the abolition of slavery. It was approved by Lincoln and actually adopted by three states. But the very limitation placed on the extension of slavery into new territory was a defeat to the principle of slavery. It was not economically successful without new lands. The pressure of the ideology of the industrial North and the free-farming West made slavery a recessive principle. The slaveowners and those who had the slaveowning mind, and others who were associated by the propagandist doctrine of states' rights, had to fight to save the central theme of their civilization or watch it perish. It has become popular to refer to the Civil War as the Second American Revolution (see Beard, *The Rise of American Civilization*), but more properly it was a counterrevolution by those already despoiled of power.

It is easy to understand why men who share in the sovereign power cannot as a rule adapt their ideas to such a crisis, why their formulae cannot be restated in the slogans of the opposition (except rarely, as when Edward I accepted the principle of Parliament advocated by Montfort, whom Edward had defeated). If those who hold the power happen to be members of the sovereign group primarily because of their economic power, they cannot switch to such new concepts as will involve the release of their economic power, for such a release of power would *ipso facto* take them out of the sovereign group. Thus the ruling group of France drove Turgot from power in 1776, because to have effected his reforms in taxation and with respect to the peasants, and to have moved to a policy of laissez faire, would have terminated the dying feudal system and Mercantilism. Revolution seemed to be a less likely finale than reform.

If those who hold power share in the sovereignty because of their control of manpower as politicians, they spend their lives evading critical issues and very rarely have either the intelligence or the temper to reverse themselves. A Joseph Fouché, one who can be cleric, Jacobin, Communist, bourgeois, police officer, imperialist, millionaire, and Bourbon, all in a lifetime, is unique. The military commander, professional armies, and police alone of the sovereign group can change their cause and hold their power because their power is not necessarily dependent upon an ideology. They deal in physical force, which is a currency that either opposition or ruler welcomes.

Consequently, when the state of society which we have described has been reached, in which there is no longer any prestige in the sovereign group or any give to its sclerotic ideology, apoplectic reactions occur. These are periods of revolution which in the Marxian sense are the only "true" revolutions. And it is idle to suppose that the opposition can be frustrated or that the transition to a new order can take place without resort to violence and the drawing of blood. It was not accidental that the disputes as to power between the king and barons, between Church and State, between merchants and monarchs (and, where such conflicts have taken place, between proletariat and bourgeoisie—the Commune of Paris, the October Revolution in Russia, the Béla Kun regime in Hungary, for example) were settled by civil wars. It is true that the vote has passed into the hands of laborers and farmers without such bloodshed; that for the most part property is no longer the criterion of the right to vote in Anglo-American governments. But the sovereign groups could afford to grant the demands of the unenfranchised in the nineteenth century; they could relieve the pressure of those interests which wanted democratic government for two reasons—because democratic government was the necessary corollary of Utilitarian freedom with its avowed end of the greatest good for the greatest number and because the economic weapons of industry in the control of the sovereign groups were increasing in power with such rapidity during the same period in which the political weapon of the ballot was being distributed that there was no real sacrifice of power by the grant of the ballot. The sovereign might be something less than dictator, but his power was ample enough to enable him to put over his "economic and political forms upon the whole of society as the only forms possible." The same is true of electoral reform in Western Europe. In most of the new nations created after World War II either there were no threatened power centers to compete with such revolutionary slogans as "democracy," "equality," and "freedom," or the dictatorship of a single party controlled substantially all the weapons of sovereignty.

Now just as sovereignty only passes from those who have held it when they have neither reputation for power nor economic weapons which they can employ, nor force itself, new groups can only achieve sovereignty by acquiring a reputation for strength based upon physical force threatened or applied; and they can only hold what they have gained by arming themselves with economic and propagandist powers, otherwise they would soon waste themselves in fighting. Moreover, without some common ideology, the revolutionists would be divided. There would either result a geographical division of power and the multiplication of small sovereigns in place of one major sovereign, as has been the situation in Western Europe during and since the decline of the Roman Empire; or there would be civil war or an indecisive division of power, as was the case in Russia in the months between the overthrow of the tsar and the triumph of the Bolshevik Party when power was divided between the ministers, the army, the old Dumas, the Soviets, and the masses demonstrating in the streets of the cities. The American Colonies could never have maintained independence of the powerful nations whose colonial empires were close to them, and the French people could not have resisted the restoration of the Bourbons, if it had not been for the unifying and stimulating effect of the seventeenth- and eighteenth-century political philosophers, English, French, and American, who afforded a vigorous and elastic formula for the new sovereigns.

At some point in the political process force must become articulate again, violence must be sublimated into new words and symbols. There must evolve a synthesis of those features of the overthrown culture which are to survive with the hopes of the new masters. The result of this synthesis must be complete enough to contain the explanation and justification of the new political and economic setup. This new ideology does not and need not at once completely unfold to cover every phase of institutional and personal life. For example, although freedom of contract was the philosophical matrix into which nineteenth-century life was set, women have not yet in many jurisdictions achieved full equality in the disposition of their property. "An ideal cannot wait for its realization to prove its validity," Santayana says in his *Reason in Common Sense*. "To deserve loyalty it needs only to be adequate as an ideal, that is, to express completely what the soul at present demands, and to do justice to all extant interests."

The creation of this new ideology, this synthesis of principle and custom, is part of "revolutionary initiative" without which revolutions cannot succeed. It is this that makes the successful revolution an orderly process, though brought about by violence, and not a mere license to freebooters. It was with this in mind that Lenin opposed "anarchistic seizures" of the land by the peasants and favored "an immediate transfer of the land to the peasants with the highest degree of organization possible." "The important thing for us," he said, "is revolutionary initiative; the laws should be the result of it." But without revolutionary energy he believed that the peasants would get neither the land nor the law which would justify their taking the land. It was the mortar of Communist philosophy which permitted Lenin to build successfully in Moscow, it was the absence of any ideology which destroyed Petlura and the other bandit barons in the Ukraine. The reason is clear. Revolutionary ideology, to survive, must give birth to a legal system that bears the brand of the revolution. Mere capricious seizure of power or property without either benefit of legal authority or a new ideology in justification —as a weapon for propaganda—will not insure the stability of the transfer of power. It can be readily reversed, for no one will rally to defend the claim of the trespasser from like seizure. On the other hand, legal sanctions will not spring into being unless the parties interested develop the energy to create legal sanctions to defend their claims. Where the claims are as contrary to existing laws or mores as the seizure of the landowners' property by the peasantry, the energy necessary to establish the new institution against the return of the old must be revolutionary energy—it must be sufficiently powerful to create a new order and defend it against the evicted sovereigns. In such a case the legal sanction must be more than a writ in the hands of a sheriff; it may require the arms of an embattled citizenry, who when triumphant give the force of law to that which was defined as treason.

> Treason doth never prosper; what's the reason?
> Why, if it prosper, none dare call it treason.
>
> Sir John Harington, d. 1612.

II

THE IDEAL OF UNITY

ONE CAN readily understand why unity has been an expressed object of sovereigns. Whatever their conception of the State and the sovereign power may have been, they have invoked the name of unity in attempts to absorb into their State (which has meant into their camp) all separatist movements, all institutions, all powers which were too strong to be destroyed or which it would have been too costly to have rewarded or subjugated.

Unity itself is psychological. It comes from the acceptance of common principles and values. Generally it is attained only by the submergence of differences, of different ends and interests in order to secure joint action for a common interest. The more inclusive the purposes, the firmer the union. The unity of the Allies aiming at the defeat of Napoleon, that of the reshuffled Allies who were joined to defeat Russia in the Crimean War, and that of the once more reshuffled Allies for the defeat of Germany was accomplished by a slight suture which disintegrated once its immediate purpose was attained; for the centripetal interests of the Allies were stronger than their bond. On the other hand the objects of the unity of the medieval

Church, of the Fascist Party in Italy, the Communist Party in Russia, even of the stockholders of the United States Steel Corporation, are more inclusive and the ties within each group are firmer. When persons make any common cause, each willing to make sacrifices for the group, as is the case with the family, they are more surely united than when each joins—as is ordinarily the case in parliamentary politics—for his personal advancement.

The ideal of unity presented by the medieval Church was perhaps the most majestic ever imagined and one of the most powerful sovereign weapons ever exercised. Extending from the Creation to the ultimate Judgment Day, the Christian Epic included in its panoply the heavens, the earth, each princeling, and every miserable serf through all eternity. As a conception of unity this is to Hegel's perfect Prussian State as the great cathedrals are to little village churches; it is as far superior to that Hegelian backwash, Hitler's corporative State, as Mont St. Michel is to an outhouse. Compare, for example, St. Augustine's *City of God* with Hitler's *Mein Kampf*.

The human mind seeking refuge in the simplicity of an all-embracing slogan has struggled with formulae of many varieties, from those of Heraclitus, Parmenides, Aristotle, Lucretius, Aurelius, through those of St. Augustine, St. Thomas, Descartes, Spinoza, Kant, Hegel, James, and Einstein and many others and attempted to apply in politics some derivative of a metaphysical concept of unity.

We cannot here consider specific theories of unity or gauge the merits of mystical as against empirical unity. It is sufficient to understand at this point the enormous cohesive force of unity in political life and its value as a weapon to submerge conflicting interests. The cliché that in unity there is strength, and the moral of Aesop's proverb of the Tiger and the Bulls: "a kingdom divided against itself cannot stand," which was adapted by Lincoln in a crucial moment where a split of sovereign power was threatened, are based on agelong experience.

The very fact that unity of action can inspire self-sacrifice in a common interest, submerge personal conflicts, and thereby release new energies has lent the tint of truth to the Hegelian State in which the General Will is the sum of all personal wills and the personality of the State is a new personality over and above the puny personalities of individuals. "Nothing short of the State," said Hegel, "is the actualization of freedom." Here is a philosophy of unity which degrades man before institution just as dogma has denied at times man's free will to set his earthly home in order. In the Hegelian State the expression of a conflicting interest would be treason, just as a deviation from Church dogma is labeled heresy. In the name of such solidarity, opposition could be ruthlessly destroyed—for the sovereign would be the judge who would give the definition of the "General Will."

The unity offered by Hegel's ideal Prussian State afforded the rationale on which Bismarck flourished Prussian paternalism as a weapon to beat off the threat of German Social-Democracy. It is in the same key as Fascism, although Hegel's all-inclusive State becomes pitifully absurd as expressed in the Aryan credo of Hitler:

> The chief aim to be pursued by a national State is conservation of the ancient elements, which, by disseminating culture, create the beauty and dignity of a higher humanity. We as Aryans can only picture to ourselves the State as the living organism of a nationality which will not only ensure that that

nationality shall be maintained, but also, by continuing to nurture its intellectual and imaginative capabilities, will lead it on to the highest freedom.

The Hegelian concept of the State is, of course, also the ancestor of the Communist State. Marx and Lenin aimed at an ideal unity to be achieved by the abolition of class struggle through the elimination of classes. This, they taught, could be accomplished through the medium of a dictatorship of the proletariat, a sovereignty as all-inclusive and dominating as that Prussian State which was to be the General Will. In contradistinction to the Hegelian State, the dictatorship of the proletariat was in theory to be a temporary phase. Under the Soviet government, the dictatorship of the proletariat has been temporary, momentary, if it could be said to have existed at all, having been succeeded almost at once, under the stress of the counterrevolutionary expeditions and the dynamics of Lenin's leadership, by a factional dictatorship as the instrument of political unity.

The successes of Communism and Fascism have been achieved insofar as the sovereigns have been able to build new group loyalties—to party, to nation, to racial stock, to cooperative, to collective. Facism failed to complete accomplishment in Italy before the ideal of unity preached by the Church and championed by the Vatican. Unity was not achieved in Nazi Germany, for a time at least, because of resistance by the Catholic Church in the south and the evangelical churches in the north and the professional army, each insisting that unity as they understand it did not involve their submergence in the State. Although the authority of Hitler and the State was accepted and internalized by the Nazi Party cadres and government officialdom, it was not accepted by all and high officers such as Roehm paid the penalty for deviance. Where it did not internalize authority, the German public was cowed by the Gestapo and SS, and nevertheless many thousands were sent to concentration camps and thousands were executed. But neither the concentration camps nor the death camps in which millions of Jews and other "non-Aryans" were starved and beaten or murdered were accepted as evidence of opposition but were considered instrumentalities by which to assure unity. How long the semblance of unity would have lasted no one can estimate with assurance, but it is unlikely it would have outlasted Hitler. Nor could Italian Fascism achieve economic solidarity. Even if a balance had been reached, as it has been for extended periods in democratic countries, so that the wages were above the minimum subsistence level and profits sufficient to attract new capital to industry—a balance which has never been achieved under Fascism—a fundamental conflict of interests remained wherever private property was held for profit: the interest of the workers is for the production of goods for wide distribution and consumption, that of the owner of the means of production is for the increase of his capital, that of the entrepreneur for profits. Thus the corporative State of Fascism could not achieve unity, though it attained managerial control temporarily sufficient to define and impose by force an artificial balance between wages and profits. In Spain, workers, students, and the lower clergy have not accepted Franco's imposed unity.

Stalin, too, attempted through terror to create a monolithic state. But the extent of his achievement can be measured by the slave labor camps to which nonconformists were sent and the immediate refusal of the Communist

Party—after his death and that of Beria, the evil man who headed his secret police—to permit anyone else to be the heir to his powers, and finally Khrushchev's exposure and condemnation of Stalin's terrorism.

It is not intended to suggest, in emphasizing the psychological weapon of unity, that united action (or inaction) is attained by the stimulus of theoretical monism alone. Only temporarily at best do people act upon the slogan that "in unity there is strength" unless there is in fact strength behind those urging the slogan of unity. Storm troops, the Red Army, secret police, and the terror and torture have been part of the process bringing about the unification of Italy and of Germany under Fascism and of Russia under Communism. But the ideology of unity, of mass solidarity, has been essential to make a degree of success possible in any State.

During the Roman Empire the conquests of the legions were consolidated by the spread of Hellenistic culture from Transjordan to Britain and by the introduction of the Roman law with its sanctions which were rooted in Rome. The world looked to Rome. The comparative peace which Rome maintained internally caused gratitude in all parts of the Empire and eventually led to the Cult of the Emperor, the deification of the Emperor at Rome as the symbol of a solidary empire: (to the same effect is the "cult of personality" in Communist States, Hitler's Germany, and Franco's Spain.) "The Cult of the Emperor seems from our modern point of view more an expression of political than of religious feeling. It was one of the main props of imperial authority and as such cultivated by Emperors, and by all supporters of the imperial regime." It became "so nearly identical with the imperial authority itself, that a denial of one was felt to be a denial of the other," says McIlwain. The refusal of the Jewish people to recognize this cult and their insistence on observing the first commandment of the Decalogue caused continual friction in Palestine and Alexandria. It was interpreted not as a sectarian preference for a local god but as political disaffection. "Render unto Caesar the things that are Caesar's" was more than a precept distinguishing the sacred from the profane: It was a revolutionary slogan challenging the Emperor as a "present god" and consequently challenging his authority.

"The Jews were a *nation;* the Christians were a *sect,*" as Gibbon has said. As a feeble nation the Jews could be politically destroyed by a mere localized treatment—fire, sword, and dispersion. But as an evangelical sect, the Christians organized a religious association which was at times secret, whose claims were exclusive, which became highly organized, and which though outlawed by the emperors nevertheless multiplied in numbers and grew in proselytizing fervor. It could not be destroyed. Its challenge was a threat to the sovereignty of the emperors. St. Paul's Epistle to the Romans urging obedience to earthly rulers, though they were pagan, is itself evidence that among the early Christians there was a tendency to ignore their sovereigns and refuse to be bound by mundane authority.

When this large body of subjects had been organized, the emperors tolerated and established the Church; they made concessions in return for the acknowledgment of their sovereignty. By act of the emperor, "the peculiar laws and institutions of this religious society are now made coextensive with the state and every member of the Empire from the highest to the lowest brought within the jurisdiction of the constituted authorities of the Christian Church." For a time this unity was harmonious. In the fourth century St. Optatus reminded the Donatists who rejected adverse decisions of the emperors that *the Church was in the State*. As the power of the Church grew and that of the Empire weakened the churchmen made claim to greater authority. St. Ambrose wrote to the Emperor Valentinian II that in matters of faith it belonged to the bishops to judge the Christian emperors, not to the emperors to judge the bishops—"*The Emperor is within the church not over it*"—and that those things which were divine were not subject to the imperial power.[1]

It is a tribute to the psychological vigor of Church unity that for more than a millennium secular rulers provided the sanctions, the weapons necessary for the enforcement of religious uniformity in return for sanctification of their rule. That papal support was a valuable weapon is evidenced by John's appeal to Innocent III. Because of his resistance to the election of the Pope's nominee, Stephen Langton, as the Bishop of Canterbury, the Pope in 1211 released the English people from allegiance to John. After Magna Carta, John made his peace with Rome, and Innocent issued a bull in which he described John's wickedness and repentance, his surrender of England and Ireland, his Crusaders' oath, his quarrels with the barons, the charter which he termed the result of a conspiracy, and he condemned "any agreement of this kind" and forbade the king and barons alike from observing or enforcing it. This was followed by another bull reminding the barons that the sovereignty of England belonged to Rome and that all acts

[1] See R. W. & A. J. Carlyle, *History of Medieval Political Theory*, pp. 148–49, 180–84.

in the kingdom required papal consent. At a Lateran Council, the Pope excommunicated those barons who had persecuted "John, King of England, crusader and vassal of the Church of Rome, by endeavoring to take from him his kingdom, a fief of the Holy See."

When Louis, the son of Philip of France, invaded England at the invitation of the barons, the Pope again interfered, and Philip in reply attempted to reduce the force of the Pope's arguments by proving a defective title in John and a color of right to the English crown in Prince Louis. These men were warrior monarchs. They would not have feared papal decrees or sought the interjection of the Pope against their enemies had the Church's power over the minds of people and over their swords not been immense. (It is difficult for us today to feel the horror of the weapon of excommunication, which deprived the one excommunicated of the opportunity to work and the society of others, unless perchance, he was a powerful nobleman. Moreover, once excommunicated, the believing Christian lost all hope of grace after death.)

For centuries political discussion centered about the right of princes to interfere with the bishops, as in the dispute over investiture, and the right of the Church to dictate to secular authorities. Physical force was largely in the hands of the princes; economic power was divided, but that of the secular rulers was generally greater; nevertheless the most powerful propagandist weapons were with the Church. So long as the doctrine persisted that "society was but one, and the State and the Church alike were only different aspects of this oneness," that all princes held their crowns as "fiefs of the Holy See," sovereign power was not free of the threat of papal and episcopal interference.

Secular rulers could not defy the Church until trade and commerce had so strengthened the burghers that they could give added economic support to the lay rulers and supply new propagandist weapons with which to meet the churchmen. In this lies the political significance of the Protestant Reformation.

We have already seen how in the field of economics the ruling group creates a class of adverse, unappeased interests which can bring about the downfall of that ruling group. We have noticed how in the use of propagandist weapons slogans of liberty which assisted the sovereign group to triumph are thrown into the discard when their sovereignty is in turn assailed. So too the weapon of unity has been blunted in the fight for sovereignty; it has been weakened as a long-term force by the necessities of immediate conflict. Thus it was Church opposition to secular rulers who would not recognize its authority which laid the foundation for the defeat of its own ideal of unity by setting up conscience against law and the individual against his State.

12

DUAL AND PLURAL SOVEREIGNTY

WE HAVE seen that the sovereign is not absolute, that though he can have no superior and no one of equal strength in his domain he is not supreme because the weapons of sovereignty are divided. We have described the political process, the method of compromise, the sublimation of force, and the ultimate resort to violence. We have seen that so long as there are conflicting interests competing for power there can be no true unity, and noted the paradox of sovereignty: that though it seeks to obtain solidarity, its very use of power creates those pressures out of which come the conflicting interests which make unity impossible.

There are other results of the division of political weapons which must be considered. At certain times and places there may be no sovereign. Merely holding the title of sovereign does not make one such; nor is sovereignty coterminous with the jurisdiction which it asserts. Bryce's comment that the Holy Roman Empire was neither holy, Roman, nor an empire illustrated that one of the most grandiose claims of sovereignty was a will-o'-the-wisp, a powerful propagandist weapon of a monarch attempting to appear greater than he was by dressing up like the Caesars. The Holy Roman Emperors were actually only local monarchs.

In Africa some years ago, a tribal chief, Tshekedi Khama, nominally independent, inflicted corporal punishment, probably justifiably, on a white British subject. The British authorities, escorted by troops, tried the chief, whose lands were under British "protection," for this offense and summarily removed him from his office. For all his title of Chief, Tshekedi Khama was no sovereign.

The great modern corporations, like the Praetorian Guards, at times make and destroy governments or determine the policies of governments (see the history of sugar- and banana-growing countries in South and Central America and the relation of the *Comité des Forges* to the French Government before World War II). To that extent their leaders are part of the sovereign group. But this is quite different from saying that because there are spheres in which governments are unable or unwilling to control or destroy property interests, the possessors of those property interests are sovereigns in those spheres in which they are free from interference.

During World War I there was no sovereign of No Man's Land, though treaties had recognized a particular area as French or Russian or Turkish and the guns of the rival armies covered it. Again, in the case of a civil war or revolution there may be no sovereign at a given moment, for the powers of sovereignty may be so dispersed as to give to no group that preponderance of power which amounts to sovereignty. In such circumstances the contending powers create a dual sovereignty—with no one group decisively in control—which is no sovereignty at all. A splendid example of this split of power leaving the ultimate control indecisive is found in the relation of the Soviet to the Provisional government after the first Russian Revolution in March 1917. General Alexieff, Chief-of-Staff, appealed to Guchkov, Minister of the Interior, not to "indulge the Soviet," which exercised power in many ways coextensive with that of the provisional government which it still recognized. To this Guchkov replied: "The government, alas, has no real power; the troops, the railroads, the post and telegraph are in the hands of the Soviet. The simple fact is that the Provisional Government exists only so long as the Soviet permits it."

During the American Revolution and immediately afterward, until the adoption of the Constitution, there was no sovereign whose power extended over all the Colonies. The British crown ruled only where its troops were quartered. Thirteen colonial governments held sovereign power over thirteen separate territories. The Continental Congress organized under the Articles of Confederation was a mere conclave of states. It had no substantial administrative power; its will prevailed only as long as thirteen sovereign entities yielded some of their sovereignty for the cause of the Revolution. "Sovereignty flows towards the centre of administration," as Harold Laski says, and a central administration only came into being with the Constitution. It was only in 1789 that the Federal government became sovereign, the power of its sovereignty being qualified by the powers still held by the states and the resistance of a revolutionary population which for decades from time to time rebelled against authority.

By conquest and occupation legitimized sovereignty may be deposed and the occupying power exercise sovereignty with no better claim to legitimacy than that might makes right. Examples are the powers exercised by the Soviet Union in the satellite states of Eastern Europe after World War II and by Israel over the Arab lands after the War of 1967. But it could hardly be said that there was dual sovereignty in these instances, for *de jure* sovereignty is no sovereignty in the face of *de facto*. Title is not the equivalent of power.

The fact that sovereignty is not absolute, that its weapons are dispersed, that local communities, churches, business enterprises, or labor organizations hold some of these weapons, has led to the conclusion that they are therefore sovereign in their particular spheres or that sovereignty should be legally recognized as subsisting in these institutions. This pluralism is convenient to the philosophy of guild socialism and syndicalism. Granting that the State has not destroyed and in many instances not even attempted to control local self-government, churches, corporations, and labor unions (although each of these institutions has at one time or another been destroyed by government), it cannot be urged that they are independent of and superior to the State; where the power to act exists, nonaction becomes action. When disputes arise among them, or between them and other interests, it is the State which ordinarily settles the matter. This is well analyzed by Professor Morris R. Cohen:

> To prevent the inconvenience of interminable conflicts, the power to terminate them by a deciding word is given to the State as the organ of the general community. The power to have the last word in any dispute is just what sovereignty is.

The wisdom of large measures of home rule or autonomy to be accorded to various local, vocational, and religious organizations, need not be questioned. But we must recognize that the community cannot irrevocably part with its power to revise such grants and that it is impossible for all the parties to a dispute to have the last word. . . . The evils of an absolute state are not cured by the multiplication of absolutes.

This magisterial superiority on the part of the State, a superiority existing in fact as well as in theory, denies to those other institutions the title of sovereign in their own spheres. Nor can they be made sovereign by the *ipse dixit* of law. We have already seen that legal doctrines do not make for sovereign supremacy, although they may afford a formula to justify the disregard of limitations which have been placed on sovereigns by other legal concepts. For example, an American state government is bound by constitutional restriction not to take private property arbitrarily, without "due process of law"; but a state, being a "sovereign entity," can declare certain private property to be contraband or can destroy private property through an exercise of police power without compensating the owners. In other words, *governments are only limited by their impotence to absorb all interests in the community and therefore to control all political weapons.*

Positive law, the law of governments, requires sanctions, penalties which must be applied by superior force. What kind of sovereignty would then be lodged in institutions which must call upon the State to use its power to settle their jurisdictional disputes with other institutions?

If we regard society as a whole it is not possible to believe in plural sovereignty. Groups in any society may resemble the whole; that is, the processes of ward politics, of church politics, of corporation politics, of labor union politics may be the same as those in national politics. Similarity of structure and function should not be confused with similarity of situation. As has already been noted, Mr. Justice Holmes has well warned us that it is sometimes degree that makes the difference. Just so with sovereignty. Given groups, because of the loyalty or self-interest of their members, have a power which is a counterweight to the power of the State, may at times even be indestructible by the whole power of the State, though the wielders of that power may desire to destroy all conflicting interests in their search for that solidarity which would leave their interest supreme. It does not follow that because such groups hold a durable power and exercise functional processes in many respects similar to those of the State itself, they must consequently possess sovereignty. Nor does it follow, as suggested by Cohen, that "the law of contract confers sovereignty on one party over another" because the courts will enforce a contract. It is more accurate to say that contracting parties and testators accept the power of the courts to declare (through their interpretation of documents) how the State will enforce them. As we have seen, a sovereign will apply its powers for the benefit of those whose interests are such that they must be protected by the ruling group in its own interest. But it would be a dissolute sovereignty which transferred its powers to individuals. Self-aid is evidence of a lack of sovereign power—not of sovereign strength.

The logic of plural sovereignty must multiply the number of sovereigns that a man has by the number of social relationships in which he is in an inferior position to some other person or group. A man may be a member of a union, an employee in a factory, a stockholder in another company, a member of a church, a citizen of a city within a state within a nation; he may owe money on a mortgage on his house and may be threatened by racketeers. In each instance he would be subject to a different sovereignty, if the doctrine of plural sovereignty were to hold. Political theorists of the Middle Ages made no such mistake. They understood the difference between sovereignty, which is the power to rule, and dominion, which is power over property, even property in persons. Economic dominion undoubtedly contributes power to the sovereign as it does to others. It may relieve the sovereign of the necessity of taxation, but it is not the same as fiscal sovereignty, nor is the power of the sovereign to dispose of his property, even of his slaves, the same as magistracy.

13

ETHICS AND IDEALS

WE HAVE noted that the business of sovereignty is the maintenance of its power, not absolute but superior power, through the political process, which is essentially a process of weighing conflicting interests, of enlisting those interests which give strength to the sovereign, and of demolishing or ignoring those which would bring less support or would weaken the sovereign. When we have spoken of weighing interests we did not mean placing moral valuations upon them. We did not mean that the sovereign's judgment was exercised in the interest of some absolute idea of right and against some moral wrong. The weighing done by the sovereign is rather a measuring of potential strength.

Although the sovereign group attempts to attain solidarity by achieving the monopoly of all of the political weapons, including those of propaganda; although it tries to embrace all symbols and institutions—the Church, the State, the schools, the press, entertainment, the means of production—in the terms of the predominant ideology (the prevailing socio-economic concept), it cannot smother forever the cries of the opposition nor bury securely in its towers the bones of those interests which it has strangled. For as Dean Pound has pointed out, men are unwilling to concede that "the magic words 'be it enacted' " and "it is considered and adjudged" give moral warrant "as well as legal efficacy to anything which follows," whether statute or judicial decree. The Duncans, regal and humble, persist in murdering sleep. The disinherited younger sons will not always remain silenced mercenaries. The symbols of right and wrong can never be monopolized by the sovereign.

Politics are imperative. Neither the sovereign nor the opposition can get sufficient perspective as a rule to measure acts and objects against a standard of ultimate wisdom or an eternal norm, but only by immediate pain and pleasure phrased in terms of power. The Socratic ideal of good as a blend of pleasure enlightened by knowledge has no reality in politics independently of the application of some form of power. Consequently, the political processes are amoral. The test is whether this or that act relieves or burdens a given interest. The task is the sophisticated one of managing the affairs of the State so as to get on—which means to acquire or hold political power.

Nevertheless this inherent hedonism must be contained in some frame for each participant, and the particular frame determines his answer in matters involving any phase of life in society. And here it must be emphasized that it is not the form of government but the functional interests of the sovereign group which determine the character in which the prevailing ideology is cast, the frame in which the sovereigns act. What may be injurious to one sovereign may be the very life blood of another. The freedom and competition of the industrial system, for instance, would have been impossible to feudalism.

It is the degree of unity and cohesiveness of the sovereign group, the extent to which the prevailing interests can mobilize the weapons of sovereignty, which determines the form of the State through which sovereignty is exercised. About this form, whether it be monarchic, theistic, oligarchic, democratic, dictatorial, is built an anthropomorphic worship of the governmental status quo. The sovereign looks at his handiwork, at the State which he has created, and declares it to be good, and all those who want faggots from his forest, pennies from his almoner, crumbs from his board, or the privilege of collecting his taxes or selling him wine likewise proclaim it good.

"Art, science, government, human nature itself, are self-defining and self-preserving: by partly fixing a structure they fix an ideal. But the barbarian can hardly regard such things, for to have distinguished and fostered them would be to have founded a civilization," Santayana said in *Reason in Common Sense*.

But once the basic ideology for the seizure and maintenance of power has been laid out, all this is incidental. Once the fetus survives, the bone structure is determined; it may be large or small, strong or weak, straight or bent, but it will harden in the pattern of a man, a monkey or a bird. The basic principles of the State are determined by the needs that demand to be respected. Out of those demands grow the moral concepts which are comprised in an ideology. "Present demands," as Santayana reminds us, "are the only material and occasions for any ideal: without demands the ideal would have no *locus standi* or foothold in the world, no power, no charm, no prerogative." The nature of political morals depends then upon the character of the demands out of which they are fashioned. A given ideology is descriptive of the interests whose needs call it forth. When those interests triumph their ideology becomes acceptable; it is pronounced by the victors to be the only adequate ideology. Slavery is moral because the dominant land economy requires it; and slavery is wicked in a society in which it is desirable to have fluid labor which need not be supported in an off season. To the Church, whose early strength lay in devotion to the democratic utopia of the City of God, slavery was evil. Before God and His vicar master and man were equal. In small communities such as the Greek states it was only through the use of slave labor that the ambitious projects of the citizens could be accomplished. They had to be free from menial labor to carry on their wars, their commerce, their religio-artistic enterprises. Aristotle accepted slavery.

Another instance is to be found in the different attitudes toward profits. In the era of petty traders and handicraftsmen, "livelihood," as Veblen said, "was the fundamental norm of business regulations; profits had but a secondary standing, if any." Industrial enterprise, on the contrary, regards the profit motif as dominant, and livelihood becomes important only to the extent that its sufficiency enhances and its insufficiency depresses profits.

Moral concepts, in addition to being part of the dominant ideology, part of the matter out of which law is fashioned, are also the first mumbled words of inarticulate opposition. As Korkunov has expressed it, law is the delimitation of interests, morals their evaluation. *Future political forms must first establish themselves in the womb of ethics; the symbolic weapons of sovereignty must first withstand tests on the forge of moral dialectics before they are accepted as apparently valid, as sufficient to arouse the sup-*

port of interests prepared to fight for them because they believe those symbols are expressive of themselves.

We have already discussed positive law as the means of defining the limits to which the sovereign will extend his power. It is, of course, impossible for the sovereign to cover in advance by legal rule every point of conflict which may arise. New objective conditions necessarily call for new rulings. A shortage of grain, a plague, the invention of a cotton gin or an automobile will upset the niceties of the balance established by previous statute and decision. The alteration of economic and physical conditions creates new social pressures, new points of friction, and the established order is disturbed, just as heat and frost will bend and crack the surface of a road. To meet these conditions the law has great zones for expansion—"India rubber sections," "safety-valve concepts," such as rules of "reason," "due process of law," "the intent of the legislator" and "police power," and such expressed objects as "the commonweal." [1] Among these flexibly applied zones the courts, in the first instance, and if they fail, legislatures can work adjustments to extend or contract the field of sovereign intervention within the ultimate boundary of the prevailing ideology.

Wurzel has shown the relation between judicial thinking and ethical influences and their dependence upon the symbolism of words. In his *Methods of Juridical Thinking* he writes:

[1] See John Austin, Lecture IV, Second Edition, p. 85: "The general happiness or good demands the institution of property: that the exclusive enjoyment conferred by law upon an owner shall not be disturbed by private or unauthorized persons: that no man shall take from another the product of his labor or saving, without the permission of the owner previously signified, *or without the authority of the sovereign acting for the commonweal.*" (Italics mine—J.M.)

That formulated rules of law could possibly be applied independently of other social groups of value judgments is improbable from the very circumstance that like the other groups it is the product of volition and intended to influence volition, as well as from the fact that it must make use of language—language, in which so many words, without change in their proper logical significance, may be applied in so many different ways according to the social valuation that goes along with them as a sort of overtone.

It is through this process of interpretation, of providing new innuendos to old phrases, that moral concepts are readily introduced into the ideology of the sovereign group and into the fabric of its law. When the judicial process fails to meet the needs of an interest which is sufficiently articulate to be respected, the more drastic action of legislation is called upon to declare the rule which the sovereign will enforce. It is not any a priori concept of good or evil which prompts legal innovation. The moral rule becomes a rule of law, in the words of Duguit, "when the social reaction produced by the violation of this rule has become energetic enough and definite enough to receive from custom or from the written law a concreteness more or less complete." A change in law is the resultant of a political conflict; it is, to quote Berolzheimer, "the result of a struggle and the victory of one part of the community over the other."

Out of the needs of groups and classes, then, there arise ethical demands which constitute part of the politico-economic ideology of those groups or classes and of all other people upon whom they can impose their philosophy. This ideology affords a reservoir from which are derived those institutions which wield the sovereign powers, including law as the principal symbol of political force and power.

In the molding of political life and organization the nature of the needs which are to be recognized is all-important. Which ideology, that is, the child of which interests is to wear the crown? Shall it be the royal court or baronial manor, the exploiter of new lands, the city merchant, the financier, the entrepreneur, the landlord, the proletarian, or the farmer whose interests are to be dominant, or shall it be a combination of two or more of these interests? *The broader the base and the more common the interests whose needs are protected the less will be the friction and correspondingly the less will be the demands, the struggles, and the readjustments of political power.*

The aim of equality of interests and powers, couched in the slogan that the least government is the best government, was the mistaken hope of democratic libertarianism, which failed to achieve its expressed purpose because people did not see or did not wish to recognize that the right to register votes is not identical with the control of sovereign weapons. Liberalism was a precious watchword, a magic incantation to those interests powerful enough to thrive on unfettered competition.

Under the slogan of a classless society it is the dream of Communism that all members of the community will have common interests and that there will be neither governors nor the governed. In such a society, rights as moral ends would supersede rights fortified by sovereign sanctions. But perhaps, as Jethro Brown suggests, the term "right" is used in these two senses as a form of wish fulfillment.

Meanwhile the statesman, the lawyer, and the legal philosopher prefer to think that rights which the sovereign is called upon to protect are not selfish privileges of the powerful but diadems along the path that moral man travels toward utopia. Special pleaders are available to every institution that will pay their price, and every State has found its defenders, as Demogue says, "to legitimatize all of its acts, even the most abominable." Common criminals are rarely so depraved as not to feel the need of some justification to themselves of their wrongdoing. Sovereigns themselves at times point to *law* as their excuse for violating *moral judgments*, making of law observance a virtue in itself. And Fichte declared that one who violated the law thereby outlawed himself until he had expiated his wrongdoing in such manner as society might decree—i.e., after the manner of the Teutonic tribes, the lawbreaker put himself beyond the protection of law and the compassion of the community. Repeatedly at the Nuremberg trials at the conclusion of World War II, the defense was offered that the barbarous acts of which the defendants were accused were merely in observance of Hitler's laws, which they accepted. To them conformity to law, whatever the law, was right.

But the very fact that people fear to have their works and the objects of their devotion described as abominable, and that they strive to paint the words "Justice" and "Good" over those blemishes that might cause rejection of their acts and the deflation of their symbols of prestige, reveals the vigor of moral aim as a material out of which power is wrought. Thus, to the sovereign, moral right is a patent of power, his deed of title. A threat to his prerogatives is a wrong; and wrong is to trespass against his sovereignty. To the governed, that is, to those interests which do not belong to the group in control, right is a proclamation to win the adherence of others similarly situated. It is a martial air, a flag to rally to; and wrong is oppression, it is power misused, it is the justification for resistance, for what Alexander Hamilton called "that original right of self-defense which is paramount in all positive forms of government."

Part II

14

THE SOVEREIGNTY OF NATIONS

WEAPONS OF SOVEREIGNTY

In treating of sovereignty we are dealing largely with the uses of power, the several weapons of power and their interaction. These are not abstractions, not idealized concepts, but dynamic forces arising out of human needs and expressed through human transactions. And as Morgenthau points out: "The main signpost that helps political realism to find its way through the landscape of international politics is the concept of interest defined in terms of power." The political processes involving the use of weapons in the exercise of sovereignty and combating it (with some important modifications which will be discussed) are the same in the international power struggle of sovereigns as in domestic power struggles.

Force

Force is present or in the background of international relations. It is mutually weighed in maneuvers of competing nations. It is considered in the adoption and prosecution of national goals beyond a nation's borders. It attracts allies, clients, and dependents, as when in war smaller nations adhere to great powers, or as when Eastern European countries were subordinated to the Soviet Union after World War II and West Germany became a client of its former enemies in the Atlantic community. Force may also repel allies, clients, and dependents, as was the case in 1954 when England, France, and Israel seized the Suez Canal and when the United States prosecuted the war of South Vietnam against rebel forces and North Vietnam and antagonized friends and allies of the United States.

War is the ultimate use of the sovereign weapon of force. The same power that controls the police internally conducts war externally. Von Clausewitz, who after a century and a half is still a classic authority on the nature of war, described it as "an act of violence intended to compel our opponent to fulfill our will." He goes on to say, "If we desire to defeat the enemy, we must proportion our efforts to his power of resistance. This is expressed by the product of two factors which cannot be separated, namely, *the sum of available means* and *the strength of the Will*." We increase our own means, our adversary does the same, and this results in "a new material enhancement which . . . must create a fresh effort towards an extreme."

This need to escalate force in war to the point at which the enemy will fulfill or submit to our will is as extravagant a use of sovereign power against other nations as the use of physical force is against domestic opposition. To make the use of war, of force, valid the cost of the consequences of its use to the user must be proportionately favorable to him. The cost of war as an instrument to extend sovereignty should therefore properly be weighed, as in the case of the use of force to extend or maintain internal sovereignty, against the use of other weapons which may not achieve the same degree of submission to the sovereign will. As Hawtrey wrote, "Fighting is but a clumsy expedient, if the desired object can be obtained without it;" i.e., if the goal can be substantially achieved by other political means. Thus the wise sovereign is more concerned with the manipulation of other forms of power than with physical force, although the latter may be a silent threat.

War is an expression of national policy; it is not independent of political intercourse but a continuation of it. The message of the sword carries a message of national policy. Force, whether by war or otherwise, induces changes in relationships which cannot be stabilized by force alone. Stabilization requires communication, even though this be the negative communication by the victor disregarding the wishes of the vanquished.

Von Clausewitz points out that the effects of the French Revolution beyond the borders of France came about "much less through new methods and views introduced by the French in the conduct of the War than through the changes which it brought in state-craft and civil administration, in the character of Governments, in the condition of the people, etc." It was a blunder of policy on the part of other governments, he maintains, for them to have endeavored "to hold their own against forces of a novel kind and overwhelming strength" with the ordinary means of warfare. This too is the lesson of the French and American struggles in Vietnam. For war not only derives from national policy, it also affects the political process of the parties.

There have been changes in the conditions in which, and

occasions on which, force has been used, and this has resulted in different applications of force. When the public treasury was regarded as the private purse of the sovereign kings, they could make wars in their private interests. Even then, however, they had to use their armies with circumspection, for once they were destroyed or dispersed they could not well raise new ones. The Middle Ages developed the feudal obligation of service, relief from which could be paid for (scutage), and this payment went into the king's treasury. Later, when the treasury came under the control of a larger sovereign group—the king and his ministers—it was deemed to be the government's but not the people's, and the people remained separated from the enterprises of war.

Von Clausewitz points out that while the people participated in and were of great consequence in the Tartar invasions and in the wars of the old republics and the Middle Ages (if restricted to those having rights of citizens), they had only an indirect influence in the conduct of war during the nineteenth century. This separation of the government and the people imposed strong limitations on the State's military power. In this century nations not only depend upon volunteers but, in times of crisis especially, on the draft of soldiers. To a large extent the latter remain civilians in uniform. In the two World Wars whole national populations were involved and the entire assets of the warring nations were committed. This does not mean that the people of the nations, no matter how democratic, had power to control war or peace. The sovereign power in each country, by the use of economic and psychological weapons, could enforce acceptance of its war goals and people's participation in the exertions of war.

Weaponry, too, changed the nature of war. Gunpowder was not only more destructive than bow and arrow, sword and spear; it also reduced physical contact and the importance of individual prowess with arms. Now long-range airplanes and missiles with nuclear warheads have further increased the physical distance of combatants, involved the whole population as targets, and for the time at least, have deterred the great powers from engaging in direct military conflict. Smaller nations feel reasonably secure against the use of nuclear weapons, for in the client systems and networks of alliances that have developed the smaller nations believe that if nuclear weapons were to be used against them by some great power, their patron or ally would threaten reprisal with nuclear weapons against the offender, the escalation of a small war into a holocaust.[1] Thus weak nations such as the Vietnams and Koreas can afford to confront each other and defy the great powers, frequently using guerrilla tactics to which armies based on great firepower find it difficult to react successfully. The little powers with mountains and swamps and resentment against the intrusion of foreigners can defiantly thumb their noses at the clumsy giants, however heavily armed those giants may be.

Nevertheless, through these wars of small nations the great powers can confront each other without their own soil being touched and even sometimes without their own personnel being seriously involved. This is what happened in the Spanish Civil War, in which the Fascist powers and

[1] However, as arguments on disarmament in the United Nations committees and Assembly have shown, nations with highly developed scientific resources (such as France, India, and West Germany) have felt uncomfortable that they had no control of the use of nuclear weapons which they were capable of developing.

some of the Western powers tested their weapons. Even in Vietnam, where the United States became deeply involved with men and equipment, there has been no direct confrontation with the Soviet Union or the People's Republic of China, but new "conventional" weapons of all these powers could be tested in war. Such military actions are symbolic of the great-power struggles for which the military feel obliged to prepare continuously. This is not the first time that symbolic expressions of hostility have occurred. Although the medieval church preached the message of love and peace, "the lust of violence asserted itself against the spiritual yoke imposed upon it; chivalry and the Crusades offered the Church the possibility of restraining and directing the love of violence and slaughter," Hans Kohn wrote. Thus in a number of ways force can be channelized without commitment of doctrine, men, or property of basic importance.

Ultimately national strength depends less on action abroad than on domestic development, the internal strength of a nation. Von Clausewitz makes this clear when he emphasizes "the strength of the Will" and "the sum of available means" in the efforts of war. In other words, morale and industrial capacity to produce materiel and to replace what has been used and destroyed are essential to the use of force in war and to a reputation for power. "Theory," he says, "must take into account the human element. . . . The act of war has to deal with living and with moral forces, the consequence of which is that it can never attain the absolute and positive."

Economic Power

Over four thousand years ago trade routes had been established by land and sea by venturous merchants, often with the support or encouragement of their rulers, who might by those traders send gifts to other rulers as a symbol of friendship or the price of peace, independence, or alliance. In more recent times sovereigns have exploited foreign trade as weapons in their international relations. In the economic field foreign trade has been an extension of national policy.

Mercantilism was a power weapon of national policy. The sovereign gave to certain favorites the monopoly to exploit commerce in specific products or regions. Its purpose was to strengthen the competitive position of the State. It was to the advantage of the home State and the disadvantage of all foreign interests. This is exemplified by the policies of colonialism which monopolized the wealth and raw products of the colonies and the markets for finished goods. Colonialism also tended to be exclusionary of cultures other than that of the colonial power itself. The language, administrative practices, sometimes educational goals and methods, and political institutions were imported from the colonialist nations. The colony was a military, economic, and cultural outpost. Mercantilism, therefore, was "of an intrinsically warlike nature."

Foreign investment has been another economic weapon affording varying degrees of power across the geographic boundaries of a sovereignty. These investments were often private, not governmental. The Lombard bankers made loans to kings, emperors, and high churchmen. Of course the powerful debtor could default. No officer of a court of law could enforce judgment against him. But, as in the case of other debtors, a default affected his credit and the possibility of getting further loans to support his court or his wars. And as Fisher said, "Even where there is no organized superior sovereign power to compel obedience, a government is not free to ignore the conduct and attitudes of those with whom it must deal." And there are, of course, people who conform to rules and customs because they believe in them and find them to their advantage without regard to their enforceability. This conformity has been necessary to establish the confidence on which a commercial and industrial society rests and requires the adherence of the sovereign to a considerable extent. Thus while the sovereign can depreciate its currency or tax its creditors, it generally permits and pays claims against it where the norms of commerce and industry are dominant in the economy.

National banking systems and international private bankers have continued to finance foreign sovereignties, often acting in the dual capacities of banker and financial adviser and so determining not only the economic but also the political policy of the client State.

The Mercantilist practices of the seventeenth, eighteenth, and nineteenth centuries, when colonial powers established corporations to set up factories (engaged in merchandising and factoring) on foreign soil, have been succeeded more recently by large corporations which have established foreign manufacturing plants and merchandising outlets, developed foreign mines, purchased controlling interests in foreign enterprises, so much so that American corporate enterprises in Europe have been described as the second most powerful economic system, second only to that of the United States itself. In smaller, less economically developed nations, this economic control has frequently made and broken the sovereign power of the State. This has sometimes been described as a new colonialism. Trade, it was said, followed the flag; but with greater frequency the flag followed trade. Naval powers defended their commercial and financial offshoots, and political policy has retaliated to interference with commercial enterprises as much as to insults to the flag. In fact interference with commerce and insult to the flag might be interchangeable, as was the case along the coast of China. Resistance to foreign enclaves led to the Boxer Rebellion by Chinese patriots against the privileges claimed by Western powers.

Under the Monroe Doctrine the United States did not permit European powers to intervene when Venezuela defaulted on its obligations; but the United States itself intervened. When as a result of the Mexican Revolution of 1913 the Mexicans seized American oil wells and refineries, the United States seized the port of Vera Cruz, and later responded to Villa's threats to Texas with an expeditionary force in northern Mexico. The seizure of American oil refineries, sulphur plants, and sugar properties by Castro's revolution in Cuba was responded to by the United States with embargoes. These were all within the United States "sphere of influence." Indonesia was not, and the American oil companies which had large investments there withdrew rather than bring pressure on the United States to intervene with economic or military power.

But government agencies have used their economic power to help American corporate interests in distant parts of the world. Funds for a Peruvian domestic "Peace Corps" were withheld to bring about a "more reasonable" attitude by the Peruvian government in negotiations with American oil companies, and the hungry people of India were threatened with an end to food shipments unless India accepted American price fixing for fertilizer produced by an American oil company. Similarly, the Soviet Union fixed prices for the exchange of its manufactured products for raw materials of the satellite nations of Eastern Europe while restricting their trade with the West. The effect of this colonial practice was to create economic dependence on the Soviet Union.

Foreign aid has been granted as an act of charity and as support to a friendly nation or defeated enemy, but always as an instrument of foreign policy or to strengthen the granting nation's economic power. Thus it is, with few exceptions, a political action. The greatest foreign aid program was the Marshall Plan following World War II. Without underrating the generosity of the United States and millions of supporters of the plan, it is doubtful whether it would have been possible except as a means of implementing national policy to help Western Europe, including West Germany, the former enemy, resist Communism. Grants were made under this plan and others sometimes in the form of outright gifts of money, credit, or material, sometimes as loans at low interest rates. They have been for economic development, social and educational improvements, and military support. And more and more they were tied in with a requirement that they be spent for agricultural and manufactured products in the United States. While foreign aid has been a conciliatory gesture it has nevertheless been an instrument of power politics.

The United States has not been unique in foreign aid. The Soviet Union and to a lesser extent other nations also have utilized foreign aid as instruments of political power. In exchange for funds and engineering skills to build the Aswan Dam and armaments against Israel the Soviet Union has obtained long-staple cotton on good terms and naval bases in Egypt. Cuba has become politically, militarily, and economically dependent on Moscow at the price of becoming the sugar producer for the Communist bloc.

There tends to be ambivalence toward these grants both in the granting and receiving nations. There may be gratitude but also a sense of humiliation at receiving "charity," and after a time expressions of gratitude decline. The economic and political price of aid may also enter into the evaluation of the aid received and arouse feelings that aid is not "charity" but economic exploitation. On the other hand, the granting nation tends to think of aid as openhandedness, generosity, and to expect gratitude. When it realizes that *Undank ist der Welt Lohn* it may react hostilely toward the object of "charity." Thus both sides pay a psychological price for the arrangement. In addition, when the aid is in military equipment it supports the sovereign power, which may be burdensome to the people of the receiving nation by giving those in power the means to overcome with force efforts toward reform. Only if both nations accept the fact that bilateral aid agreements are given and received as instruments of power, not as charity, will such transactions be realistically evaluated.

Like Mercantilism and foreign investment, foreign aid on a unilateral basis can be economic penetration of a weaker nation and reduce its power. Moreover, as Hawtrey said, "The multitude accept the policy of economic nationalism as axiomatic. If their support is to be gained for a policy, they must be convinced that it is for their own benefit." Moral sentiment and international goodwill will not be long supported at economic cost, or expenditure of lives, unless the public believes it is receiving an economic or strategic benefit.

Multilateral aid, such as is given by agencies of the United Nations, presents no such problems of ambivalence. It is neither granted nor received for purposes of power; and, whether or not the receiving nation contributes to the fund, as a member of the United Nations it shares in granting as well as receiving. It is not humiliated by an expectation of gratitude.

Certain governmental acts affecting international transactions may involve a mixture of physical force, economic power, and psychological influence. This would include tariffs, export duties, restrictions on monetary transactions, currency manipulation, encouragement or limitation of immigration and emigration, control of travel within a country or across its borders, and boycotts. These may be for political or economic purposes, but in either event they can be weapons of aggression or defense. They are aggressive weapons when they are used discriminatorily, favoring some regions, nations, races, or cultures and injuring or prejudicing others. Censorship of publications, moving pictures, radio, or television programs is a weapon against the dissemination of information and ideas threatening to the sovereign power. Dictatorships or other highly autocratic societies which dread adverse criticism are more likely to install strong censorship and be exclusionary as to ideas. Thus the Soviet Union behind Stalin's iron curtain jammed foreign broadcasts and several Communist countries punished their citizens for publishing abroad books, articles, or poems critical of a Communist regime.

Some of the political powers, the powers of sovereignty, just discussed may be utilized by private organizations, labor unions in particular. In a number of lands longshoremen, for example, have refused to handle goods coming from an "enemy" country even in time of peace. An international organization of airline pilots threatened to refuse to fly planes to Algeria if that country did not release the crew and passengers of an Israeli plane that had been hijacked and landed in Algeria. There have been boycotts by cultural institutions which have refused audience to the music of "enemy" composers or to speakers or performers who they feared might contaminate their own culture.

Some nations are more favored than others by environment and culture to develop economic strength and institutions which contribute to their power. The tendency is for those nations so favored, the "have" nations, to gain in power compared to the "have-not" nations. Leninist doctrine says that because capitalism cannot profitably invest within the limits of its economy—profit yields becoming less as the economy advances—it has to export its capital to less developed areas for resources and markets. This has not been happening.[2] Capital has been principally invested abroad (oil and minerals excepted) in nations economically more advanced. And foreign aid by the United States tended to be in the form of grants to the wealthy nations and in the form of interest-bearing loans to the poorer. A United Nations survey found that the developing nations were returning to the "donors" more than half they had received. Because capital and industry multiply themselves, assuming the people of the nations are dynamic and motivated to produce, this not only accentuates differences in standards of living but also makes possible increased firepower, the power to use physical force, both quantitatively and comparatively.

To the moralist this will appear wrong, unjust, immoral. But political realists, in the words of Morgenthau, "think and act in terms of interest defined as power." Power be-

[2] Mao Tse-tung, on the other hand, sees in imperialism the front of the richer nations, whether capitalist or Communist, "the Cities of the World," against the poorer, the rural, or agrarian.

ing amoral, such judgments are irrelevant, except as they become symbols about which domestic and international factions may rally, and except further, as in a world of alliances and client States, they may lead to power confrontations.

Words and Symbols

As in the domestic political process, words and other symbols are used by sovereign power or against sovereign power to increase or diminish its influence. They are used internally and among friendly nations to gain support for national policy and to avoid or substitute for more costly physical and economic conflicts.

People tend to support a strongly aggressive position against what they consider a threat from a foreign power for several reasons. In times of crisis they need the support of their own community, their in-group against outsiders. In such times people, too, are likely to distrust their own judgment (we don't have the facts; the government does) and will more readily follow the dictates of those in authority. Milgram has shown that a large proportion of people will tend to obey the commands of one whom they consider to be legitimate authority even to doing cruel acts. This is especially true in the presence of the authority figure and when they have no contact with and do not see the suffering of the persons hurt, which is the case in war. For today only ground troops have direct contact with their enemy, not the gunners, the bombers, or the staff officers, who do not see or hear the anguish of their victims. Even the feeling of hatred may be wanting until one is subjected to the combat itself, when, as Von Clausewitz points out, there will be excited "in us a desire to retaliate and be revenged upon him [who attacks us] sooner than on the superior power at whose command the act was done." To the sovereign power hostility is divorced from physical reality and becomes symbolic.

Finally, people can express normally repressed aggression on an opponent whom they define as evil, not just as different or wrong or who has other needs and perceptions. A child is "good" when he obeys orders and "naughty" when he disobeys. This becomes symbolized so that when he grows up and becomes a person with authority he tends still to define as "good" "those who obey its [his] orders and the 'bad' as those who defy it." Thus conditioned the adult reacts in this pattern to political factions and governments, to religions and ideologies.

An ideological base has always made it possible for sovereigns and their people to blot out awareness of ethical questions arising from the uses of power and discover righteous justification in the role of God's avenging angels destroying the idols of the heathen. The concept of nationalism is such a base. It is, as Hans Kohn has said, "a state of mind." Nationalism developed with the nation-state. It had little relevance to the tribal governments, the city-state, the ancient empires, the Holy Roman Empire, or the Catholic Church. "Nationalities are created out of ethnographic and political elements when nationalism breathes life into the form built by preceding centuries." As a state of mind nationalism is incorporated in the value systems of a majority of the people of a nation. Its political forms, its cultural satisfactions and economic standards become the lens through which it views all other nations.

In public affairs—and to an exaggerated degree in international affairs—stereotyping of in-group and out-group prejudices, semantic and linguistic misinterpretations, and pressures to maintain prestige images increase the difficulties of receiving feedback, evaluating it, and determining appropriate conduct. Of the Emperor Justinian it was said, "He did not think that the slaying of men was murder unless they happened to share his own religious opinions." When the Turks were threatening to take over Constantinople and the Church of Rome had sent an emissary, a high Orthodox churchman exclaimed, "It is better to see in this city the power of the Turkish turban than that of the Latin tiara," and Petrarch said, "The Turks are enemies but the Greeks [the Orthodox Eastern Empire] are schismatics and worse than enemies."

Each sovereignty tends to interpret another's diplomatic communications in terms of its own culture and expectations and often projects its own intentions onto the other. Failing to find the real meaning may have disastrous results. An example which will be discussed later (in Chapter 16) is the problem of the United States interpreting two conflicting communications from Khrushchev during the missile crisis in 1962. Other examples are Khrushchev's statement, "We'll bury you," which appeared as a threat of war to many people in the United States but had a different meaning in the idiom of the Russians. During the Russo-Japanese War an American correspondent said of a Japanese general, "He's a brick." For this he was penalized by the general, to whom it meant not a compliment but a cake of mud. Moseley has written that "one of the difficulties of the Soviet-Russian vocabulary is that the word 'compromise' is not of native origin and carries with it no favorable empathy. It is habitually used only in combination with the adjective 'putrid'!" Even a minor concession "makes a Bolshevik-trained negotiator feel that he is losing control of his own will and is becoming subject to an alien will."

Hostility toward other nations and peoples is often expressed in popular idioms. In his joyous book *Naming Day in Eden* Jacobs recounts how syphilis was called the Corinthian disease by the Greeks; the English called it Spanish gout; the Germans referred to it as the French disease, and the French described it as Florentine or Neopolitan. The Dutch said that one infected by it had seen Spain and the French said that he had gone to Sweden or Bavaria. Similarly, fleas and cockroaches were described as being citizens of other nations and the German Jews of the Rhineland described all Polish Jews as *ganufs* (thieves).

All communication is blurred by our different interpretations of language resulting from our different experiences, but this is more pronounced when the symbolic concepts must be viewed through different cultures. This is illustrated by the different views of "democracy" among the nations appearing in a publication of UNESCO, *Democracy in a World of Tensions*. Other terms bearing different ideological emphases today are "scientific," "materialistic," "communistic," "capitalistic," "atheistic," "racist," used as symbols to condemn other nations or in justification of one's own hostility. In Muller's words, "one man's holy mystery is another man's primitive superstition. . . ."

Once the opposing power has committed itself to arms in support of its cause, it is too late for a sovereign to meet sword and passion with arguments or even concessions. For force and the passions it stimulates freeze positions so that generally one or the other demands "unconditional surrender" which in itself freezes resistance. Those who feel the breath of the opponent who threatens them must respond by fighting or die, like the King of the Wood, for it is not possible to tell an escaped slave who has seized a branch of the tree of life to refrain from fighting his cause. At the beginning of the Spanish-American War, Spain attempted to appease the United States at the time the latter was boiling to engage in the war. France and England sought to appease Hitler at Munich but one year later he broke his agreement because he had prepared Germany to seize the sovereignty of Russia, Western Europe, and England. Xenophon describes the speech of Clearchos to Tissaphernes to induce him to discuss face to face their respective suspicion of each other and the rumors which had generated them. In his speech Clearchos said:

For I know it has often happened that either from slander or from suspicion men have been frightened of each other, and wishing to get in first before they suffer, they have done incurable mischief to others who were not intending to do anything of the sort, nor indeed wishing to do it. I think such misunderstandings are best ended by meeting face to face; so here I am, to assure you that you have no reason to distrust us.

But it was too late. Tissaphernes was committed. While he consented to Clearchos' proposal he induced Clearchos to produce his officers so that the guilty sources of the rumors could be pointed out to him. Then when Clearchos did so Tissaphernes promptly slew all of them and Clearchos himself.

An approach of face-to-face discussion has to be continuous and in ordinary situations should avoid physical conflict; but it is questionable whether such a process would often prevail against a foe drunk on its ideology. It was not Christian charity but the arms of Charles Martel that stopped the Islamic power, which was offering the unconverted only the choice of the crescent or the sword. The maneuvers of the *ancien régime* could no longer save the Bourbons from the fury of the people of France in revolt. Nor could the concessions of England quiet the American Colonists once they were aroused to demand control of their own fortunes. But compare the later dismemberment of the British Empire when demands for freedom were met in the spirit of Burke's principle of magnanimity in politics and most of the independent colonies remained in the British Commonwealth. Though the bond of sovereignty was cut and the restraining power of force dissolved, economic and psychological interchange afforded continuous dialog with the mother country.

The sovereign has greater sources of information than the people, although individuals and particular groups may have more in specific cases, as may a foreign power. The sovereign has greater visibility than his people and his statements therefore will reach a larger audience than those of others and have greater weight with other sovereigns. There is the tendency too for the news media, in the effort to be timely, to accept as fact what a government says without subjecting it to careful analysis. Where there is little or no freedom of the press careful analysis may be a passport to imprisonment. Because he has greater information than others the sovereign can more readily distort meaning and value and the people will be none the wiser; and because military and diplomatic information especially is in large measure secret, he can select items for publication which will more readily fit his purposes. Secrecy is a form of distortion, and, as Hilsman puts it, "Where information is an asset, command over information is the power to grant or withhold that asset. . . ." For "Political leverage is power. Information is power. Secrecy is power. Speed in communication is power." The sovereign, consequently, has great power to manipuate symbols and exercise psychological controls.

Finally, through the extension of their culture to foreign peoples, nations have solicited friendship and created readiness to accept their version of transactions which may be international or may be internal but have international results. Nations have supported the exportation of their arts and the exchange of scholars and performers. They have maintained abroad schools conducted in their language, libraries and cinema and lectures about their own system and culture. Libraries have performed a dual function of presenting a culture and being the scapegoat of patriotic passion against the nation maintaining the library by offering the opportunity to express hostility through wrecking the library or burning the books. Furthermore, the United Nations Educational, Scientific and Cultural Organization (UNESCO), which organized to facilitate free cultural exchanges and promote educational, scientific, and cultural development (which it has in considerable measure done) has been used frequently to promote national political goals and its constitution has itself been amended to endorse this usage. Members of the governing board are no longer representative citizens of their countries but are now government representatives. Sovereigns have made of UNESCO another psychological instrument of power.

Reference has already been made to the tendency of a people to support authority, especially in times of crisis. The power of sovereignty over words and symbols cannot well be matched by dissidents where the sovereign is involved in or creates an international crisis. There have been exceptions such as: (1) when war has weakened the sovereign power and it is overthrown by an antiwar regime as occurred when the Mensheviks and then the Bolsheviks took over the sovereignty of Russia from the tsar and his court; and (2) when expression of opinion and the power freely to evaluate acts of sovereignty by the people are maintained as in the United States during the Vietnam War which after years appeared to them to be fruitless. Nor is counterpropaganda by foreign sovereign power likely to be accorded equal value to the words of domestic sovereignty; for not only will it meet with sentiments of patriotic solidarity hostile to the enemy, but cultural differences may conceal unfamiliar meanings and concepts which are made all the more unacceptable by inferences and suspicions. These inferences and suspicions are frequently untested and equally often there appears to be no desire to evaluate them. The result is that people who wholeheartedly desire peace expect war. "The indispensable condition of war," Gordon Allport has said, "is that people must expect *war* and must prepare for war, before, under war-minded leadership, they make war. It is in this sense that 'wars begin in the minds of men.'" It is this psychological process of expectation, which in so large measure determines behavior, which neither UNESCO nor the other organs and agencies of the United Nations have been able to modify successfully. Expectation of war affects the way of life of a nation. It also can strengthen the power of sovereignty by the very fears and dependence which it precipitates.

We are conditioned by our education and other experience to *expect* win-lose situations, that is, that one side must win and the other must lose. This is particularly so in political life, nationally and internationally. As a matter of fact where there are wars, revolutions, and serious riots the situation is usually one of lose-lose. There are and can be win-win situations where both parties win something, if not everything, and both may lose something, though not everything. But the expectation is that both can win, and this expectation is mutually accepted. While we do not usually think in terms of win-win, we have built into life the rudiments of such expectations. For example, although one side will be the winner of an election, the elective process is a recognition that both sides win by avoiding armed conflict between factions.[3] And in spite of great claims to sovereign supremacy a treaty has been approved renouncing the deployment of arms in outer space.

On the other hand, the very existence of a nation's sovereignty may be denied by another State but they may have transactions beneficial to both. The United States has refused to recognize the People's Republic of China. This is a win-lose posture by the United States. Nevertheless, there have been hundreds, if not thousands, of informal meetings between diplomats of the two countries in Warsaw and other places. This is a recognition that whatever goes on

[3] In the Second Book of Samuel in the Bible it is said: "And David executed justice and righteousness [charity] towards all people." The Babylonian Talmudic commentary on this passage says that where there is strict justice there is no charity and that where there is charity there is not justice. The commentators say that justice is done toward one by giving him his due whereas it is charity toward the other by removing his ill-gotten gains from his possession. So here was a case of moral win-win, though one may wonder whether he who was "charitably" relieved of his ill-gotten gains believed this a victory as the scholarly moralists evidently did.

over the table, under the table there is the mutual expectation that both nations will win something by communication.

When nations have been blocked on a win-lose position as between themselves, they have frequently tried the win-win approach by negotiations through third parties. The intervention of a third party as mediator may be an effective way to preserve prestige and make possible positive solutions. Many wars have been avoided and many ended by the mediation of third parties who have brought about solutions that did not impose the will of one upon the other in a clear win-lose situation. There have also been instances in which two nations have agreed to terms which were to the benefit of a third nation, not a party to the agreement, and which were enforcible by the third nation.

Although litigation is in the main a win-lose relationship, and the use of physical force aims at win-lose, parliamentary processes, management-labor negotiations, and international conferences commonly result in win-win resolutions of conflicts. This is what Max Adler has referred to as "creative bargaining." The result may not be a compromise but a new community of effort.

Thus, through the use of psychological weapons, hostile confrontation can be reduced by modifying expectations that one side to a dispute must win and the other must lose. Such a change in expectations automatically affects behavior.

15

LIMITATIONS ON SOVEREIGNTY OF NATIONS

BY ONE STATE ON ANOTHER

Bodin conceived of the idea of sovereignty to strengthen the Valois kings. This was a useful concept for rulers who wanted to concentrate power in their own hands and it supported the political weapon expressed in the idea that kings were God's anointed. Sovereigns of that day were well acquainted with the thought of St. Thomas that a ruler "had a primary responsibility to God who was the author of the law upon which the ruler's authority rested." And in the eighteenth century Louis XV could still proclaim: "It is only in my person that the sovereign power resides. . . ."

But the folly of the theory of absolute sovereignty even for domestic purposes (as discussed earlier) is magnified when it is applied to foreign relations. Powell, referring to John Dickinson's discussion of sovereignty, said, "He showed how it happened that folks got to thinking about sovereignty and that what they thought about it *for* was what made them think about it the way they did. . . . So if the idea was made up just to cover things all inside a country, you shouldn't try to make believe that the idea has anything to do with things between two countries."

Starke, writing on territorial sovereignty in international law, quotes the decision of the arbitrator in the case *Island of Palmas Arbitration*: "Independence in regard to a portion of the globe is the right to exercise therein, to the exclusion of every other State, the functions of a State." When we speak of "sovereign States" we are really talking of States with the power of self-government (at least to the extent that other "sovereign States" do not interfere with it). Those that cannot govern themselves have little sovereignty beyond the title. An example of this is the Congo when it first became independent of Belgium. Nor are sovereign States, even the powerful ones, independent of foreign sovereignties because the latter exert pressure and limit the freedom of action of other sovereignties and affect their goals and internal affairs.

Just as in the medieval Italian towns wealthy men spent fortunes to build towers as high as or higher than their neighbors' to obtain prestige, or for defense, and tried to match each other with the number and bravado of their *conditieri*, so nations try to match or surpass the military power of others within their economic capacity. Since the cold war began, after World War II, the United States and the Soviet Union have adopted budgets to assure themselves weapons that could match if not overcome the other. Production of consumer goods in the Soviet Union and improvement of city slums, education, and other welfare measures in the United States were curtailed or postponed in the interest of maintaining military prestige. *Each nation felt itself forced by the other to limit or modify its internal goals. Each, then, restricted the sovereignty of the other.* Communist China's assault along the northern Indian border in 1962 interfered with India's progress toward increasing industrialization, improving agriculture, and raising the standard of living of hundreds of millions of hungry, illiterate people. Israel and its Arab neighbors have spent large proportions of their budgets on military equipment which might better have gone to improving economic, and, in the Arab states, educational development and conditions of public health. Where military force is the coin of power a sequence of escalations affects the independence of nations to solve their problems. In this way sovereigns are limited in the exercise of their sovereignty, just as competing interests may limit sovereignty domestically.

After the Communist Revolution, Soviet Russia modeled its State after the highly mobilized war-States of the West, controlling the minds and bodies of men and planning their future as a general staff might plan a battle. And indeed in the late 1920s and 1930s Stalin's struggles to enforce collectivization of farms and eliminate rival politicians were as sanguinary as warfare. Stalin could maintain power by stimulating the psychology of a war-alert. The model was later taken over by Mussolini and Hitler. "And Russia's single-minded cult of power after 1917," Stillman and Pfaff wrote, "its demonstration that violent action can remake a nation, was to prove the most important influence that the new Russia would exercise upon the other awakened non-Western societies." It was this "Soviet vision of naked power" displayed so bloodily by the Stalin-Beria team that contributed to the change of the United States from a power relying principally on economic and psychological weapons to one that placed increasing dependence on force by way of the Truman Doctrine, Korea, and Vietnam. It also raised the power of the military in relation to the civil government, through what President Eisenhower called the military-industrial complex, to the highest point in American history.

A sovereign State may also be limited by another in the very territory of its sovereignty. The French claims to Alsace-Lorraine were denied between 1870 and late 1918 by the threat of German arms. Neither India nor Pakistan has been able to exercise sovereignty over the whole of Kashmir. The English kings could not successfully assert their title to the sovereignty of France in the Middle Ages. It need scarcely be mentioned that imperial designs on the territory of others to which there was no title by prior conquest or possession have been frustrated, as in the case of Russia's attempts under the tsars and the Soviets to expand to warm-water ports on the Gulf of Arabia and the Mediterranean.

The power of the State relates to geography and grows less with the distance from its power center. Its power becomes, as Russell said, "in equilibrium with that of some other state, and there the frontiers will be, unless the force of tradition interferes." Only war or a negotiated treaty can overcome the status of frontiers and extend the geographical boundaries of sovereign power.

The power of the sovereign was inversely related to the power of the satraps and proconsuls of old as the physical distance between them increased, and so too more recently the relations of the sovereigns to naval and military bases. For although modern communication techniques have made information and directions more readily transmissible, the ultimate power of force diminishes with problems of logistics. Thousands of miles still cause national flags to flutter more than fly.

In their power struggles stronger nations may impose their political maneuvers on neutral or new nations which had hardly any contact with them. This may be in terms of military, economic, or psychological power or a mixture of them. In recent times the United States, Great Britain, the Soviet Union, France, and Communist China have each tried to woo smaller nations as clients or dependents.

Sometimes institutions other than the State may enter upon foreign soil and exercise the powers of a sovereign. Thus the British East India Company operated as a sovereign in India but nevertheless was subject in many respects to the sovereignty of England, as witness the trial of Warren Hastings for his cruel administration in India. The United Fruit Company controlled or manipulated governments in Central America. Nevertheless it was subject to American antitrust laws. Around the sixteenth century the Jesuits representing Portugal and the Franciscans representing Spain tried to win the Japanese people to their faith and their cause. The Jesuits and their converts destroyed Buddhist temples and persecuted Buddhist priests. When a revolt occurred by the followers of these foreign orders the *shogun* decided that the country had had enough of foreigners and that the missionaries were what today we would call fifth columnists for imperial Portugal and Spain. Japan was then closed to all foreigners until the middle of the nineteenth century when it was opened by American threats of force and British guns.

In all of these instances domestic rule, sovereign power, was overcome, reduced, or distorted by foreign power.

Even more direct control of the independence of one

State by another occurs. Repeatedly in European history nations fought wars of succession to determine who would sit on a throne and exercise sovereign powers. For almost a century England, without asserting colonial dominion over Egypt, controlled its government so as to assure that the imperial lifeline through the Suez was secure. With varying excuses the United States has sent military forces to control Haiti and Santo Domingo until governments satisfactory to it were securely in power. Sometimes interventions in Latin America were to protect commercial interests, sometimes they were decked in ideological terms to preserve "democracy" from "Communist" inroads, always to preserve power in the sphere of influence of the United States.

In Eastern Europe Stalin imposed solutions and forms on the nations in that area which would solidify domination by Moscow and establish its enduring hegemony. He helped (even stimulated) revolutions, but, Djilas says, "only up to a certain point—up to where he could control them—but he was always ready to leave them in the lurch whenever they slipped out of his grasp." For Stalin recognized that "every revolution, simply by virtue of being new, also becomes a separate epicenter and shapes its own government and state," in other words, assumes sovereign powers.

Although after his death Stalinism was rejected by the Russian Communist Party, it maintains the policy of limiting the sovereignty of Communist nations at its borders. For example, the Soviet Union reacted strongly to the growth of independence in Czechoslovakia. Its power center was threatened by the growing freedom of speech and press in the Czech nation and the latter's drift toward closer political and economic relations with the West. This trend was a bad example for those other satellite nations within the Soviet Union's sphere of influence. If it were followed, they might all in time slip out of the grasp of the Kremlin's power structure. This would not only weaken the Communist alliance militarily, economically, and psychologically, but also indicate to the Russian people that its dictatorial authority had only limited sovereign power after all and that this might be challenged by free speech and press at home.

The invasion of Czechoslovakia was a defense against such threats to sovereign power. This invasion was explained by *Pravda* in an article entitled "Sovereignty and International Duties of Socialist Countries" as conforming to Communist ideology.

> Just as, in Lenin's words, a man living in a society cannot be free from the society, a particular socialist state, staying in a system of other states composing the socialist community, cannot be free from the common interests of that community.
>
> The sovereignty of each socialist country cannot be opposed to the interests of the world of socialism, of the world revolutionary movement. . . .
>
> Discharging their internationalist duty toward the fraternal peoples of Czechoslovakia and defending their own socialist gains, the U.S.S.R. and the other socialist states had to act decisively and they did act against the antisocialist forces in Czechoslovakia.

This concept is, of course, nothing new. Individuals, States, religions, and other groups in their own interests have time and again moved to save others from themselves regardless of the price paid by the "saved." It is clear that the interaction of States, the international political process, expands and contracts the respective power of States with relation to each other.

INTERNATIONAL LAW

Whether there is such a thing as international law has been the subject of massive scholarly discussion. Excellent examples are the articles by Scott and Morgenthau in *Essays on International Law*. To those who treat international law as being, in fact, law, it bears a closer resemblance to Hobbes' social compact than to Austin's positive law. "International law is a consensual legal system" according to Katz, not in the sense of social contract, however, he continues, but "in a practical operational sense." Certainly it is not law in the same sense as national (municipal) law, for it is neither made nor enforced by a sovereignty. It does not describe the limits within which a sovereign will exercise power as domestic law does. It is far more in the nature of customs, conventions, or contracts which serve the interests of a State. To speak of international law in the same sense that we speak of domestic law is wishful thinking at best. It is romanticism or semanticism. It can be called law but that does not make it law. Jessup, who believes that there is a body of international law, himself admits that national interests dictate national views on what are the rules of international law.

There can be a legal right only if there is a legal remedy and there is law only to the extent that it provides an enforcible remedy, i.e., that it is positive. The success of the common law has been its ability to find new writs to protect new rights, and when the King's courts were inadequate his chancellor could intervene, sitting in equity. As sovereign power has no authority to make or enforce international law, international law depends on acceptance by national States and that can be obtained only voluntarily, except as the result of the *force majeure* of an act of war. International law cannot be enforced against a State contrary to its will except through the action of another State to enforce its own will.

The most crucial issues between sovereignties are power struggles which are not justiciable. No court could determine the issues involved in the cold war between the Soviet Union and its allies on the one hand and the Western powers. Nor could the conflicts between Germany and her enemies have been litigated in 1870, 1914, or 1939. Even internal power struggles that develop into civil wars may not be litigable. Thus before the Civil War the South's insistence on the sanctity of states' rights, even at the expense of destroying the Union, as against the North's insistence that maintenance of the Union was paramount, could not have been effectively adjudicated.

When one party to a treaty regards the provisions to be unfair or no longer relevant it cannot force another sovereign to modify the treaty. It can only effectuate its own interest by action which violates the treaty or abrogates it. No legislative or judicial body can reform it. No concept of "sanctity" can preserve it. This is different from the situation in domestic law where "the possibility of amendment or repeal by the political organs of government is always present." Nevertheless, treaties and other international expressions of norms do have strong psychological power. Thus, as Kaplan and Katzenbach have pointed out, "Quite a bit has to be at stake, and a state has to be quite sure of its ability to 'get away with it,' before it will overtly violate norms which are generally accepted."

The invasion of Belgium by the German Empire in 1914 was a violation of the treaty between Belgium and Germany. The treaty violation was brushed off by the German Chancellor Bethmann-Hollweg with the statement that treaties were scraps of paper. The shock of the immorality of the invasion was compounded by the shock of realizing that treaties *were* scraps of paper if there was neither the will nor the capacity to enforce them. Germany had no will to respect the treaty. Belgium and the other Allied Powers at that time had no capacity to enforce it. Domestic (municipal) laws may also be scraps of paper unless expectation, dictated by experience, that they will be enforced by the sovereign causes people to observe them, or observance serves their self-interest. If they are not observed from self-interest or enforced by the sovereign or observed by the people with the expectation that if disregarded they will be enforced by the sovereign, there can be no law or, in that area, sovereignty.

What is called international law is a mixture of contractual arrangements (treaties, covenants, charters, etc.), customs, impositions by a superior power on a weaker, court decisions, and resolutions and declarations by international bodies which are not self-enforcing. The important difference between what is called international law on the one hand and domestic or municipal law is that the latter, but not the former, can be made and modified by legislative action which is binding, whether or not consented to, and can be enforced by the power of administration.

For the most part law observance among States comes about voluntarily because it appears to be in the national interest. For, lacking a successful war or the threat of war by a superior power, economic and psychological weapons for enforcement will prove ineffective, with rare exceptions. More likely there will be support of the defaulter by another nation; or, as in the case of the League of Nations' sanctions against Italy for making war on Ethiopia, the self-interest of the enforcing nations will omit from the prohibited goods such items as oil and steel.

OBSERVANCE FROM SELF-INTEREST

Contractual arrangements such as the fixing of postal rates by the Universal Postal Union are of a standing interest to the various parties. Each party tends to observe its undertakings in order to assure performance by the other parties.

There has long been a custom among nations, even before treaties to this effect, that foreign ambassadors should be treated with respect and neither they nor their embassies subjected to physical harm. Of course an ambassador and his staff could be easily imprisoned or manhandled by an angry State to which they were accredited. They could be fined for traffic violations, but they are not, for they enjoy diplomatic immunity from legal process. Here again mutual self-interest affords the protection of this custom, this "international law."

When a particular ambassador or a member of a diplomatic mission is found to be unacceptable by the nation to which he is accredited, he must leave that country. In reprisal the second nation usually finds the ambassador or a member of his mission accredited to it to be unacceptable and requests his withdrawal. This is a kind of ritual dance expressing hostility, permitting face saving, and avoiding direct confrontation.

If voluntarily agreed to, treaties fixing national boundaries are customarily observed; but this is not likely to be so when they are imposed by a conqueror on the vanquished. The acquiescence of the vanquished nation is felt by it to be consent given under duress, a humiliation to be redressed when the vanquished nation recovers power and prestige. This has been the sustenance of irredentism. Examples are easy to find, such as France with respect to Alsace-Lorraine after 1870, Germany and the Sudetenland after 1919, the claims to nationhood of Poland and the Baltic States, and the two-millennia-long desire of the Jews culminating in the establishment of Israel (which in turn has stimulated Arab irredentism). Humiliation or territorial deprivation or both have in all ages been *causa belli.*

Whereas duress may be a defense in municipal law, it is not a defense in international law, for to legitimize abrogation of treaties between conqueror and conquered would illegitimize a large proportion of the world's national boundaries and create international disequilibrium almost everywhere in the world. The Polish and Czech borders fixed by the Versailles Treaty were not acceptable to Germany between the World Wars and their rectification in 1938 became the first stage in Hitler's drive for conquest. But frequently the pressures to stabilize borders result in the voluntary submission of border disputes to arbitration, which is a way of consenting to border changes and at the same time saving face. By such a process the solution becomes no longer that of the sovereign. He is not responsible for the outcome, as he would be in case of war.

The charter adopted by the Allies authorizing the Nuremberg trials was an *ex post facto* definition of war crimes and no different from the imposition of norms and penalties upon the conquered which has occurred throughout history (except that at Nuremberg this was phrased in legal terms). For the Allied conquerors made the laws and had the power to pass judgment and enforce the judgment. This is not to criticize the sentences of the courts or the findings of guilt, but to point out that the "law" applied was the law of the triumphant.[1]

RETRIBUTION

In preliminary stages of the development of domestic or municipal law, retributive justice was common practice. A clan or tribe, one of whose members had been killed or otherwise harmed, could freely retaliate against the clan or tribe a member of which had done the harm. Even after sovereigns began to establish courts of their own, retributive justice continued for many centuries; and it is the rule today among States because of the absence of positive international law.

An interesting custom in the field of international law was that of *letters of reprisal.* If in the sixteenth, seventeenth, and eighteenth centuries the fleet of a foreign power seized a merchantman, the owner might apply to his sovereign for letters of reprisal. This authorized him in legal phraseology to go and seize ships of the other power, say Spanish, Dutch, or English ships, of equal value in order to compensate the shipowner for his loss. If pur-

[1] This discussion refers to "war crimes" not to the other offenses for which the defendants were tried, which applied the common norms of criminal law.

suant to the letter of reprisal the shipowner seized Spanish ships of a value in excess of his damages, the balance had to be turned over to his government, which in turn paid the excess over to the other government. (The practice lapsed when navies substituted for private reprisal.) "The remarkable fact is," says Jessup, "that the requirements of this law of reprisal were observed with all the punctilio of the *code duello*." This is another example of how self-interest induced observance of an otherwise unenforceable norm, even in a situation of reprisal, although the greater self-interest of maintaining peace could not be satisfied.

PEACE PACTS

A different kind of situation exists in such treaties as the Kellogg-Briand Pact renouncing war as an instrument of international policy and agreement not to seek the settlement of any dispute or conflict except by peaceful means. This was hailed as a great step toward peace in 1929 when it was ratified by sixty-three nations and Secretary of State Frank B. Kellogg was garlanded with the Nobel Peace Prize. It was a psychological commitment of importance, but its importance was a function of interobservance by the parties. Three of the signatory nations—Germany, Italy (1939), and Japan (1941)—made war in violation of the Kellogg Pact. France and England joined in the war, not to enforce the treaty, but to preserve themselves. Soviet Russia sat on the sidelines until invaded by Hitler. The United States rationalized its assistance to the Allies, before it became a belligerent, by the fact that the treaty had been violated by illegal resort to war. It is difficult to believe that the United States would not have aided the Allies, before it entered the war, even without such legalism.

The United States' abandonment of neutrality has also been declared legal in reliance on Grotius' classic: "It is the duty of those who stand apart from a war to do nothing which may strengthen the side whose cause is unjust, or which may hinder the movements of him who is carrying on a just war, and, in a doubtful case, to act alike to both sides. . . ." Such a rule calls for a value judgment of who is just and who unjust, and as no neutral court gives the evaluation it is left to the decision of each sovereignty as to which interpretation will best serve its national self-interest.

INTERNATIONAL LAW AS THE LAW OF THE LAND

Of course a State may include something designated as international law, such as a treaty or covenant, as part of its own domestic (municipal) law and enforce it as such. It then becomes part of the "law of the land" and is implemented in the same manner as any other law of the land. But it is the State, not any international power, which implements such international agreements. For "the ultimate decision as to whether and how to engage in a law-enforcing action," Morgenthau makes clear, "lies within the individual State." This "enforcing agent is identical with sovereignty in the judicial field. . . ."

While decisions of the International Court of Justice and its predecessor, the Permanent Court of International Justice, have in general been observed, this is not because of sovereign power used to enforce the decisions but rather because the parties to the case have committed themselves in advance to acceptance of the decision, and commitment is a built-in self-enforcer. It is in relatively unimportant disputes, moreover, that sovereigns will make such a commitment, which also accounts for the good record of observance of decisions. Critical issues affecting power or prestige are not likely to be adjudicated.

While commitment to accept the decision strengthens the chance that the international court's judgment will be adopted, the international judicial system is weak for the very reason that jurisdiction must be accepted by all the parties. This is well stated by Morgenthau: "The individual State remains the supreme party for deciding whether and under what conditions to submit a dispute to international adjudication, and no other State can summon it before an international court without its consent." In other words, the State itself determines whether a judgment of an international court will be enforced, just as it determines whether a domestic court decision will be enforced.

RECOGNITION

Another custom which Lauterpacht calls "a fundamental rule of international law" is that every independent State is entitled to representation by a government internationally, and that "to deny that right to a state is to question its independence." Consequently one sovereign is not normally concerned with changes in the form or membership of another sovereignty. However, difficult questions may arise when the replacement of one government by another involves revolution or civil war. This requires a determination of fact as to whether there is a government in power and inevitably involves political value judgments which may run counter to international law. International scholars such as Lauterpacht like to believe that the structure or composition of a government is an internal question and that a foreign sovereignty has no right to interfere even by raising the question of granting or refusing recognition. He says: "to admit that the grant or refusal of recognition to an authority claiming to be the government of an independent State is a matter of mere political discretion is to concede that some vital aspects of international relations, normally governed by international law, are subject to the vicissitudes of arbitrariness and of changing circumstances of expediency." Is such a concession not necessary if one is to view realistically the practices of States regarding recognition? International law may require the recognition of the People's Republic of China but United States commitment to the Republic of China in Taiwan, its opposition to Communism, and the constitutional problems relating to the Chinese veto power in the United Nations Security Council are more determinant of recognition than any "rule of international law." Many nations have refused to recognize the government of East Germany for several decades out of deference to the sensibilities of West Germany, or as a bargaining point with the Soviet Union.

ALLIANCES

Alliances have all the weaknesses and temporal characteristics of factions in the domestic political process. So long as it is to the common interest of the members of an alliance to pursue a policy or resist the forces of others, they feel obligated to mutual effort; but the relation tends to be unstable. After the cause which they were organized to meet has been dealt with, the allies become more involved in their respective national policies and needs for prestige, which become priorities. While psychological and economic pressures may be used to some effect in the name of the alliance, the likelihood that military force will support the alliance becomes with time less certain and more attenuated.

The Versailles Treaty prohibited Germany from exercising sovereignty over part of the Rhine Valley. Seventeen years later Hitler violated this provision of the treaty and no attempt was made by the victorious Allies of 1918 to enforce it. The United States had not ratified the treaty and had lost interest in Europe. Mussolini in Italy was allied with Hitler. France and England were not united on enforcement. The "law" of the Versailles Treaty therefore lapsed.

Economic partnerships are a form of alliance with greater promise of stability than politico-military alliances. The European Coal and Steel Community, Euratom, and the European Economic Community involve joint planning of economic development and production and reduce national competitiveness in their respective fields. The treaties setting up these organizations provide for community courts to settle disputes. To those courts have been delegated part of the sovereign judicial powers of the member States, which have guaranteed the execution of its judgments by the courts of those States. There may be conflicts between the community and national courts and these must be left to political agreements, for the law of the Coal and Steel Community, for example, is not sovereign law. The Community's law still requires and depends upon the action of each nation; but the functional nature of the partnership of these international economic institutions tends to remove disputes from the battlefield of the international power struggle to an area of cooperation in the ruling bodies of these organizations. This does not mean that there are no disagreements, but their settlement is less likely to be the result of the threat of force, for the bonds among the parties are functional. What Jessup has noted and quoted in another connection is valid here: "'. . . the legislative process of compromise, rather than the judicial process of victory-defeat, is considered more suitable to the resolution of disputes in . . . relatively new and uncharted paths of economic cooperation among nations.'"

THE UNITED NATIONS AND SOVEREIGNTY

It is sometimes argued that the United Nations is to international law what the national State is to national law. Undoubtedly the United Nations does exercise power over national States. This is a psychological power for the most part. Its good will is desired; its antagonism is to be avoided; membership and participation help national prestige; support or nonsupport—as by a promise of help or resistance to aggression by other nations—is sought at least as a psychological weapon. But the United Nations has neither legal nor judicial powers that are binding on nonconsenting States, and its enforcement powers other than those having a psychological effect are limited by the veto in the Security Council; and by the power of the States to refuse to contribute to United Nations peace forces or economic sanctions which might compel compliance. There has been unwillingness to apply the penalties prescribed in the United Nations Charter against nations failing to pay their assessments.

Furthermore, it appears that the United Nations cannot maintain a peace observation team on the soil of a sovereign State without that State's consent. Thus in 1967 when Egypt was preparing for war against Israel, it demanded that the United Nations remove its observers from Egypt. U Thant, the Secretary General, thereupon withdrew the United Nations observers. Certainly the United Nations forces were not sufficient to overcome the belligerent powers of Egypt if the latter had chosen to put them out physically. So the "law" followed the power reality. What the effect on other nations would be if a nation which is host to a United Nations observer team physically removed that team is uncertain. It would probably differ in various situations, depending upon a power alliance configuration in that area; but the very uncertainty of reaction to the removal or disarming of a United Nations force must have a strong psychological effect. This independent power of States demonstrates not only that international law of the United Nations is not positive law, but that it must break down into no law when it is not accepted by a particular State.

A comparison can be made to the Articles of Confederation at the end of the Revolution of the American Colonies against Great Britain. Each of the thirteen colonies, now states, sent delegates to the Congress. Regardless of population, each state had one vote. As Beard described the Congress, "It was in effect little more than a council of diplomatic agents engaged in promoting thirteen separate interests, without authority to interfere with the economic concerns of any." It had no executive, though a committee of thirteen sat when Congress was not in session. It had no system of courts. It could not raise an army or collect taxes except through the states "to which it had to assume the role of a beggar, hat in hand, at the capitals of the several commonwealths." The Confederation had no sanctions or power of coercion, which caused Madison to write: "Under form of such a constitution, it is in fact nothing more than a treaty of amity and of alliance between independent sovereign states."

While the United Nations Charter has the same weaknesses as the Articles of Confederation had, nevertheless the Assembly and the Security Council offer far-reaching platforms for psychological pressures. Although those organs have little practical power of economic sanctions, the collaborative actions by the United Nations agencies—as distinguished from competitive-political—exercise great economic as well as psychological power.

But it would be a mistake to assume that an international government could have and apply police power similar to that of a State to prevent violent power conflicts. For no international forces could be strong enough to intervene between great powers or even subdue or restrain a single great power. In the case of smaller nations there is the likelihood that a big power would become involved in support of the little State which it might need to help secure balance of power or superiority. The theory of the organization of the Security Council requiring unanimity of the big powers therefore makes sense with reference to weapons of force. However, if the Security Council wished to apply the sovereign weapons of economic or psychological power, the same argument for unanimity would not necessarily be relevant. Nor should the United Nations be underrated as a political battleground where symbols of force are used but force itself is not required. A nation's prestige in the United Nations may not be in terms of its war potential because the small States and the weaker ones have equal voting rights with the large and powerful, and alignments may have little reference to military power.

As the framers of the United Nations Charter recognized the realities of the application of force to the great powers and provided for what we know as the "veto," i.e., required their unanimity in the Security Council, they also realistically gave recognition in Article 51 to "the inherent right of individual and collective self-defense." In other words, if collective security could not be organized against major powers through the United Nations, then pragmatically a sense of security might be attained by a balance-of-power system, however vaporous and unreliable that might be in an age of nuclear armaments.

In practice the major powers have been loathe to engage in collective security. The Soviet Union and France have refused to contribute to the United Nations peace-maintenance forces, preferring freedom of diplomatic maneuver and alignment and support of subversion in troubled areas. The United States regarded as "unthinkable" the acceptance of the Soviet Union's suggestion to join in the enforcement of the United Nations demands against the United Kingdom, France, and Israel in the Suez crisis of 1956, for this would have given the Soviet Union military entry into the Middle East (which it later obtained bilaterally in Syria and Egypt). Nor was the United States willing to risk a general war in that year by intervening in the suppression of Hungary by the Soviet Union.

So far the nuclear powers have recognized that direct

military confrontation would precipitate the use of nuclear weapons, and that this must result in a lose-lose situation for both sides, that there could not be a win-lose result, and that only by restraint and accommodation could both sides win.

DIPLOMACY

When Woodrow Wilson in his Fourteen Points demanded open covenants openly arrived at he was voicing popular objection to international commitments by sovereigns which secretly bound their States without public notice or discussion. Secret diplomacy is a power weapon unsuited to an open society, a democratic State, for it leads to demands by the sovereign power group on the people of a nation for which they may be unprepared. It can be an arbitrary use of power. Therefore, secret diplomacy may also be ineffective as a psychological weapon of sovereignty because arbitrary power can stimulate resistance to the sovereign. This would not necessarily be so in the case of autocratic governments, as witness the Soviet-German treaty in 1939 which awarded the Baltic States to Stalin's Russia and gave Hitler a free hand to war against the West.

On the other hand, openness may also be an ineffective diplomatic technique. When the world plays kibitzer to both parties it is difficult to play the diplomatic game of negotiation to the best effect, whether that effect be the increase of power and prestige or reaching an accommodation.

For when the sovereign power speaks it is addressing some audience. This audience may be an opposing State, or neutral or hesitant nation whose support is desired; or more especially the words may be aimed at home consumption, i.e., maintaining sovereign power domestically. This is exemplified by nations at war, or the belligerence and posturing in anticipation of war. Such public commitments tend to freeze positions and make adjustment of differences impracticable. Whether relationships become frozen by secret undertaking or public pronouncement, the freezing process reduces fluidity for negotiation.

As Elmore Jackson has pointed out, there are international disputes suitable to judicial settlement before a court or arbitrator (such as treaty interpretations), and didactic statements of the case need be no bar to judicial settlement if they do not block submission of the issues. Other disputes, he says, are politico-economic and may involve more significantly vital national interests, including matters of sovereign power and prestige. In such matters States want to control both the forms and method of settlement. In these cases the mediation or intervention by the United Nations or some other third party can be seriously hampered by premature definition or freezing of positions.

"Conflicts," Jackson says, "are usually accompanied by strong emotional overtones, and the reduction of individual and group emotion is at least partially a problem in human relations, as well as being a problem in substantive settlement." Settlement is more likely to be effected if one or both parties perceive a risk in failure to reach an agreement than if neither does. And it is important that both parties be enabled to preserve prestige.

Maintenance of prestige may be a problem too for the United Nations or one of its organs or a State if they act as mediators and fail. Individual mediators selected by the United Nations or a State are therefore more likely to have greater freedom of operation.

INDIVIDUALS VERSUS FOREIGN STATES

Individuals have no remedies in international law except as their own government grants in its own courts a remedy against another State (usually against its property), or as a State undertakes to prosecute the cause of an individual in an international forum as a matter of State policy. Individual claimants against foreign sovereigns are in a position similar to those of individuals against sovereigns in medieval law. In the time of Edward I, the author of *Mirror of Justices* advocated that an English freeman, if his rights under Magna Carta were denied, "ought to recover damages by an assize of novel disseisin," but, says McIlwain, "unfortunately, as Bracton said, 'No writ runneth against the King.' The complainant has at most only an opportunity to petition for royal grace." But to whom, in the present state of international relations, can the individual petition if some sovereign does not undertake his cause?

Nevertheless, individuals have acquired psychological weapons of considerable power in *The Universal Declaration of Human Rights* and Covenants adopted by the United Nations and its agencies. Many national courts have made their provisions the law of the land, even in States that are not signatories to the Covenants and even without an international treaty based on the Declaration. But as yet individuals are without remedies in international forums and are likely to remain so while nationalism jealously withholds international status from the rights of individuals. If the United Nations creates the proposed position of Commissioner of Human Rights to receive and report on individual complaints of deprivation of human rights, this might give the individual a psychological weapon of value. But it is hard to conceive in the present state of national claims to sovereignty that the United Nations would or could enforce the rights of individuals except as the offending sovereign was amenable to the assumption of United Nations jurisdiction.

Finally, in the international as in the domestic field, the power of words and symbols will persist and grow. Slogans like freedom, equality, and justice, ethical appeals to conscience, the application of reason to the solution of problems, and a developing sense of community will affect power relationships. Words and symbols have always been a threat to arbitrary and autocratic uses of physical force and economic power and will increasingly threaten them in the international arena where the self-interest of the greatest holders of such powers demands restraint.

16

PRESTIGE

SOVEREIGNS ARE men; they react and interact with others as men; and they depend on the ideas and feelings of those whose support they require. As men who need the support of men, they must have prestige, that reputation for power which has already been considered in an earlier chapter. Prestige is not only associated with reputation for power, but also with such sentiments as admiration and respect, as Heider points out. Admiration and respect lead to alliances, partnerships, at times; but it is principally prestige based on a reputation for power that affects the political process. Whatever the origin of prestige (whether power or sentiment), opinions, values, and attitudes tend to follow the opinions, values, and attitudes of a person or institution with higher prestige.

To sustain sovereign power requires the constant maintenance of prestige. For those holding sovereign powers, as for any group of people, this is a psychological power need, which preserves in reserve and intact the more costly expenditures of force and economic power. The sovereign and group needs for prestige are derived from our needs as individuals for a sense of social power. This is an ego need which must be satisfied if we are to maintain balance or equilibrium, a homeostatic condition, within ourselves and in our transactions with others. We become hostile when another person or group causes us to have a sense of lost social power. As the business of sovereigns is to maintain, enhance, and exercise power, prestige (or social power) is of the essence of sovereignty. When the maintenance, enhancement, or exercise of power is reduced or threatened by some other force, hostility is stimulated. The same is true if there be aggrandizement of a rival's power which appears threatening to the sovereign, that is, is sensed by him to be a reduction of his own power. For power, never being absolute, must always be relative to that of others, and the pursuit of power must inevitably involve conflict.

When, therefore, it is said that war is necessary for the vital interests of a country, or to meet its obligations, what is meant is that the war is necessary in order to enhance or protect something which contributes to national strength. An example is to be found in the Peloponnesian War, brought on by the fear of Athens and Sparta and their allies that anything short of war, any concession necessary to maintain peace, would damage their prestige, weaken their respective alliances, and open them up to attack by the other. After years of war Athens, to increase her power and reduce that of Sparta, engaged in the self-destructive campaign to conquer Syracuse, a miscalculation with "patriotic" motives which ended in the annihilation of her forces in Sicily, the conquest of Athens, and domestic dictatorship.

The conflict to excel in power is illustrated by the manner in which World War I developed out of checkerboard moves by nations to preserve or enhance their prestige, each escalating a move by another until they were all driven to economic ruin or loss of prestige or both. The imperial plans of Austria-Hungary, Serbia, and Russia had been blocked in the Balkans. France still suffered from the defeat of 1870 and the annexation of Alsace-Lorraine to Germany. Germany had been blocked by England and France in Morocco in its ambition to compete with them for colonial hegemony in Africa. France, Germany, Austria-Hungary, Serbia, and Russia were suffering from depreciated prestige. And England felt its power to be threatened, especially by the growth of Germany's navy.

In this atmosphere of ailing prestiges came the murder of the heir to the throne of Austria-Hungary at Sarajevo. Austria-Hungary moved by threatening Serbia, Russia by threatening Austria-Hungary, Germany by threatening to support the latter, France and England by threatening to support Russia. Italy, an uncertain member of the Triple Alliance with Germany and Austria, wavered and finally opted for the Entente (England, France, and Russia). Lord Grey on the eve of the war told Parliament of his fear of "all of Western Europe opposite us . . . falling into the domination of a single power," i.e., Germany. England, he said, must take her stand "against the unmeasured aggrandizement of any power whatsoever." All the great powers of Europe, and some of the lesser, had thrown their prestige on the kindlings of Sarajevo. And as Lord Grey said, the lights of Europe went out one by one as Germany drove her armies against Belgium, France, and Russia. In the end they all lost prestige, for in military, human, and economic resources they were depleted—all except Serbia, which gained in area, population, and Mediterranean Coast under a more arbitrary and cruel sovereign than the Hapsburgs had been. The stage was then set for the rebuilding of prestige and new hostilities derived from new threats to power.

By means of war the stronger forces its will on the weaker sovereignty, so that in effect the latter may lose its sovereign power. This is what happened when the French kings increased their rule from a small domain to the sovereignty of all France, when the United States took over the richest land of Mexico, and when after World War II the Allies took over Germany and ruled it for some years. Even after much of the power of sovereignty has been restored to West Germany, the presence of the Soviet Army in East Germany, the armies of the Allies in West Germany, and the segregated position of a divided Berlin in the midst of Communist East Germany remain as symbols of the limits of Germany sovereignty. If both Germanys were to seek union they could not achieve it against the wills of their conquerors, except perhaps by precipitating another world war, for vital political interests of the power patrons of each Germany are involved.

If the relative strength of sovereigns is known, it need not be tested, for the weaker will yield to the stronger or the stronger may find other means to impose its will, as by the use of economic or psychological weapons. But this is not always the case. Ethiopia did resist Italy to keep independence, and Spain fought the United States. (Although Spain offered to pay an indemnity to the United States to avoid the war, the United States pursued war and some show of fight by Spain was essential to maintain a last vestige of prestige.)

The difficulty is that it is often impossible to measure

the relative strength of nations, i.e., the valence of their prestige, because this depends not only on ascertainable facts but also on their evaluation. If the relative power of hostile sovereignties could always be determined with definiteness, conflicts of force could be eliminated. But there are many imponderables, particularly in the field of the psychological forces of the apparently weaker power. Both Napoleon and Hitler misjudged the patriotic self-sacrifice (as well as climate in the case of Napoleon) of the Russian people. The Imperial German Army overestimated the military power of the tsar although perhaps if the German General, Von François, had not disobeyed his orders and delayed entering the Battle of the Masurian Lakes the Russians would have seriously damaged the fighting power of the Kaiser's army on the Eastern Front. It is interesting to ruminate on the difference this act of insubordination may have made in Marshal Von Hindenberg's reputation and thus in history. Hitler's misjudgment of the power of the Royal Air Force and the spirit of the British blocked his plans to invade England. This emphasizes too, as in the case of Russia, that psychological forces may have the weight of legions and must be assayed in estimates of power. Out of "social condition," Von Clausewitz said, "and its relations War arises, and by it War is subject to conditions, is controlled and modified."

There is another psychological facet to the miscalculation of prestige value. A nation, or its leaders, may misjudge the *possibility* that it may lose prestige by not using force and assume this to be a *probability*. Because Mao Tse-tung once referred to the United States as a "paper tiger" (a verbal attempt by a weak China to boost its prestige by humiliating the United States), this became a psychological factor in moving the United States to accelerate its participation in the civil war in Vietnam to show that it could conquer the dissident rebels and defeat the army of the Northern part of that country, even though the cost of the American intervention created dissidence and economic disequilibrium at home, that is, weakened the very basis of its military power and prestige. A folly which depletes a nation's power will not compensate for a demonstration that it is no paper tiger.

Cruelties committed in war have not long affected prestige. (Hitler's death camps are attributed not to war but to his madness and Nazi racism.) Generally some new cruelty in some other struggle replaces the old in public interest. Sometimes cruelties have even enhanced prestige at home, as was the case of the Crusaders who returned (when they did) boasting of the infidels they had slaughtered and the spoil they had seized.

Another argument is made in justification of intervention in another State to the effect that failure to do so would be defaulting on a nation's treaty obligations. Of course failure to honor military agreements would damage a reputation for reliability or responsibility, just as any breach of contract would and therefore would depreciate prestige. But even if a sovereign power were bound by treaty to intervene in a war, perhaps such an intervention would not be supported by the other treaty nations if they were not getting economic benefits from the purchase of military supplies from them at the cost of small contributions of men or material of their own.

Economic power makes possible physical power, the creation and replacement of the instruments of armed force in preparation for a showdown and to inflate prestige. Economic and psychological power create the capacity to maintain a war.

In this sense the economy of a nation is the base of its prestige; and the moral strength, that is, the psychological attitudes and will of its people, supports its prestige. Reference has been made to the impossibility of accurate self-evaluation by a nation of its psychological power of resistance, measurement of its prestige, and reliable evaluation of the power of resistance or prestige of another nation. But in the final analysis the capacity to use force effectively is the weapon to which all else contributes.

As in domestic situations the political process involves the choice of fight, compromise, or withdrawal. To keep this power strong for a possible conflict basic to national interest may at times dictate the surrender or deprecation of a claim to sovereignty which is less vital. It is true that to other nations compromise or withdrawal may appear evidence of a consciousness of weakness, it may be an injury to prestige, but if it secures the strength and availability of sovereign weapons for possible conflicts of more vital concern, then it is a sacrifice worth making. Athens' failure to disengage itself in Sicily made its defeat by the Spartans inevitable, Rome's unreadiness to liquidate its extended empire in the face of a weakened economy, and the dynamic assaults of the Germanic tribes cost it its Western empire and the sovereignty of Rome itself. On the other hand France, by disengaging itself from Southeast Asia and Algeria (which it had long considered part of Metropolitan France), gained more prestige than it lost, for it stopped a great drain on its economy and manpower and a serious division in popular support. The economy of Great Britain, however, was so depleted by two wars that the liquidation of its empire could not restore its prestige. Retreat under necessity is more damaging to prestige than a tactical retreat.

Hostility that is implict in a threat to sovereignty and its prestige encourages the projection of the sovereign's hostility to others. A sovereign may attribute greater strength and aggressiveness to the opponent than it possesses and find the mirror image of the sovereign's own hostility in the words and acts of the opponent. This projection is facilitated by the secrecy maintained about armaments and war plans generally which stimulates rumors of aggressive plots. For we fill in the gaps of knowledge with rumors and many a fantastic and threatening concept.

Feeling that a war may become necessary to rectify the balance of prestige, to prove its prestige, a nation frequently accuses another nation of preparing for offense. It is probable that many wars as well as domestic crises of sovereigns have resulted from the self-fulfilling prophecies that hostile actions would be commenced by an opponent. The feeling of the inevitability of a war, the expectation of war, affected the minds of Englishmen and Germans before World War I.

Before that war England was preparing for war with Germany, which was threatening England's century-long naval supremacy and demanding a place in the select club of colonial imperialists. The German claim that it was encircled by enemies determined to destroy it led it to the offensive of both World Wars. (Switzerland, however, equally encircled, projected no such hostile feelings on its neighboring nations and used them for its economic advantage. The uses of economic power were more suitable than force to establish its prestige.)

Boulding suggests that, though it is not necessary always to execute threats to make them effective "they must be carried out on a sufficient proportion of occasions," so that they are taken seriously. The psychology of this threat process is described by Rapoport in discussing "brinkmanship," the threat of war which depends for its fulfillment on the opponent's response. Brinkmanship, he says, is telling the opponent:

This is an issue on which we must have our way or else we go to war. We know that we may stand to lose everything in a war. But so do you. You will lose much less if you yield on this issue than if you fight. Therefore it is in your interest to yield. . . .

The effectiveness of this gambit depends entirely on how firmly the opponent believes what you are saying. If he disbelieves you, both you and he lose. Effective communication (the ability to communicate so as to be believed) is essential in any policy based on threats.

If threat to a sense of power arouses hostility, that is, an attempt to redress the balance of power, then it should be apparent that to avoid war or any other hostile behavior it is more effective to give the opponent an opportunity to save face, to keep prestige, not to challenge his power more seriously than the reality of the situation (not its flamboyant psychological offshoots) demands. Reston says that "the major governments are beginning to adapt their action to the realities of power and geography. They talk tough, which is the respect they pay to the political assumptions and attitudes of the past [the myth of the supremacy of national sovereignty], but they act prudently, which is the respect they pay to the destructive nuclear power of the present." It would seem wisdom that a power should permit an opposing power to escape humiliation or a threat to its national sovereignty, however restricted the latter may be. The rebellious barons in medieval England went through the ritual of attacking not the king himself but his "wicked advisers" and removing them. Thus the king, who might really be at fault, did not have to defend his dignity or power to maintain prestige although in fact his power was challenged. Only when his crown, his title, was threatened did a confrontation with arms become inevitable. Senator Robert F. Kennedy has given further supporting details.

THE CUBAN MISSILE CRISIS AS A MODEL

A good example of sensitivity to an opponent's possible humiliation in a modern power struggle between States was the Cuban missile crisis. We have detailed descriptions of this in the synoptic accounts of Sorensen, Schlesinger, and Hilsman, all of whom participated in one way or another in the planning or the execution of the plan on the American side.

In the summer of 1962 reports came from several sources—routine shipping intelligence, reports from Cuban refugees, and reports by intelligence agents in Cuba—that Russian missiles were being installed there. Although there was risk involved—especially after America's loss of face when a high-flying reconnaissance plane had been shot down over Russia two years before, resulting in Khrushchev's cancellation of a planned summit conference with President Eisenhower—President Kennedy decided to have high-flying U-2 planes reconnoiter and photograph possible missile sites in Cuba. The photographs proved to be convincing evidence of a threatening situation, for they showed missile installations in various stages of completion only a few miles from the American coast. These missiles when fully installed would have been within firing distance of all but one major city in the United States and would have increased the Soviet destructive power against the United States by fifty per cent, "enough to erode the American capacity to strike back." The missiles and their installations were being delivered and set up in secrecy, which in itself increased threat. When Russia learned that the United States knew something about the installations, high Russian officials insisted that only defensive weapons were involved in order to prevent an American invasion of Cuba. Foreign Minister Gromyko made such a statement to the President, who already knew the truth, at the end of a talk in which Gromyko had made threats about the position of the Western allies in Berlin.

Here in Cuba was a threat to American power and prestige that could not be overlooked. It was addressed to a vital interest of the nation. Would the threat of removal of the missiles by force represent a similar threat to Soviet power and prestige? Could the American position be firm without freezing either its own or the Soviet's position so that prestige maintenance could only be accomplished through war, in this case a nuclear war? How could support be obtained from the American people, the NATO powers, the Organization of American States, and the United Nations without tipping American hands (destroying *its* secrecy) in advance and possibly creating dissension and reducing needed support? How could the Soviet Union be given an opportunity to save face? Similar questions in one form or another are present in all confrontations between nations.

On a world level the positions of the Soviet Union and the United States had changed in the preceding year or so. The Soviets were having more difficulty than anticipated in dealing with underdeveloped nations. The Sino-Soviet dispute had got out of hand. It could no longer be patched up or swept under the carpet. The Soviet Union was having economic difficulties domestically. In the United States President Kennedy after more than a year's experience felt more secure in the presidency. He could act firmly on Berlin. There was greater unity in the Atlantic community, and the United States had definitely gained military supremacy, particularly through its nuclear power. That it realized it had this supremacy it let the Soviet Union know by indirection, in this case through a speech by an undersecretary of defense. (Important information is frequently given by such indirection, apparently because in the atmosphere of conflict a direct statement may be regarded as propaganda or a declaration by a more highly placed person may be more likely to freeze the diplomatic position of the nation.)

Cuba was a sensitive subject. The revolutionary government of Castro was demanding military protection from its sponsors in the Soviet Union; and the United States, the President in particular, was smarting under loss of prestige as a result of the failure of the Cuban refugee invasion of Cuba at the Bay of Pigs the year before which had been supported by the Central Intelligence Agency.

The Soviet decision to install missiles in Cuba was made in an attempt to resolve some of these problems, to redress the power balance, and to capitalize on the Bay of Pigs blunder. It is apparent that the Soviet Union considered this tactic in its world political context as a leverage on the

Berlin situation, as a threat of war which might damage the unstable NATO Alliance, encourage other Communist revolutions in Latin American, weaken the power and prestige of the United States, and impress China with the Soviet's aggression against the leading capitalist country.

The prestige of both the Soviet Union and the United States was being tested by this Cuban confrontation. Cuba's prestige was not much considered at that moment. It only became an issue later when Cuba refused to permit United Nations inspection of the missile sites which were to be abandoned pursuant to the settlement reached by Kennedy and Khrushchev. (Presumably the Soviet officials knew in advance that this would be Cuba's position.)

What the political pressures were in the Kremlin we do not now know. But it is reasonable to assume that there were those who wanted to take a firm stand, to shoot it out if necessary, and those who were more alive to the dangers of a nuclear war and were ready to write off the Cuban venture as a lost gamble even at the cost of some lessened prestige. On the American side, there were pressures to take no action—especially in view of the Bay of Pigs fiasco with its loss of prestige the previous year—by people who felt it not worth taking the risk of bringing two countries to the edge of nuclear war. Such people included some members of the general public, Congress, the press, and possibly allies on both sides of the Atlantic. Then there were the chiefs of staff of the military forces who were for drastic military action to remove the missiles and installations promptly by force. And it was anticipated that there would be those congressmen (there already were senators), part of the press, and the general public demanding strong military action when the facts became known.

There were also those who wanted action limited to diplomacy directly and through the United Nations; and finally some who sought a middle-ground approach. So part of the political process was to keep the facts hidden as long as possible, to go about the business of government seemingly as usual while determining policy, to inform the allies in the Atlantic Organization and the Organization of American States, to inform the United Nations, and to brief leaders of Congress and the press—and to tell the Russians. The President then had to present dramatically to the world the facts that he had about the Cuban missiles and how he proposed to deal with the problem.

Among the President's closest advisers there was division, and some probably were not convinced of the rightness of his decision. Some believed no action to be necessary. Others preferred formal diplomatic approaches directly to Khrushchev or through the United Nations or the Organization of American States. Some preferred to take out the missiles by military force without warning (like the Japanese action at Pearl Harbor in spite of the world's horror at such an assault and the danger of Russian nuclear retaliation). And finally, a few at first, were those who wanted the tactic of a blockade (called by the President "quarantine" because it sounded less belligerent, less like an act of war). The decision was to "quarantine" (blockade) Cuba against the entry of all Russian ships containing armaments or war materiel and to board all Russian ships outside of Cuban waters. Though the President's statement to the world was firm on the removal of the threatening missile bases, it offered the Soviet Union a way out. This plan began with the use of force at the lowest level, leaving open further levels of force to be applied if necessary.

There was, of course, a risk of Russian resistance and retaliation, but the Russians had a chance to withdraw, to save face before irretrievable acts of violence occurred. This, as the President expressed it, reduced the possibility of a "spasm" reaction.

The President's intention was to be firm but to space events so that his opponents could always preserve a measure of prestige if, facing the probable consequences of escalation, they stepped back. So on Monday he announced his plan of blockade. Only on Tuesday, after receiving approval from the OAS, did he issue his proclamation, which was not to become effective until the next day. The two ships stopped (one boarded) were permitted to proceed to Cuba because they carried no weapons, although one was an oil tanker.

On Friday, through an unofficial contact (a correspondent of an American television network), not diplomatic channels, the Russian Embassy asked and immediately received the United States' terms for Soviet withdrawal. The next day came a long cable from Khrushchev to Kennedy. According to Hilsman and Robert Kennedy, a key passage read: ". . . we and you ought not to pull on the ends of the rope in which you have tied the knot of war, because the more the two of us pull, the tighter that knot will be tied. And a moment may come when that knot will be tied so tight that even he who tied it will not have the strength to untie it, and then it will be necessary to cut that knot, and what that would mean is not for me to explain to you, because you yourself understand perfectly of what terrible forces our countries dispose." No better symbolic argument against the escalation of international disputes could be given, no better way of saying that the alternative to war was lessened tension through joint participation in a solution.

On Saturday Khrushchev broadcast what appeared to be a reversal of position and offered to trade removal of the Soviet missiles in Cuba for removal of the American missiles in Turkey. President Kennedy refused to make such a trade under pressure (ironically, the American missiles in Turkey were obsolete and the President had ordered their removal some time before, but the military had failed to follow instructions). The Russian ships and the escorting submarines had meanwhile stopped short of the blockade line but one ship detached itself and moved toward Cuba. Each side was testing the will of the other.

How were these contradictory signals to be treated? Were Friday's superseded by Saturday's? The President's brother, Robert Kennedy, suggested that the Saturday version be ignored and Khrushchev's Friday cable, together with the informal presentation of the American terms made through the correspondent, be accepted as the solution.[1] To the Friday communications, therefore, the President replied and broadcast his reply (with a contemporaneous communication through diplomatic channels of the urgency of reaching agreement). Then Sunday morning Khrushchev announced that the weapons would be dismantled and returned to Russia; and the President, sensitive to the need for the Soviet Union to maintain prestige in the interest of lessening tensions, urged his administration not to gloat or claim victory.

[1] This became known as the "Trollope Ploy." In the novels of Anthony Trollope, when a girl's hand has been squeezed by a young man she frequently interprets it as a proposal of marriage. Thus the United States chose to treat Khrushchev's Friday signals as a "proposal of marriage."

Here we can see a confrontation of the two most powerful nations possessing the most lethal weapons resolved (with the defeat of the Soviet Union, it is true, but without humiliation) with sensitivity to the need to handle with care, as explosive, that reputation for power, the loss of which would stimulate hostility. The tactic used permitted the opponent to withdraw without humiliation at any step of the way and at each pause to weigh the ultimate costs in terms of escalation by either side which might result in a "spasm response" with nuclear warheads.

The failure to restrain the escalation of force, to make withdrawal without humiliation, without offering to opponents a sense that their psychological power will not be severely damaged but will be respected, was the mistake of the several powers before World War I and of the United States in its involvement in Vietnam, to cite two examples.

Where the confronting nations can join in an enterprise tensions can best be reduced, and the making of the treaty barring above-ground nuclear tests a few months after the missile crisis further reduced the tension between the United States and the Soviet Union. The Cuban missile crisis demonstrated that firmness can be respectful of the opponent's pride and strength, can withhold or graduate the application of force. It is true that the presence of missiles in Cuba was of greater importance to the vital interests of the United States than to those of the Soviet Union. Had the prestige and power values of the presence of missiles in Cuba been the same to both nations, deescalation would have been more difficult if, in fact, it would have occurred.

In personal confrontations, laughter is a great easer of

tension; but laughter unfortunately is regarded as weakness by sovereign nations, seriousness as a sign of determination. For when the holders of power are anxious because they are uncertain how others esteem their power, they fear humor which may be directed at them and threaten them with humiliation. They appear unable usually to free themselves of this dread and share laughter. Hurt pride reduces mobility even more than threatened prestige. The king's jester served a purpose by ritualizing comic relief.

PRIDE

If prestige is the reputation in which a person or nation is held by others or the regard in which they are held, the corollary is pride, or self-esteem. Both prestige and pride are ego needs, and a threat to either, especially when prestige and pride are focused on power, may cause a lessening of self-confidence and politically may entail a loss of support. When, therefore, a sovereign takes a strong position in support of or against another power, his position tends to become frozen and his pride to block an admission of error. This is sometimes called loyalty to friends or sticking to a principle, but in either case it becomes a block to accommodation.

Three items illustrating this appeared in *The New York Times* on the same day. There is a barren island about one-third of a square mile lying between India and Ceylon. It has no fresh water or inhabitants and has been used occasionally by smugglers and fishermen. Even the spelling of this island's name was uncertain. Ceylon ran up its flag and thus proclaimed the island to be under its sovereignty. This created an uproar by the opposition party in the Indian

Parliament and they accused the government of minimizing what they called a territorial crisis. Pride was impeding negotiations.

The second incident was a letter alleged to have been written by the crew of a United States intelligence ship captured by the North Koreans, who claimed the ship had entered its territorial waters and held the crew prisoners. The crew purported in its letter to ask its government frankly to admit "that we intruded into territorial waters of the Democratic Peoples Republic of Korea and committed hostile acts, and sincerely" apologize "for these acts and" give "assurances that they will not be repeated." Whatever the merits, the crew with the consent or at the instigation of their North Korean captors were asking the United States to admit violation of international law, to do an act which would humble its pride.[2]

Third, President Nasser of the United Arab Republic (Egypt), suffering from a third military defeat by Israel, repeated his refusal to negotiate peace face to face with Israel because no Arab leader dared to engage in such negotiations. Not only might his government fall, but he might be assassinated because Arab pride had been humiliated by a small nation with a small population. Israel, too, had frozen its position by insisting on face-to-face talks. Its pride required its enemies to sit down with it as an equal.

When it is in the interest of national policy and does not endanger a sovereign power, pride may be disregarded. In the same interview, for example, Nasser admitted that he had been in error in accusing the United States, whose assistance he now courted, of sending its air force to the as-

[2] It was different for the United States to admit intrusion in the process of negotiating with North Korea.

sistance of the Israelis in the recent war. He said his accounts were based on error, but pride still prevented an apology. (The "error," incidentally, may have been a psychological weapon to whip up the passions of the Arabs in Egypt and other lands and to court the intervention of the Soviet Union. A personal telephone call between the White House and the Kremlin committed the United States and the Soviet Union mutually to refrain from intervention.)

Both prestige needs and pride tend to inhibit rational solutions. Satisfaction of prestige needs may tentatively avoid the use of power where the mere threat of power suffices to achieve recognition or reinstatement of prestige. This may provide little space for maneuver; and, where violence, war, or other physical force are conceived as the principal and most likely weapons to redress the prestige balance, ego defense by demonstration of power risks overcompensation with deathly results. This is especially so when action is influenced by sick personalities or mobs or whole populations in hysteria or panic.

CONCLUSION

PEOPLE WHO are not dependent or docile have certain needs which they may call democracy, equality, freedom, or something else. These needs, whatever they are called, include being respected by others and not being dominated or pushed around. People also want to participate in some way, to have some voice in determining their condition; they want to be able to assess what the sovereign power or any other authority has done which affects them. They want to be free from arbitrary acts which reduce their sense of self-esteem, their sense of social influence, and their prestige, however lowly it may be, however scanty on the scale of power. Finally, they want the power to take action to have these needs fulfilled. They want the sovereign or the sovereign's court to see them, to hear them, and to listen to them. This is the essence of such symbols as democracy, equality, and freedom which the opposition uses against, what Fulbright has called, the arrogance of power, an arrogance not only of sovereigns in their pursuit of domestic policies, but also internationally. It is in this symbolic sense that "democracy," "equality," and "freedom" are used here.

The essence of democracy, then, is not the representative

or parliamentary form of government with which it is often confused. Of course, this confusion is aided and abetted by refusal to face the ugly fact that political, economic, and social equality do not exist and that democracy is therefore an ideal, rather than a reality, that in its political aspects democracy is only ritualized equality. In democratic countries it is as bad manners to question the realities behind formal democratic institutions as it would be to challenge the fact and condition of marriage of your aunts and uncles. And in the "people's democracies" of the Communist world the question has led to the firing squad or exile, and still may close the prison doors behind the questioner.

No substantial democracy can be achieved nor, being brought about, can long endure unless the mass of the people, as a whole or singly or by groups, can canvass the acts, the words, and other symbols of all who have economic or physical power over others, and express prompt and open approval or disapproval.

What we call a democratic State as compared to an autocratic State requires such a balance among the holders of political weapons of force and wealth as will enable freedom of expression to exist. Politically, freedom of expression is the right not only to state one's own view but to challenge and assess the views of others. *For the first equalizer is the question, that question which searches the reason or justice of some specific application of power.*

It is the question that initiates what Mills calls "the free ebb and flow of discussion." It is the role of the mind, of reason, to attack myth and hokum and "to define reality adequately and in a publicly relevant way." There can be no democracy or equality or freedom where force can be arbitrarily applied or where economic power can be exerted without accounting. The bully and the terrorist do not recognize the needs of others less powerful. They do not perceive or, perceiving, acknowledge that others need a sense of social power, some chance to question their condition; or if they perceive these needs, they fear them and attempt to destroy those who express them. The same is true of holders of great accumulations of wealth. They want no equal competitor, no challenge of their power whether from government, labor, consumer, or another holder of strong economic power weapons, although openly or covertly they may combine with the latter in cartels. "Democracy has no more persistent nor insidious foe than the money power. . . . The enemy is formidable because he works secretly, by persuasion and deceit rather than by force and so takes men unawares," Viscount Bryce says in *Modern Democracies*. And today the "money power" whether in the form of private enterprise or state operation controls the most powerful media of information and opinion, that is, psychological power.

In the concentration of economic and psychological power, great corporations not only strongly influence the sovereign power, or even are an important part of it, but they can control the lives of workers, except as limited by labor bodies and the influence of the latter on legislation. But for such matters as take home pay and hours of labor, on which standards of living and upward social mobility depend, the laboring class in highly industrialized nations tends to merge with the middle class and thus to outdate the Marxian confrontation of proletariat and bourgeoisie. The relative increase in employment in service industries (including government) compared to production industries (more than half the laboring force in the United States is in the service field today) accelerates this change in relationship. Nevertheless, conflicts of interest persist and in an age of dislocation of work opportunities and obsolescence of skills due to rapid technological development, power relationships have a new relevance. A more highly skilled and better educated work force, feeling its way into middle-class culture, will be less docile, less willing to accept a position of little or minimum influence, than the unskilled and semiskilled workers of traditional industry. So we find a tendency to involve workers in the changes brought on by advancing technology, including their own training to adapt to new skills. We find, too, a developing trend to instruct management in the human relations aspects of industrial operation, i.e., the better use of psychological power and less reliance on arbitrary economic power in the motivation of workers. Where, especially in government, management has not developed in this way, labor organizations have tended to force acceptance of greater worker participation.

Where great masses of people are involved, they feel a distance from the authorities who make the decisions and purport to control their lives without giving them a chance to influence the manner in which *their* institutions are operated.

"One feature of modern existence which tends to convert aggression into hate is the size and complexity of civilized institutions," Storr writes. "When a man is, or feels himself to be, an unimportant cog in a very large machine, he is deprived of the chance of aggressive self-affirmation, and of a proper pride and dignity." It is not only in industrial and government bureaucracies that conflict has developed out of people's sense of distance from and lack of influence on policy making and adjustment to change. There have been demands by students to control university education, by local communities to control their local schools, and by slum populations to take over the management of institutions aimed at improving their condition. This movement to push controls down to the people affected has been called "participatory democracy."

Participatory democracy has been successful in the New England town meeting in Colonial times and in the kibbutzim in Israel, that is, in small, easily defined communities. But in large fluid communities it is questionable to what extent and for how long people will democratically participate except when specific, emotion-laden issues are involved. Technical issues not subject to electoral processes will more likely be incompletely dealt with and there will be the tendency of the community after the first flurry of participation no longer to participate. Most likely is the use of mechanisms of participatory democracy by power factions within and overlapping the community, whether they are political, ethnic, racial, or ideological. Marx advocated participatory democracy on the basis of the short experience of the Paris Commune. Lenin and his Bolsheviks used the Soviets of soldiers and workers to accomplish their revolution but then rapidly discarded them. This does not mean that *participation* in policy making cannot reduce conflict and increase motivation when it is functional, as in university management, parent-and-teacher participation in the organization of schools, and bringing about change in industrial organizations and governmental bureaucracies.

Although the art of sovereignty lies in the satisfaction of adverse interests (when they cannot be eliminated), it is not within the power of sovereigns dealing with so variable a species as mankind to obliterate all conflicting interests, or to weave into a single pattern the differentiated needs and demands of the human race. Thus, theories looking to the complete elimination of the State are only propagandist dreams. We have also seen that the broader the base of the sovereign group and the more inclusive the synthesis of conflicting interests into a dominant ideology, the greater will be the equilibrium of society and the less need will there be for power in the State to enforce the sovereign will. In other words, the fewer or weaker the outstanding interests which are not incorporated in the group holding power, the fewer or weaker will be the disaffected interests and consequently the less call will there be on the sovereign group to make distribution of its economic substance or apply its repressive forces.

In primitive societies, variation of type, of background, and of economic need was slight and any marked deviation from culturally accepted norms was immediately punished by the elders, or by secret societies who enforced conformity to the will of the ancestral shades in whose names they spoke. Thus substantial equality was maintained—of course subject to those elders. But this is not possible in a complex industrial society, the very technological needs of which demand creative enterprise. The ghosts of saints and sinners cannot be permitted to slow the industrial assembly line except at the price of economic dislocation. The very life of an industrial society demands the continued application of scientific method, the creation of new conditions of disequilibrium, of new demands which cannot be at once, if ever, completely satisfied.

Technological advances continuously result in change, change which demands the reassortment of personal relationships. The management of changed roles and relationships by computer must result in alienation and alienation will be the broth, the culture, within which will be bred resistance and hostility. Any reassortment of relationships will tend to increase tension and resistance to change unless the people affected are involved in the process of planning those areas of change which directly concern their relationships to others, that is, their amended roles. This is a democratic process that Bennis and Slater suggest "becomes a functional necessity whenever a social system is competing for survival under conditions of chronic change."

Any ideology, to have validity, must effect a synthesis between the need for an inclusive sovereign group, and the centripetal effects of scientific development which will constantly upset the niceties of social and economic balance. It must find a place also for the formula that industrial development requires science and that the scientific mind and method are sceptical, inquiring, logical; that the scientific mind cannot live without free thought which is crystallized into words, into symbols that reach beyond pure science and become the leaven for doubts and the leverage for a new motion of things. The Communist countries have been able for a time to compartmentalize this freedom of scientific method and thought; but other compartmentalized areas could not be expected to continue indefinitely oblivious to the freedom of scientists and barred from interacting with them. Poets and other writers require freedom, too, and they have in all ages been able at last to force their symbols into the political process.

Congenital inequalities and psychic storms which originate in the nursery have a disintegrating social effect. This is so whether they be expressed or concealed if they have not been successfully compensated or sublimated in adult life. Even the well-housed and well-fed derive insecurity and dissatisfaction from these conditions. The inmates of hospitals, prisons, and asylums for the mentally ill at one extreme, and megalomaniacs who, more often than we recognize, hold political or industrial power at the other, bear testimony to this. Lasswell says that "political movements derive their vitality from the displacements of private affects upon public objects. . . . The state is a symbol of authority, and as such is the legatee of attitudes which have been organized in the life of the individual within the intimate interpersonal sphere of the home and friendship group. . . ."

A political philosophy which is not autocratic and whose goal is to minimize power differences must provide for a State implemented by powers which are widely distributed. It must be alive to the fact that power is volatile or, as James Madison expressed the idea in *The Federalist*, "power is of an encroaching nature, and . . . ought to be effectually restrained from passing the limits assigned to it." This is not to be achieved by the simple device of the Constitution of the United States, the sharing of the formal machinery of the State among the executive, legislative, and judicial branches of government. That simply leaves the State machinery or one or more of its arms open to capture. "The moral is," Russell says, "that a democracy, since it is compelled to entrust power to elected representatives, cannot feel any security that, in a revolutionary situation, its representatives will continue to represent its wishes. . . . If Parliament, in such circumstances, can rely upon a preponderance of forces, it may thwart the majority with impunity." The framers of the Constitution had a realistic sense of such a possibility, so they also provided mechanisms to offset the arbitrary will of the propertyless majority; and the First Congress adopted the Bill of Rights to restrict the arbitrary powers of the Federal government. It was only at the end of the nineteenth century, and especially during the presidencies of the two Roosevelts, that finance and industry began to be seriously controlled. (But note that some of the controlling agencies, such as the Interstate Commerce Commission, the Federal Power Commission, and the Federal Communications Commission, as well as their counterparts in the states, have tended to strengthen great private enterprises rather than protect the public in whose interest they were created.)

But while it has been the boast of Anglo-American political theory that we are a government of laws, not of men, can law be more than norms of comparative justice, freedom, equality, and authority to be interpreted and applied by men in accordance with their experiences, needs, and hopes? That this is so is demonstrated by the history of legal systems. Parliaments and the highest courts have reversed themselves when their old norms came under pressure of new demands.

DIFFUSION OF POWER

Limitation of power is only to be achieved through a diffusion of physical force and economic power. Some weapons of physical power are already diffused. They may not always be effectively timed or appropriatly used. The strike is now centuries-old. So are demonstration and boycott. In our own time nonviolent civil disobedience has been added to the arsenal of effective force against authority. But when these weapons are accompanied by violence, or should their use appear to threaten the supremacy of sovereign powers, counterviolence will be enacted by the police or the military. Other factions may also feel threatened and respond with violence or bring pressures on the sovereign to use force against the strikers or other demonstrators.

Under capitalism the only hope of diffusing economic power is to maintain a balance between finance and industrial management, organized labor and consumers. Otherwise the State, the machinery of the sovereign power, will be seduced or captured by the stronger power.

The mere transfer of economic power to the government through government ownership, that is, State socialism, will not accomplish this diffusion of force and power, for bureacuracy will then only substitute for plutocracy or some form of oligarchy. State socialism can at best be only a temporary advance over the concentration of private ownership. It must result in a losing race for equality, for the satisfaction of those individual needs already mentioned, as against bureaucracy. In a socialist society, the end can only be achieved through direct control of industry by each industrial group, leaving to the State the settlement of conflicts, overall planning and financing, and foreign and defense affairs. But such residual powers themselves may enable the sovereign group to diminish free expression and the freedom to canvass sovereign behavior. Such limited independence of industrial enterprises, a sort of diluted syndicalism, appears to be the developing pattern in Yugoslavia, where, subject to overall planning, each plant or commercial establishment makes its own plans and competes with other similar plants and commercial operations. This should ideally have two immediate results: first, the diffusion of economic power and its consort propaganda—neither the State bureaucracy nor finance capital could then have a dominant monopoly as to economic weapons or could monopolize the weapons of propaganda. Second, there would be a lessening of the role and therefore the power of the central bureaucracy. But while there is any kind of centralism resting in the police or the military or industrial bureaucracies, can the challenging questions be publicly asked? And where technological developments change personal relationships, can stability be achieved under any system that is autocratic?

The great stumbling block to the diffusion of power is war, even the threat of war, which requires a mobilization of physical force and brings internal as well as external dangers from such concentration of power. For an army may be as dangerous to the sovereign group as an enemy and needs as careful watching lest it be the vehicle of a transfer of sovereign powers. Praetorian Guard, Reichswehr, or Red Army—none is to be trusted. And General Eisenhower, in his farewell Presidential address, warned the United States against its "military-industrial complex," a power—often a secret one—within the government.

This combine of military (force) and industrial (economic) power greatly influences the government bureaucracy and restricts its role as a balancing force among the various interests and factions of the people. It controls communication (psychological power) by the prestige and financial assets of its members and their capacity to give rewards. Its psychological power is enhanced by the tendency of great conglomerate corporations to combine war-related industries with the control of publishing houses and other mass media.

The fear of war, however justified, induces hysteria, and hysteria is oblivious to its own lack of balance, is blind to trenches it has dug for itself. The warning of Alexander Hamilton is clear:

> The violent destruction of life and property incident to war, the continual effect and alarm attendant on a state of continual danger, will compel nations the most attached to liberty to resort for repose and security to institutions which have a tendency to destroy their civil and political rights. To be more safe, they at length become willing to run the risk of being less free.

For when a people fear or expect war they will support their sovereign power in preparations against invasion and treachery and to avoid them will be ready to find security in the restrictions of an armed camp and the suspicions of the police mind. The "military-industrial complex" will become the sovereign power.

Examples are not difficult to find. During the American Civil War the writ of habeas corpus was suspended and censorship imposed by so great a libertarian as Lincoln himself in violation of the First Article and First Amendment, respectively, of the Constitution. After the Japanese attack on Pearl Harbor in 1941 one of the most disgraceful pages of American history was written when in hysteria first-, second-, and third-generation Japanese, citizens as well as residents, were herded into "relocation"—concentration —camps. During both the World Wars, censorship, espionage acts, and sumptuary laws cracked down on civilian populations throughout the world. The threat of war has created armed camps and destroyed civil rights in most of the land between the North Sea and the Pacific. Even in the comparatively isolated United States, before World

War II, bills were introduced in Congress which on the coming of war would deny the people free speech, free press, and the right to strike. At the same period, France adjourned parliamentary procedure and the parties of the left, in the shadow of a dictatorship, were compelled to accept Daladier's partial suspension of the forty-hour working-week legislation which was a basic part of their program. A pattern was set for the Vichy government. This and more were made possible by German mobilization and Hitler's threats to Czechoslovakian sovereignty. The hysteria deriving from the threatened danger of war has led the world repeatedly to pawn individual freedom of action and expression which was won by centuries of effort and the sacrifice of millions of lives.

Our perceptions of sovereignty are influenced by our expectations of the roles of the sovereign, which, as in the case of our expectations in everyday life, are based on our experience. So long as our experience has emphasized the use of threat of force as a principal role of the sovereign in relation to those subject to his sovereignty as well as to other sovereigns, our expectations will be centered around the uses of potential force. It is worth repeating what Gordon Allport has said, that "what *people expect determines their behavior*. . . ." and "the indispensable condition of war is that people must expect *war* and must prepare for war, before, under war-minded leadership, they make war. It is in this sense that 'wars begin in the minds of men.' "

But such expectations need not be. They can be changed over time. They can be reoriented here and there in specific situations. We have seen this occur among the Scandinavian nations, and, in fact, almost all European nations and the Soviet Union are composed of formerly warring States. So, too, in Colonial days miniscule wars occurred between American Colonies. This illustrates how earlier win-lose expectations have become expectations of community in which all the original parts become the winners.

While the concept of force remains in the background and has not been eliminated from expectations in the case of domestic sovereignty, the other weapons of sovereignty including institutions symbolic of physical force have been introduced and have found acceptance. Lorenz has shown that among certain species of fish and birds ritualized expressions of aggression have substituted for fighting and have made possible the protection of areas claimed by fish or fowl as well as the perpetuation of the species. Symbolic expressions of aggression are psychological weapons and need development, but this cannot be achieved unless the expectations of those controlling sovereign powers are prepared for it. In this connection it has been urged that disarmament will of itself change expectations and attitudes by reducing reliance upon force as an appropriate mode of settling disputes or reestablishing equilibrium. This certainly has been the story of disarming private people who through the ages had carried arms and used them to settle disputes.

The more that satisfying arrangements for settling disputes without force can be instituted, the less will be the importance of the use of force and feelings of prestige relative to force. It is just possible—and surely necessary—that in an age of nuclear weapons national interest may be perceived in terms of avoidance of use of force.

While force lurks around the corner or behind some arras of noble words in all political situations, it is pragmatically avoided in the political process in normal times.

The uses of economic and psychological weapons are more practicable; but as they can be applied inequitably, arbitrarily, and cruelly they may create disequilibria which lead to resort to force. This is so both domestically and internationally.

It follows that only as international equilibrium can be established through the elimination or at least the substantial reduction of conflicting interests (whether between sovereigns or between sovereigns and their people) can there be a diffusion of the weapons of physical force. No democratic, no egalitarian ideology can, therefore, be complete which does not encompass the entire world. Salvation cannot be national nor can freedom from domination and humiliation be provincial. Until all people have power in addition to voting to participate in making decisions that affect their lives (at least on a local level or where their roles and relations to others are seriously affected) and until all people have the power to challenge sovereign power, to ask the questions that search the integrity and wisdom of authority, the first whispered complaints of the unrequited will become again and again the roar of hate from a new wave of rebels (to be crushed or purchased) or of conquering revolutionaries—or a new explosion of armed power. Then each time dissent will once more subside to be crystallized into the ideology of a new system with more or less unwilling adaptation to changed relationships by those whose needs are not met and whose expectations may be disappointed by the changes that have occurred.

One must remain skeptical as to whether equality and freedom can ever be wholly achieved; but one can envision a world less torn by the struggle for power between irreconcilable interests. "The issue," as Inis Claude has formulated it, "will never be whether power exists; it will always be whether power is subject to effective management." This can only happen with the increase and diffusion of psychological power, i.e., of words and symbols, in relation to the other weapons of power, physical force, and economic power. Values can be changed. They are constantly, if not always noticeably, changing. So too is it possible to change expectations from win-lose (one side must win, the other lose) to win-win (both sides can win something) in the relationships of sovereigns to those subject to them and in the relationships of nations.

BIBLIOGRAPHY

CHAPTER 1

FRAZER, JAMES, *The Golden Bough.* New York, The Macmillan Company, 1923.

CHAPTER 2

Bailey v. Alabama. 211 U.S. 452 (1911).

BOUVIER, JOHN, *Law Dictionary*, 3d ed. Kansas City, Mo., Vernon Law Book Company, 1914.

CARDOZO, BENJAMIN N., *The Paradoxes of Legal Science.* New York, Columbia University Press, 1928.

CHARMONT, JOSEPH, "Conflict Between Law and the Individual Conscience," *Modern French Legal Philosophy.* The Modern Legal Philosophy Series, Vol. VII. Boston, Boston Book Company, 1916.

DICEY, ALBERT V., *Law and Public Opinion in England During the Nineteenth Century.* London, 1905.

———, *Introduction to the Study of the Law of the Constitution.* London, The Macmillan Company, 1902.

LASKI, HAROLD, *The Foundations of Sovereignty.* New York, Harcourt, Brace and Company, 1932.

MACHIAVELLI, NICCOLO, *The Prince.* New York, Everyman's Library, 1932.

McIlwain, C. H., *The Growth of Political Thought in the West.* New York, The Macmillan Company, 1932.
McKechnie, W. S., *Magna Carta.* Glasgow, James Maclehose & Sons, 1914.
Markby, William, *Elements of Law.* New York, H. Froude, 1905.
Rosenthal, Joel T., "The King's 'Wicked Advisers' and Medieval Baronial Rebellions," *Political Science Quarterly*, LXXXII, 4 (1967).
Story, Joseph, *Commentaries on the Constitution of The United States.* Boston, Little, Brown and Company, 1905.
Swindler, William F., *Magna Carta: Legend and Legacy.* Indianapolis, Ind., Bobbs-Merrill, 1965.
Trotsky, Leon, *The History of the Russian Revolution.* New York, Simon and Schuster, 1932.
United States v. Sprague, 282 U.S. 716, 733.
Wolfe, Martin, "Jean Bodin on Taxes: The Sovereignty-Taxes Paradox," *Political Science Quarterly*, LXXXIII, 2 (1968).

CHAPTER 3

Jackson, Elmore, *Meeting of Minds.* New York, McGraw-Hill Book Company, 1952.
Machiavelli, Niccolo, *The Prince.* New York, Everyman's Library, 1932.
Trotsky, Leon, *The History of the Russian Revolution.* New York, Simon and Schuster, 1932.
Witte, Count Serge, *Memoirs.* Garden City, N.Y. Doubleday Page and Co., 1921.

CHAPTER 4

Adamic, Louis, *Laughing in the Jungle.* New York, Harper & Brothers, 1932.
Berle, Adolph A., *The Three Faces of Power.* New York, Harcourt, Brace & World, 1967.
———, *Power Without Property.* New York, Harcourt, Brace and Company, 1959.

———, and Means, G. C., *The Modern Corporation and Private Property*. New York, Commerce Clearing House, 1932.

Cohen, Morris R., "Philosophy and Science," *Columbia Law Review*, XXXII, 1122 (1932).

Cushing, Harvey W., *From a Surgeon's Journal*. Boston, Little, Brown and Company, 1936.

Demogue, René, "The Notion of Law," *Modern French Legal Philosophy*. The Modern Legal Philosophy Series, Vol. VII. Boston, Boston Book Company, 1916.

Dennis, Lawrence, *Is Capitalism Doomed?* New York, Harper & Brothers, 1932.

Dewey, John, *Liberalism and Social Action*. New York, G. P. Putnam's Sons, 1935.

Galbraith, John Kenneth, *The New Industrial State*. Boston, Houghton-Mifflin Company, 1967.

Kaufman, Bel, *Up the Down Staircase*. Englewood Cliffs, N.J., Prentice-Hall, 1964.

Kozol, Jonathan, *Death at an Early Age*. Boston, Houghton-Mifflin, 1967.

Liebknecht, Karl, *Militarism*. New York, B. W. Huebsch, 1917.

Markby, William, *Elements of Law*. New York, H. Froude, 1905.

Newton, Jesse Homer, *Educational Administration as Social Policy*. New York, Charles Scribner's Sons, 1934.

Ponsonby, Arthur, *Falsehood in War-Time*. New York, E. P. Dutton & Company, 1928.

Rathenau, Walther, *In Days to Come*. London, George Allen & Unwin Ltd., 1921.

Reider, Joseph, "The Origin of Deuteronomy," *Jewish Quarterly Review*, XXVII, 366 (1937).

Riegel, Oscar W., *Mobilizing for Chaos*. New Haven, Conn., Yale University Press, 1934.

Sakharov, Andrei D., "Thoughts on Progress, Peaceful Coexistence and Intellectual Freedom," *The New York Times*, July 22, 1968.

Von Ihering, Rudolf, *Law as a Means to an End*. The Modern Legal Philosophy Series, Vol. V. Boston, Boston Book Company, 1913.

CHAPTER 5

American Banana Co. v. United Fruit C., 213 U.S. 347, 358.

ARNOLD, THURMAN, "The Role of Substantive Law and Procedure in the Legal Process," *Harvard Law Review*, XLV (1932), 617.

ASCH, SOLOMON E., *Social Psychology*. New York, Prentice-Hall, 1952.

AUSTIN, JOHN, *Lectures on Jurisprudence*. London, J. Murray, 1869.

Baker v. Carr, 369 U.S. 186 (1962).

BERLE, ADOLPH A., *The Three Faces of Power*. New York, Harcourt, Brace & World, 1967.

BREHM, JACK W., and COHEN, ARTHUR R., *Explorations in Cognitive Dissonance*. New York, John Wiley & Sons, 1962.

Brown v. Board of Education of Topeka, 347 U.S. 483 (1954).

CARDOZO, BENJAMIN N., *The Paradoxes of Legal Science*. New York, Columbia University Press, 1928.

———, in *People v. Defore*, 242 N.Y. 13.

DEMOGUE, RENÉ, "The Notion of Law," *Modern French Legal Philosophy*. The Modern Legal Philosophy Series, Vol. VII. Boston, Boston Book Company, 1916.

FISHER, ROGER, "Bringing Law to Bear on Government," in Saul H. Mendlovitz, ed., *Legal and Political Problems of World Order*, preliminary ed. New York, The Fund for Education Concerning World Peace through World Law, 1962.

GARDINER, JOHN H., *The Bible as English Literature*. New York, Charles Scribner's Sons, 1906.

GAREIS, KARL, *Introduction to the Sciences of Law*. The Modern Legal Philosophy Series, Vol. I. Boston Book Company, 1911.

Gitlow v. New York, 268 U.S. 652.

HOLLAND, THOMAS E., *The Elements of Jurisprudence*. Oxford, The Clarendon Press, 1888.

Jacobus v. Colgate, 217 N.Y. 235.

LINCOLN, ABRAHAM, "First Inaugural Address," *Abraham Lincoln's Speeches and Letters*, 1832–1865. London and New York, Dutton and Company, 1907.

McIlwain, C. H., *The Growth of Political Thought in the West.* New York, The Macmillan Company, 1932.

Maine, Henry James S., *Dissertations On Early Law and Custom.* New York, Henry Holt and Company, 1883.

———, *The Early History of Institutions.* New York, Henry Holt and Company, 1888.

Markby, William, *Elements of Law.* New York, H. Froude, 1905.

Massell, Gregory J., "Law as an Instrument of Revolutionary Change in a Traditional Milieu," *Law and Society*, II, 179 (1968).

Post, Charles Gordon, *The Supreme Court and Political Questions.* Baltimore, The Johns Hopkins Press, 1936.

Sherif, Muzafer, *The Psychology of Social Norms.* New York, Harper & Brothers, 1936.

Trotsky, Leon, *The History of the Russian Revolution.* New York, Simon and Schuster, 1932.

Von Ihering, Rudolf, *Law as a Means to an End,* The Modern Legal Philosophy Series, Vol. V. Boston, Boston Book Company, 1913.

Williams, Michael, *The Catholic Church in Action.* New York, The Macmillan Company, 1934.

Wilson, Francis G., "A Relativistic View of Sovereignty," *Political Science Quarterly*, XLIX, 394 (1934).

CHAPTER 6

Cohen, Morris R., "Property and Sovereignty," *The Cornell Quarterly*, XIII (1927), 8.

Gardiner, John H., *The Bible as English Literature.* New York, Charles Scribner's Sons, 1906.

Gareis, Karl, *Introduction to the Science of Law,* The Modern Legal Philosophy Series, Vol. I. Boston, Boston Book Company, 1911.

McIlwain, C. H., *The Growth of Political Though in the West.* New York, The Macmillan Company, 1932.

CHAPTER 7

Adkins v. Children's Hospital, 261 U.S. 525.

AUSTIN, JOHN, *Lectures on Jurisprudence*. London, J. Murray, 1869.

Henningsen v. Bloomfield Motors, Inc. 32 N.J. 358, 161 A. 2d 69 (1960).

MCILWAIN, C. H., *The Growth of Political Thought in the West*. New York, The Macmillan Company, 1932.

MARKBY, WILLIAM, *Elements of Law*. New York, H. Froude, 1905.

VON IHERING, RUDOLF, *Law as a Means to an End*, The Modern Legal Philosophy Series, Vol. V. Boston, Boston Book Company, 1913.

Wilkinson v. Leland, 2 Peters U.S. 627 (1829).

CHAPTER 8

DEMOGUE, RENÉ, "The Notion of Law," *Modern French Legal Philosophy*. The Modern Legal Philosophy Series, Vol. VII. Boston, Boston Book Company, 1916.

DEWEY, JOHN, *Liberalism and Social Action*. New York, G. P. Putnam's Sons, 1935.

JOAD, C. E. M., *Guide to Modern Political Theory*. Oxford, The Clarendon Press, 1914.

LASKI, HAROLD, *The Foundations of Sovereignty*. New York, Harcourt, Brace and Company, 1932.

LENIN, V. I., "The State and Revolution," *A Handbook of Marxism*. New York, International Publishers, 1935.

MCILWAIN, C. H., *The Growth of Political Thought in the West*. New York, The Macmillan Company, 1932.

MACHIAVELLI, NICCOLO, *The Prince*. New York, Everyman's Library, 1932.

MARKBY, WILLIAM, *Elements of Law*. New York, H. Froude, 1905.

TROTSKY, LEON, *The History of the Russian Revolution*. New York, Simon and Schuster, 1932.

WELLS, H. G., *The Outline of History*. 3d ed. New York, The Macmillan Company, 1921.

CHAPTER 9

ADORNO, THEODOR W., et al, *The Authoritarian Personality*. New York, Harper & Brothers, 1950.

ARGYRIS, CHRIS, *Personality and Organization*. New York, Harper & Brothers, 1957.

Brown v. Board of Education of Topeka, 347 U.S. 483 (1954).

CARTWRIGHT, DORWIN, and ZANDER, ALVIN, eds., *Group Dynamics*. Evanston, Ill., Row, Peterson, and Company, 1953.

COHEN, ARTHUR R., "Upward Communication in Experimentally Created Hierarchies," *Human Relations*, 11, 1 (1958).

KIRCHHEIMER, OTTO, "Private Man and Society." *Political Science Quarterly*, LXXXI, 1 (1966).

LIKERT, RENSIS, *New Patterns of Management*. New York, McGraw-Hill Book Company, 1961.

RICE, ALBERT K., *The Enterprise and Its Environment*. London, Tavistock Publications, 1963.

WHYTE, WILLIAM FOOTE, *Men at Work*. Homewood, Ill., Dorsey, 1961.

CHAPTER 10

BEARD, CHARLES A., *The Economic Basis of Politics*. New York, Alfred A. Knopf, 1945.

———, and BEARD, MARY R., *The Rise of American Civilization*. New York, The Macmillan Company, 1927.

BERLE, ADOLPH A., *The Three Faces of Power*. New York, Harcourt, Brace & World, 1967.

DEMOGUE, RENÉ, "The Notion of Law," *Modern French Legal Philosophy. The Modern Legal Philosophy Series*, Vol. VII. Boston, Boston Book Company, 1916.

DICEY, ALBERT V., *Law and Public Opinion in England During the Nineteenth Century*. London, 1905.

FRAZER, JAMES, *The Golden Bough*. New York, The Macmillan Company, 1923.

Fulbright, J. William, *The Arrogance of Power.* New York, Random House, 1966.

Hawtrey, R. G., *Economic Aspects of Sovereignty,* 2d ed. London, Longmans Green & Company, 1952.

Kropotkin, Prince Pietr A., *Ethics: Origin and Development.* New York, Dial Press, 1924.

Laski, Harold, *Karl Marx, an Essay,* London, The Fabian Society, 1925.

Lewin, Kurt, *Field Theory in Social Science.* New York, Harper & Brothers, 1951.

Madison, James, "Vices of the Political System of the United States (1787)," in Gaillard Hunt, ed., *The Writings of James Madison,* Vol. II. New York and London, G. P. Putnam's Sons, 1901.

Marx, Karl and Engels, Friedrich, *The Communist Manifesto.* New York, Russell and Russell, 1963.

Merriam, Charles E., *Political Power.* New York, McGraw-Hill Book Company, 1934.

Rathenau, Walther, *In Days to Come.* London, George Allen & Unwin Ltd., 1921.

Recent Social Trends in the United States, Report of President Hoover's Research Committee on Social Trends. New York and London, McGraw-Hill Book Company, 1933.

Rosenthal, Joel T., "The King's 'Wicked Advisers' and Medieval Baronial Rebellions," *Political Science Quarterly,* LXXXII, 4 (1967).

Santayana, George, *Reason and Common Sense.* New York, Charles Scribner's Sons, 1917.

Trotsky, Leon, *The History of the Russian Revolution.* New York, Simon and Schuster, 1932.

Zweig, Stefan, *Joseph Fouché.* New York, The Viking Press, 1930.

CHAPTER 11

Carlyle, R. W., and Carlyle, A. J., *A History of Medieval Political Theory in the West.* London and Edinburgh, William Blackwood & Sons, 1903–36.

Charmont, Joseph, "Conflict Between Law and the Individual

Conscience," *Modern French Legal Philosophy*. The Modern Legal Philosophy Series, Vol. VII. Boston, Boston Book Company, 1916.

HEGEL, GEORG W. F., *Lectures on the Philosophy of History*. New York, Humanities Press, 1963.

HITLER, ADOLF, *My Battle*, trans. by E. T. S. Dugdale. Boston and New York, Houghton-Mifflin Company, 1933.

McILWAIN, C. H., *The Growth of Political Thought in the West*. New York, The Macmillan Company, 1932.

McKECHNIE, W. S., *Magna Carta*. Glasgow, James Maclehose & Sons, 1914.

CHAPTER 12

COHEN, MORRIS R., *Reason and Nature*. New York, Harcourt, Brace and Company, 1931.

LASKI, HAROLD, *The Foundations of Sovereignty*. New York, Harcourt, Brace and Company, 1932.

TROTSKY, LEON, *The History of the Russian Revolution*. New York, Simon and Schuster, 1932.

VON IHERING, RUDOLF, *Law as a Means to an End*, The Modern Legal Philosophy Series, Vol. V. Boston, Boston Book Company, 1913.

CHAPTER 13

AUSTIN, JOHN, *Lectures on Jurisprudence*. London, J. Murray, 1869.

BEROLZHEIMER, FRITZ, "The Perils of Emotionalism," *The Science of Legal Method*. The Modern Legal Philosophy Series, Vol. IX. Boston, Boston Book Company, 1917.

DEMOGUE, RENÉ, "The Notion of Law," *Modern French Legal Philosophy*. The Modern Legal Philosophy Series, Vol. VII. Boston, Boston Book Company, 1916.

KORKUNOV, NIKOLAI M., *General Theory of Law*, The Modern Legal Philosophy Series, Vol. IV. New York, The Macmillan Company, 1922.

Merriam, Charles E., *Political Power.* New York, McGraw-Hill Book Company, 1934.

Pound, Roscoe, "A Comparison of Ideals of Law," *Harvard Law Review,* XLVII, 1, 14 (1933).

Santayana, George, *Reason and Common Sense.* New York, Charles Scribner's Sons, 1917.

Veblen, Thorstein, *The Theory of Business Enterprise.* New York, Charles Scribner's Sons, 1919.

Wurzel, Karl Georg, "Methods of Juridical Thinking," *The Science of Legal Method.* The Modern Legal Philosophy Series, Vol. IX. Boston, Boston Book Company, 1917.

CHAPTER 14

Allport, Gordon W., "The Role of Expectancy," in Hadley Cantril, ed., *Tensions That Cause Wars.* Urbana, Ill., University of Illinois Press, 1950.

Clausewitz, Carl Von, *On War,* rev. ed., Vols. I and III, trans. by J. J. Graham. New York, E. P. Dutton and Company; London, Kegan, Paul, Trench, Trubner and Company, 1940.

Fisher, Roger, "Bringing Law to Bear on Government," in Saul H. Mendlovitz, ed., *Legal and Political Problems of World Order,* preliminary ed. New York, The Fund for Education Concerning World Peace Through World Law, 1962.

Fulbright, J. William, *The Arrogance of Power.* New York, Random House, 1966.

Harrington, Michael, *American Power in the Twentieth Century.* New York, League for Industrial Democracy, 1967.

Hawtrey, R. G., *Economic Aspects of Sovereignty,* 2d ed. London, Longmans Green & Company, 1952.

Hilsman, Roger, *To Move a Nation.* Garden City, N.Y., Doubleday and Company, 1967.

Jacobs, Noah Jonathan, *Naming Day in Eden.* New York, The Macmillan Company, 1958.

Kohn, Hans, *The Idea of Nationalism.* New York, The Macmillan Company, 1944.

McKeon, Richard, ed., *Democracy in a World of Tensions.*

UNESCO Symposium. Chicago, University of Chicago Press, 1951.

MILGRAM, STANLEY, "Some Conditions of Obedience and Disobedience to Authority," *Human Relations*, XVIII, 1 (1965).

MORGENTHAU, HANS J., *Politics Among Nations*, 3d ed. New York, Alfred A. Knopf, 1960.

MOSLEY, PHILIP E., "Techniques of Negotiation," in Raymond Dennot and Joseph E. Johnson, eds., *Negotiating with the Russians*. Boston, World Peace Foundation, 1951.

MÜLLER, HERBERT J., *The Uses of the Past*. New York, Oxford University Press, 1952.

WEDGE, BRYANT M., "Nationalism and International Communication," in Milton Schwebel, ed., *Behavioral Science and Human Survival*. Palo Alto, Cal., Science and Behavior Books, 1965.

XENOPHON, *Anabasis—The March Up Country*, trans. by W. H. D. Rouse. New York, New American Library, 1959.

CHAPTER 15

BEARD, CHARLES A., and BEARD, MARY R., *The Rise of American Civilization*. New York, The Macmillan Company, 1927.

DJILAS, MILOVAN, *Conversations with Stalin*, trans. by Michael Petrovich. New York, Harcourt, Brace & World, 1962.

Essays on International Law from the Columbia Law Review. New York, Columbia University Press, 1965. See especially: James B. Scott, "The Legal Nature of International Law"; Hans J. Morgenthau, "The Problem of Sovereignty Reconsidered"; H. Lauterpacht, "Recognition of Governments: I"; and Morton A. Kaplan and Nicholas deB. Katzenbach, "Law in the International Community."

JACKSON, ELMORE, *Meeting of Minds*. New York, McGraw-Hill Book Company, 1952.

JESSUP, PHILIP C., *A Modern Law of Nations*. New York, The Macmillan Company, 1948.

———, "Diversity and Uniformity in the Law of Nations," in Andrew E. Cordier and Wilder Foote, eds., *The Quest for Peace*. New York, Columbia University Press, 1965.

Katz, Milton, *The Relevance of International Adjudication*. Cambridge, Mass., Harvard University Press, 1968.

Madison, James, "Vices of the Political System of the United States (1787)," in Gaillard Hunt, ed., *The Writings of James Madison*, Vol. II. New York and London, G. P. Putnam's Sons, 1901.

McIlwain, C. H., *The Growth of Political Thought in the West*. New York, The Macmillan Company, 1932.

Morgenthau, Hans J., *Politics Among Nations*, 3d ed. New York, Alfred A. Knopf, 1960.

Powell, Thomas Reid, "A Comment on Professor Sabine's 'A Pragmatic Approach to Politics,'" *Political Science Quarterly*, LXXXI, 1 (1966).

Russell, Bertrand, *Power*. New York, W. W. Norton and Company, 1938.

Schachter, Oscar, "The Enforcement of International Judicial and Arbitral Decisions," *The American Journal of International Law*, LIV, 1960.

"Sovereignty and International Duties of Socialist Countries," from *Pravda. The New York Times*, September 27, 1968.

Starke, Joseph G., *An Introduction to International Law*, 5th ed. London, Butterworth & Company, 1963.

Stillman, Edmund, *and* Pfaff, William, *The Politics of Hysteria*. New York and Evanston, Ill., Harper & Row, 1965.

CHAPTER 16

Allport, Gordon W., and Postman, Leo, *The Psychology of Rumor*. New York, Henry Holt and Company, 1947.

Boulding, Kenneth E., *Conflict and Defense*. New York, Harper and Brothers, 1962.

Fulbright, J. William, *The Arrogance of Power*. New York, Random House, 1966.

Hawtrey, R. G., *Economic Aspects of Sovereignty*, 2d ed. London, Longmans Green & Company, 1952.

Hayakawa, S. I., "Meaning, Symbols, and Levels of Abstraction," in T. M. Newcomb and E. L. Hartley, eds., *Reading in Social Psychology*. New York, Henry Holt and Company, 1947.

HEIDER, FRITZ, *The Psychology of Interpersonal Relations*. New York, John Wiley and Sons, 1964.

HILSMAN, ROGER, *To Move a Nation*. Garden City, New York, Doubleday and Company, 1967.

HORWITZ, MURRAY, "Psychological Needs as a Function of Social Environments," in Leonard D. White, ed., *The State of the Social Sciences*. Chicago, University of Chicago Press, 1956.

KENNEDY, ROBERT F., *Thirteen Days—A Memoir of the Cuban Missile Crisis*. New York, W. W. Norton and Company, 1969.

RAPOPORT, ANATOL, *Fights, Games and Debates*. Ann Arbor, Mich., University of Michigan Press, 1961.

RESTON, JAMES, "Washington: The Law of Compensation in Korea and Vietnam," *The New York Times*, January 31, 1968.

ROSENTHAL, JOEL T., "The King's 'Wicked Advisers' and Medieval Baronial Rebellions," *Political Science Quarterly*, LXXXII, 4 (1967).

SCHLESINGER, ARTHUR M., JR., *A Thousand Days*. Boston, Houghton-Mifflin Company, 1965.

SORENSON, THEODORE C., *Kennedy*. New York, Harper & Row, 1965.

CONCLUSION

ALLPORT, GORDON W., "The Role of Expectancy," in Hadley Cantril, ed., *Tensions That Cause Wars*. Urbana, Ill., University of Illinois Press, 1950.

BENNIS, WARREN G., and SLATER, PHILIP E., *The Temporary Society*. NewYork, Harper & Row, 1968.

BRYCE, JAMES, *Modern Democracies*, Vol. II. New York, The Macmillan Company, 1921.

CLAUDE, INIS L., JR., "The Management of Power in the Changing United Nations," in Saul H. Mendlovitz, ed., *Legal and Political Problems of World Order*, preliminary ed. New York, The Fund for Education Concerning World Peace Through World Law, 1962.

CLAUSEWITZ, CARL VON, *On War*, rev. ed. Vols. I and III, trans. by J. J. Graham. New York, E. P. Dutton and

Company; London, Kegan, Paul, Trench, Trubner and Company, 1940.

FULBRIGHT, J. WILLIAM, *The Arrogance of Power.* New York, Random House, 1966.

HAMILTON, ALEXANDER, *The Federalist.* New York, Modern Library, 1937.

LASSWELL, HAROLD D., *Psychopathology and Politics.* New York, Viking Press, 1960.

LIKERT, RENSIS, *New Patterns of Management.* New York, McGraw-Hill Book Company, 1961.

LORENZ, KONRAD, *On Aggression.* New York, Harcourt, Brace & World, 1966.

MADISON, JAMES, *The Federalist.* New York, Modern Library, 1937.

MILLER, E. J., and RICE, A. K., *Systems of Organization.* London, Tavistock Publications, 1967.

MILLS, C. WRIGHT, "Mass Society and Liberal Education," in Irving L. Horwitz, ed., *Power, Politics and People.* Oxford and New York, Oxford University Press, 1967.

RUSSELL, BERTRAND, *Power.* New York, W. W. Norton and Company, 1938.

STORR, ANTHONY, *Human Aggression.* New York, Atheneum, 1968.

WHYTE, WILLIAM FOOTE, *Man and Organization.* Homewood, Ill., R. D. Irwin, 1959.

THUCYDIDES, *The Complete Writings of Thucydides,* trans. by R. Crawley. New York, The Modern Library, 1934.

TUCHMAN, BARBARA W., *The Guns of August.* New York, The Macmillan Company, 1962.

WURZEL, KARL GEORG, "Methods of Juridical Thinking," in *The Science of Legal Method.* The Modern Legal Philosophy Series, Vol. IX. Boston, Boston Book Company, 1917.

XENOPHON, *Anabasis—The March Up Country,* trans. by W. H. D. Rouse. New York, New American Library, 1959.

ZWEIG, STEFAN, *Joseph Fouché.* New York, The Viking Press, 1930.

ACKNOWLEDGMENTS

I want to thank Professor Robert Engler and Mr. Sidney Liskofsky for their advice on my manuscript, Mr. Seymour Spolter for his research assistance, Mrs. Miriam S. Frank, my secretary, and two friends who are no longer living: Justice Benjamin R. Cardozo and Professor Max Radin for their suggestions, when this book was first published, in the then unlikely event of a revised edition. Especially, I want to thank Professor H. H. (Hube) Wilson for urging me to revise and republish the book for the use of a new generation of his students.

For permission to quote from copyright material the author thanks the following publishers:

The Clarendon Press: C. E. M. Joad, *Modern Political Theory.*

Columbia Law Review: vol. xxxii (1932), p. 1122.

Harcourt, Brace and Co.: Morris R. Cohen, *Reason and Nature.*

International Publishers: V. I. Lenin, *State and Revolution.*

Little, Brown and Co.: Harvey Cushing, *From a Surgeon's Journal.*

Longmans Green and Co.: R. G. Hawtrey, *Economic Aspects of Sovereignty.*

The Johns Hopkins Press: O. G. Post, *The Supreme Court and Political Questions.*

The Macmillan Co.: A. A. Berle and G. C. Means, *The Modern Corporation and Private Property.*

———: René Demogue, *The Notion of Law.*
———: Karl Gareis, *Introduction to the Science of Law.*
———: Rudolf von Ihering, *Law as a Means to an End.*
———: C. H. McIlwain, *The Growth of Political Thought in the West.*
———: Karl George Wurzel, *Methods of Juridical Thinking.*
G. P. Putnam's Sons: John Dewey, *Liberalism and Social Action.*
Charles Scribner's Sons: Jesse Newlon, *Educational Administration as a Social Policy.*
———: George Santayana, *Reason and Common Sense.*
Simon and Schuster: L. D. Trotsky, *History of the Russian Revolution.*
The Viking Press, Inc.: Stefan Zweig, *Joseph Fouché.*

INDEX

Abrams v. United States, 71 n.
Absolutism, 5, 6, 7, 8, 12, 14
Academic freedom, 50, 53
Adamic, Louis, 40
Adams, John, 132
Adler, Max, 193
Areopagitica (Milton), 96
Aesop, 145
Africa, 154, 222
Agamemnon, 41
Aggression, 112, 253
Alexander III, Pope, 19
Alexandria, 149
Alexieff, General, 155
Algeria, 182, 183, 226
Alliances, 210–212
Allied Powers, World War I, 203
Allport, Gordon W., 191, 252
Alsace-Lorraine, 197, 205, 222
America, 34, 122, 129, 197, 198
  cities, 131
  civil liberties, 97
  Colonies, 34, 38, 71, 81, 136, 140, 155, 213–214, 244, 253
  Colonists, 23, 189
  courts, 61
  farmers, 24, 29
  government, 65
  immigration, 56
  investment in Europe, 136, 178
  journalism, 46
  landowners, 101
  philosophers, 82, 140
  property, 136
  Revolution, 38, 96–97, 100, 155, 213–214
  see also Civil War (American), Constitution, United States
American Law Institute, 75
Antipater, 39
Anti-Semitism, 121
Antitrust laws, 198
Anxiety, 108
Arab lands, 156
Arab states, 119, 205, 238, 239
Arabs, 196
Arbitration, international, 217
Are American Teachers Free? (Beale), 50
Aristotle, 15, 52, 53, 80, 94–95, 117, 144, 163
Armaments, 227
Articles of Confederation (U.S.), 155, 213, 214
Aryan credo, 13, 145–146, 147
Asch, Solomon E., 64
Asquith, Herbert Henry, 132
Aswan Dam, 180
Athenian law, 67
Athens, 39, 221, 226

Attila, 39
Attitudes, 220
Aurelius, Marcus, 144
Austin, John, 6, 26 n., 57, 164 n., 201
Austria, 222
Authoritarian personality, 105, 106
Authoritarianism, 49
Authority, 54, 104–110, 112, 113, 117, 155, 184, 185, 190, 220, 247, 254
  institutional, 106, 107
  interpersonal, 106, 107, 108
  symbols, 253
Autocracy, 119

Baker v. Carr, 62
Balance of power, 114, 228, 231
Balkans, 222
Baltic States, 205, 216
Banking, 178
Banque de France, 30
Barker, Ernest, 96
Bay of Pigs, 231, 232
Beale, Howard K., 50
Beard, Charles A., 137, 213–214
Bebel, August, 102
Belgium:
  and the Congo, 195
  German invasion of, 203, 222
Bennis, Warren G., 246
Bentham, Jeremy, 6, 26 n., 80, 86, 99
Beria, Lavrenti, 148, 196
Berle, Adolph A., 34, 35, 56, 122
Berlin, 230, 231
  divided, 223
Berolzheimer, Fritz, 165
Bethmann-Hollweg, Theobald von, 203
Bianchi, Michele, 86
Bible, 26–27, 37, 77, 97, 98, 192 n.
Biddle, Nicholas, 30
Bill of Rights, 97, 248
Bismarck, Otto von, 121, 145
Black Hundreds, 38
Blackstone, William, 6
Blanc, Louis, 24
Bodin, Jean, 5, 8, 9, 94, 194
Bolingbroke, Henry, 7
Bolsheviks, 140, 186–187, 191, 244
Boulding, Kenneth E., 228
Boundary disputes, 205
Bourbons, 122, 140, 189
Boxer Rebellion, 179
Boycotts, 23, 30, 38, 123, 182, 183, 248
Bracton, Henry de, 5, 218
Bribery, 30, 31
Britain, *see* Great Britain
British coal industry, 24
British Commonwealth, 189
British Empire, 189
British General Strike (1926), 24, 33
British East India Company, 198
Brown, Jethro, 166
Brown, John, 128
Brown v. Board of Education of Topeka, 57, 62, 114
Bryce, Viscount James, 153, 242
Buddhism, 198
Building codes, 125
Burke, Edmund, 59, 71, 189

Caesar, 149
Caius, 71
Calvin, John, 52
Canterbury, Bishop of, 150
Capital, 147, 183
  control, 35
  and finance, 29, 30, 34, 36, 44, 45, 83, 122
  see also Finance
Capitalism, 35, 43, 84, 85, 86, 134, 183, 249
  and finance, 14, 129
  see also Finance
Carlyle, R. W. and A. J., 150 n.
Castellio, Sébastien, 52
Castracani of Lucca, Castruccio, 27

Castro, Fidel, 179, 231
Catholic Church, *see* Roman Catholic Church
Caveat emptor, 44, 99 n., 100
Censorship, 182
  during World Wars, 45, 46, 251
Central America, 154, 198
Central Asia, 58
Central IntelligenceAgency, 231
Ceylon, 237
Chamber of Deputies (France), 132
Charles I, King, 37
Charter, adopted by Allies, 205–206
China, 179, 224, 232
  Communists, 196, 198
  People's Republic of, 176, 192, 196, 210, 231, 232
  Republic of (Taiwan), 210
Chinese Revolution, 100
Choate, Joseph H., 42
Christianity, 144, 188
Christians, 149, 151
Church, 11, 27, 82, 84, 94, 138, 144–146, 149–152, 163, 176
  see also Roman Catholic Church
City of God (St. Augustine), 144, 163
Civil:
  disobedience, 38, 84, 131, 248
  liberties, 61, 97, 98, 99
  rights, 38, 101, 251; *see also* Freedom
Civil war, 16, 137, 138, 140, 154, 202, 209,
  American, 28, 30, 71, 136, 202, 251
  Spanish, 175
Claude, Inis, 254–255
Clausewitz, Karl von, 172, 173, 176, 184, 224
Clearchos, 188
Cohen, Morris R., 25, 78 n., 156–157, 158
Cold War, 195, 202
Collectivization, 13, 196
Colonialism, 23, 177, 178, 179, 180, 199
Commissioner of Human Rights (UN), 219
Communication, 45, 187, 190, 193
Communism, 85, 89, 130, 146, 166, 180, 210
Communist bloc, 180
Communist China, *see* China, Communist
  see also China, People's Republic of
Communist countries, 134, 182, 246
  law in, 67
Communist dictatorship, 13, 93
Communist Manifesto, The, 53
Communist Party, 67, 111, 144, 147–148, 199
Communist philosophy, 141
Communist Revolution, 196
Communist Society, 85
Communists, 39, 108
Compact, social, 10, 79–81, 83–85, 97, 201
Compromise, 16–19, 123–126, 127, 130, 186, 212, 226
Conciliation, 123–126
Conciliation with the American Colonies (Burke), 71 n.
Confederation, 214
Conflict, 221
Conflict of Interests, 117–121, 243
Congo, 195
Congregation of the Holy Office, 56
Congress, *see* United States, Congress
Conservative Party (England), 132
Constantine, 76
Constantinople, 186
Constitution (U.S.), 12, 18, 29, 30, 84, 97, 155, 157, 247, 248, 251
  see also specific amendments

Constitution (Story), 5
Constitutional doctrine, American, 6
Continental Congress, 155, 213–214
Coronation oath, 10
Cossacks, 69
Courts, 25, 44, 56, 57, 60, 61, 63–66, 74, 75, 81, 164, 209, 211, 214, 218, 248
 see also Law *and* Supreme Court
Courts of claim, 74
Courts of Justice, 63
Crimean War, 143
Crook, Willard Harris, 33
Cruelty, 184, 225
Cruelties in war, 225
Crusades, 150, 176, 225
Cuba, 17, 18, 29, 179, 180, 229
Cuban missile crisis, 47, 186, 229–237
Cult of the Emperor, 148
Curia, 10
Cushing, Harvey W., 42, 46
Custom, 9–12, 57, 58, 65, 75–78, 201–209
Cybernetics, 44
Czechoslovakia, 205, 252
 invasion of by Soviet Union, 199–200

Daladier, Édouard, 252
Darwinism, 97–98
Decalogue, 149
Declaration of Independence, 110
De Gaulle, Charles, 47, 132
De haereticis (Castellio), 52
Democracy, 14, 50, 80, 111, 121, 139, 187, 242, 244
 essence of, 241
 participatory, 244
Democracy in a World of Tensions (UNESCO), 187
Demogue, René, 25, 26, 93, 123, 124, 126, 167
Demosthenes, 39
Deodand, 22
Dependence, 104
De Republica (Bodin), 5
Descartes, René, 81, 144
Desegregation, 57, 114
Deuteronomy, 37, 77
Dewey, John, 21, 31–32, 41–42, 92
Dialectical materialism, 54
Dialectics of Power, 126–127
Diana of the Wood, 3
Dicey, A. V., 123
Dickinson, John, 194–195
Dictatorial governments, 47
Diffidatio, 11, 78
Diplomacy, secret, 216–218
Discrimination, 114, 182
Discussion, 188
Disobedience, 59
Distortion, 189
Divine Right, 54
Djilas, Milovan, 199
Donatists, 150
Draft, of soldiers, 174
Due process of law, 98, 134, 157, 164
 see also Law
Duguit, Léon, 165
Duma, 140
Duress, 205

Early Law and Custom (Maine), 26 n., 63
Eastern Europe, 156, 172, 180, 199
Economic Aspects of Sovereignty (Hawtrey), 28 n., 128
Economic partnerships, 211
Economic power, *see* Power, economic
Education, 114, 120, 177, 180, 191, 195, 196, 244
 as instrument of sovereignty, 48–54
Educational Administration as Social Policy (Newlon), 50
Edward I, King of England, 137, 218
Egypt, 180, 199, 213, 215, 238, 239

Eighteenth Amendment, 29, 30, 72
Eighteenth Brumaire of Louis Bonaparte, The (Marx), 99
Einstein, Albert, 144
Eisenhower, Dwight D., 197, 229, 250
Elements of Law (Markby), 13
Emancipation Proclamation, 30
Engels, Friedrich, 85, 89, 90, 91, 102
England, 10, 139, 187
and Church of Rome, 150–151
Conservative Party, 132
education in, 48
and India, 23, 198
and International Law, 206
kings of, 5, 197, 229
Labour Party, 47
landowners, 101, 132
laws of, 6, 66, 248
Liberal Party, 132
Magna Carta, 218
peasant revolts, 33
political and commercial influence overseas, 47
political philosophers, 6, 81, 140
Puritan Revolution, 71
and Suez Canal crisis, 172, 199
and United States, 189
and Versailles Treaty, 211
and World War I, 222, 227
and World War II, 188, 224
see also Great Britian
Entente, 222
Equality, 54, 104–114
before the law, 111, 112, 122
in primitive societies, 245
verbal, 109–110
as weapon, 112
Espionage acts, 251
Essays on International Law (*Columbia Law Review*), 201
Estates-General, 9, 95
Ethelred, King, 10
Ethics, 26, 54, 65, 111, 160–168
Ethiopia, 204, 223
Etruscans, 56
Euratom, 211
Europe, 85, 122, 130, 139, 140, 156, 172, 178, 179, 180, 188, 199, 211, 222, 252
European Coal and Steel Community, 211
European Economic Community, 211
Evangical churches, 29, 146
Evangelical ministers, 13
Excommunication, 22, 151
Expectations, 105–114, 186, 191–193, 252–255
Experience, 25–26, 104–113, 191

Face-saving, 127, 205, 228, 229, 230, 234
Farmers and farming, 23, 24, 38, 46, 81, 138, 166, 196
Fascism, 100 n., 145–146, 147, 148
Fascist dictatorship, 93
Fascist Party, 86, 144
Fascist powers, 175
Fascists, 22
Federal Communications Commission (U.S.), 47, 248
Federal government, 6, 12, 15, 18
Federal Power Commission, 248
Federalist, The, 24, 42, 101, 117, 247
Feedback, 135, 186
Feudalism, 7, 11, 32, 35, 43, 67, 77, 78, 84, 117, 134, 161, 174
Fichte, Johann, 167
Fight or Compromise, 16–19
Fighting, 16–19, 188, 226, 253
Finance, 97, 249
and capital, 29, 30, 34, 36, 44, 45, 83, 122, 136
capitalism, 14, 129
corporate, practices of, 129
see also Capital *and* Capitalism
First Amendment, 251
First Article (U.S. Constitution), 251

First Inaugural Address (Lincoln), 69
Fisher, Roger, 74, 177–178
Florentines, 27, 95
Force, 171–176
  limits of use, 62
  military, 250
  physical, *see* Power, physical
  uses of, 128–133
Force Field Theory (Lewin), 121
Foreign aid, unilateral and multilateral, 181–182
Foreign investment, 34, 136, 177, 178, 179, 183, 199
Foreign relations, 194
Fouché, Joseph, 138
Fourteen Points, 216
Fourteenth Amendment, 15, 57, 97
France, 24, 47, 98, 132, 137, 140, 154, 173, 175 n., 187, 188, 198, 205, 207, 211, 215, 223, 252
  and Alsace-Lorraine, 197, 205, 222
  Constitution of 1848, 98, 99
  and English kings, 197
  Metropolitan, 226
  and Morocco, 222
  people of, 189
  political writers in, 81, 140
  Revolution of 1789, 34, 38, 71 n., 100, 173
  seizure of Suez Canal by, 172
  small landowners in, 101
  and Southeast Asia, 226
Franciscans, 198
Franco, Francisco, 147, 148
Franklin, Benjamin, 69
Franks, 10
Frazer, Sir James, 3
Freedom, 92–103
  of the press, 45, 189
  of thought, 53
Fulbright, J. William, 118, 240

Gandhi, Mohandas K., 23, 38
Gangsters, 131
Gareis, Karl, 72–73
General Will (Hegel), 101, 145–146
Genseric, 39
George III, King, 38, 71
Georgia, State of, 71
German Empire, invasion of Belgium, 203
Germanic kings, 14
Germanic law, 76
Germanic states, 101
Germanic tribes, 10, 77 n., 79, 226
Germany, 29, 145, 187
  and African colonies, 222
  annexation of Alsace-Lorraine, 205, 222
  Catholic Church, 13
  East, 210
  economy, 33
  election of March 1933, 21, 39
  Evangelical ministers, 13
  Franco-Prussian War (1870), 202
  Gestapo, 147
  under Nazis, 51, 100, 146, 148
  partition after World War II, 210, 223
  and Russia, Treaty of 1939, 216
  and Sudetenland, 205
  as threat to England, 227
  and United States, 180
  and Versailles Treaty, 205, 211
  and World War I, 197, 202, 222, 224, 227
  and World War II, 143, 172, 188, 202, 207, 227, 252
  see also Fascism, Hitler, Nazis
Gibbon, Edward, 149
Gitlow v. New York, 70
Goals, 107, 109, 110, 113, 195, 196
Goebbels, Joseph Paul, 42
Golden Bough, The (Frazer), 3, 4
Great Britain, 148, 154
  courts, 64
  foreign relations, 198
  and Israel, 24

journalism, 46
Royal Air Force, 224
supremacy in world affairs, 46–47, 226
and United States, 6, 23, 38, 71, 136, 155, 213
see also England
Greece, 186, 187
Greek states, 80, 163
Grey, Lord, 222
Gromyko, Andrei, 230
Grotius, Hugo, 208
Growth of Political Thought in the West, The (McIlwain), 77 n.
Guchkov, Aleksandr, 155
Guelphs, 27

Haiti, 199
Hamilton, Alexander, 24, 132, 251
Hamilton, Walton H., 99 n.
Hampden, John, 16, 96
Hapsburg, House of, 223
Harper v. Virginia, 28
Harper's Ferry, 128
Harington, Sir John, 142
Hastings, Warren, 198
Hawtrey, R. G., 28 n., 128, 173, 181
Hegel, Georg W. F., 93, 101, 102, 144, 145, 146
Heidelberg, University of, 42, 51
Heider, Fritz, 220
Heine, Heinrich, 38
Hellenistic culture, 148
Henry Plantagenet, law of, 56
Henry II, King of England, 11
Henry III, King of France, 8, 9
Heraclitus, 144
Herdonius, Turnus, 39
Hilsman, Roger, 189, 229, 234
History of Medieval Political Theory (R. W. and A. J. Carlyle), 150 n.
History of the Russian Revolution (Trotsky), 15, 17
Hitler, Adolf, 21, 23, 39, 40, 109, 146, 147, 148, 167, 196, 205, 207, 216, 224, 252
Aryan credo, 145
corporative state, 144
and death camps, 225
at Munich, 188
violation of Versailles Treaty, 211
Hobbes, Thomas, 55, 201
Hohenzollern autocracy, 121
Holders of the Weapons, 133–135
Holland, 49, 187, 206
Holland, T. E., 55, 58
Holmes, Oliver Wendell, 33, 71 n., 158
Holy Roman Empire, 153, 154, 185
see also Roman Empire
Holy See, 151
Hostility, 105, 112, 113, 176, 184–185, 190, 205, 221, 223, 224, 227, 228, 236, 246
toward other nations, 187
Hughes, Charles Evans, 69–70
Humanism, 52
Humiliation, 229
Hungary, 138, 215, 222
Husting, 20, 56, 76, 80, 132

Iconoclasm, 37–38
Ideals, 160–168
Identification, 107
Ideology, 246
Idiomatic differences, 187
Ihering, Rudolf von, 26, 32, 37, 68, 83, 99 n.
Imperial German Army, 224
In Days to Come (Rathenau), 33
India, 23, 38, 57, 179, 196, 198, 237
and Kashmir, 197
Warren Hastings administration in, 198
Individuals, 220
versus Foreign States, 218–219
Indonesia, 179
Industrial Revolution, 35, 97
Innocent III, Pope, 150, 151

Institutions, as safety valves, 112, 113
International Court of Justice, 208
International law, 195, 201–204, 238
  and individuals, 218
  as law of the land, 208–209
Interstate Commerce Commission, 248
Investment, foreign, 177
Ireland, 7, 34, 150
Islamic power, 189
Island of Palmas Arbitration, 195
Israel, 24, 156, 180, 182, 196, 213, 238, 244
  creation of, 24, 205
  and Suez crisis, 172, 215
Italy, 13, 19, 22, 100, 122, 144, 146, 147, 148, 204, 211
  corporative state in, 13
  and Ethiopia, 233
  and Kellogg-Briand Pact, 207
  medieval towns in, 195
  and Triple Alliance, 222
  see also Fascism
I.W.W., 40

Jackson, Andrew, 28
Jackson, Elmore, 217
Jacobs, Noah Jonathan, 187
James, King of England, 97
James, William, 144
Japan, 34, 186, 198, 233, 251
  and Kellogg-Briand Pact, 207
Jefferson, Thomas, 97, 132
Jerusalem, 77
Jessup, Phillip C., 201, 207, 212
Jesuits, 198
Jews, 57, 147, 149, 187
  and establishment of Israel, 205
Jewish law, enforcement of, 57
Joad, C. E. M., 102
John, King of England, 11, 12, 34, 71, 150, 151
Johnson, Lyndon B., 129
Joseph Fouché (Zweig), 116
Josiah, 77
Jurisprudence (Holland), 55
Justinian, Emperor, 56, 186

Kant, Immanuel, 144
Kaplan, 202–203
Kashmir, 197
Katz, Milton, 201
Katzenbach, Nicholas deB., 202–203
Kaufman, Bel, 50
Kellogg, Frank B., 207
Kellogg-Briand Pact, 207
Kennedy, John F., 47, 229–235
Kennedy, Robert F., 234, 235
Keynes, John Maynard, 47
Khama, Tshekedi, 154
Khazars, 8
Khrushchev, Nikita S., 39, 148, 186, 229, 232, 233, 234, 235
King, Martin Luther, Jr., 38
King of the Wood, 3, 4, 62, 116, 188
King's court, 66, 201
Kirchheimer, Otto, 108, 111
Kohn, Hans, 176, 185
Korea, 175, 197
  Democratic People's Republic of, 238
Korkunov, N. M., 163
Kozol, Jonathan, 50
Kremlin, 56, 200, 232
Kropotkin, Prince Peter A., 116
Kun, Béla, 138

Labor market, free, 14
Laissez-faire, 84–85, 122, 138
Land ownership, 119
Langton, Stephen, 150
Laski, Harold, 68, 95, 116–117, 155
Lasswell, Harold E., 247
Lateran Council, 151
Latin America, 119, 199
  and Communist revolutions, 232

Lauterpacht, 209–210
Laughter, 236–237
Law, 5, 6, 8–10, 54, 55–74, 75–78, 163, 164, 167
 commercial, 60
 criminal, 60
 due process of, 98, 134, 157, 164
 enforcement, 201
 positive, 201
 property, 60
 of reason, 10
 and social values, 67
 see also International Law
Law and Opinion in England (Dicey), 123
Law as a Means to an End (Ihering), 99 n.
Laws, sumptuary, 251
 tenement house, 125
Leadership, institutional and informal, 106–107
League of Nations, 24, 204
Legal jurisdiction, 66
Legal remedy, 201
Legislation, judicial, 56
Legislatures, *de facto* and *de jure*, 62
Lenin, 18, 41, 54, 85–91, 127, 141, 146, 183, 200, 244
Leo I, Pope, 39
Letters of reprisal, 206, 207
Lewin, Kurt, 121
Liberalism and Social Action (Dewey), 21–22, 41–42, 92
Liberty, 54, 92–103
Libri Feudorum, 76
Lincoln, Abraham, 30, 69, 137, 145, 251
Litigation, 193
Livy, 39
Lloyd, George, David, 132
Lobbyists, 36, 38
Locke, John, 97
Lombard bankers, 177
London, 46
Long Parliament (England), 96
L'Opposition Universelle (Tarde), 123
Lorenz, Konrad, 253
Louis XII, King, 19
Louis XIV, King, 5
Louis XV, King, 194
Louis XVI, King, 37
Louis, Prince, 151
Lucretius, 52, 144

Macedonia, 39
Machado, Gerardo, 17
Machiavelli, 8, 9, 10, 19, 59, 95
McIlwain, C. H., 77 n., 149, 218
McKechnie, W. S., 10, 11
McKinley Tariff Act, 29
Madison, James, 42, 101, 117, 118, 214, 247
Magna Carta, 11, 12, 150, 218
Magna Carta (McKechnie), 10
Maine, J. S., 26, 57, 63
Manifesto of October 17, 1905, 17
Mann, Horace, 49
Mao Tse-tung, 13, 183 n., 224
Markby, William, 6, 7, 8, 13, 57, 99, 100
Marshall, John, 6
Marshall Plan, 136, 180
Marsiglio of Padua, 94
Martel, Charles, 76, 188
Marx, Karl, 86, 89, 99, 146, 244
Marxian doctrine, 83, 85, 100 n., 138, 242
Marxian Philosophy, 120
Massachusetts, 49
 colony of, 38
Massell, Gregory J., 58–59
Masurian Lakes, Battle of, 224
May, Samuel J., 49
Mayflower Pact, 83
Means, G. C., 34, 35–36
Mediterranean Sea, 197, 222
Mein Kampf (Hitler), *see My Battle*
Mensheviks, 191

Mercantilism, 138, 177, 178, 181
Methods of Juridical Thinking (Wurzel), 164
Mexican Revolution (1913), 179
Mexico, 179
  religion in, 51
  and the United States, 223
Middle Ages, 9, 10, 27, 43, 44, 71, 76, 94, 159, 174, 197
Middle East, 215
Milgram, Stanley, 184
Military-industrial complex, 197, 250, 251
Mill, John Stuart, 95, 99
Mills, C. Wright, 241
Milton, John, 96 n.
Minnesota Moratorium Case, 69–70
Minority groups, 114, 121, 125
Mirror of Justices, 218
Missouri Compromise, 17
Mobilizing for Chaos (Riegel), 46–47
Modern Corporation and Private Property (Berle and Means), 34, 35, 36
Modern Democracies (Bryce), 242
Modern Political Theory (Joad), 102
Monroe Doctrine, 179
Mont St. Michel, 144
Montesquieu, 95, 97
Montfort, Simon de, 137
Montgomery, boycott in, 38
Morgenthau, Hans J., 171, 183, 201, 208, 209
Morocco, 222
Mosaic law, 67
Moscow, 141, 180, 199
Moseley, Phillip E., 186
Muller, Herbert J., 187
Mummery of the Middle Ages, 43
Munich, 188
Muslim ethnic groups, 58–59
Mussolini, Benito, 196, 211
My Battle (Hitler), 40–41, 144
Naming Day in Eden (Jacobs), 187
Naples, 19
Napoleon, 143, 224
  law of, 56
Napoleon, Louis, 98, 99
Napoleon III, 24
Nasser, Gamal, 238
National Association of Manufacturers, 51
National Industrial Recovery Act, 36
National Recovery Administration, 18
National Savings Certificates, 47
Nationalism, 185, 218, 219
Nations, "have," and "have-not," 183
NATO, 172, 230, 232, 233
Natural rights, 10
Naval powers, 178
Nazi:
  dictatorship, 13
  era, 6 n.
  Party, 146
Nazis, 21, 22, 23, 38, 51, 109, 225
Needs, 105, 118, 171, 185, 220, 240
Negroes, 15, 71, 110, 123, 130
Netherlands, *see* Holland
Neutrality, 208
New Deal legislation, 24, 129
New Economic Policy, 18
New England, 79
  town meetings, 244
New York, 66, 124, 125
New York Times, The, 237
Newlon, Jesse, 50
Nicholas II, 13, 17, 37, 140, 189, 224
Nicholas of Cusa, 94
Nobel Peace Prize, 207
North Vietnam, 172, 175
  see also South Vietnam *and* Vietnam

Notion of Law, The (Demogue), 25–26
Nuremberg trials, 167, 205–206

OAS, *see* Organization of American States
October Revolution (Russia), 138
"On the Crown" (Demosthenes), 39
Opinions, 220
Opportunity, equal, 111–113
Orestes, 41
Organization of American States, 230, 233, 234

Pactum (agreement), 10
Paine, Thomas, 97
Pakistan, and Kashmir, 197
Palestine, 24, 149
Paris, Commune of, 24, 138, 244
Parliament (England), 71, 95, 96, 136, 137, 222, 247, 248
Parmenides, 144
Pascal, Blaise, 26 n.
Peace pacts, 207–208
Pearl Harbor, 233, 251
Peasant revolts, 13, 33
Peasantry, 13, 137, 141, 142
Peers and peer groups, 104, 105, 108, 109, 113, 134
Peloponnesian War, 221
Pensées (Pascal), 26 n.
Peonage, 14
People's Republic of China, *see* China
Pericles, law of, 56
Permanent Court of International Justice, 208
Personality, 105, 110
Peru, 179
Petition of Right, 96
Petlura, Simon, 141
Petrarch, 186
Petrograd, 17
Pfaff, William, 196
Philip of France, 151
Physical force, *see* Power, physical
Pippin, 76
Pisa, 95
Plato, 14, 15, 48
Poland, 205
polis, 94
Political process, 115–142
Political weapons, 20–54
poll tax, 28
Popular sovereignty, *see* Sovereignty, popular
Portugal, 198
Positive law, 157
Posse comitatis, 58
Post, Charles Gordon, 62
Pound, Dean Roscoe, 161
Powell, Thomas Reid, 194
Power, 9, 24, 86, 104–117, 120, 139, 179–189, 196–204, 220–228, 239–255
  dialectics of, 126–127
  diffusion of, 248–255
  economic, 21, 23, 26–37, 38, 68, 86, 106–108, 176–184
  physical, 20–26, 27, 28, 30, 31, 36, 37, 38, 55, 56, 57–74, 81, 86, 130–132
  psychological, 21, 23, 30, 37–54, 73, 79–91
  vacuum, 122–123
Praetorian Guard, 154, 250
Pravda (USSR), 200
Preamble of the U.S. Constitution, 12
Prestige, 77, 105, 128–133, 138, 186, 193, 195, 205, 209, 211, 216, 217, 220–239, 240, 250, 253
Pride, 237–239
Prince, The (Machiavelli), 19
Private organizations, 182–183
Propaganda, 20
  as a political weapon, 37–54
  see also Power, psychological
Property, 9
  confiscation of, 22

Property and Sovereignty (Cohen), 78 n.
Protestant Reformation, 38, 96, 152
Prussian state, 93, 144, 145, 146
Psychological power, *see* Power, psychological
Public law, 73
Punishment, 107, 108, 179
see also Rewards
Punjab, 57
Puritan Revolution, 71, 96

Rapoport, Anatol, 228
Rathenau, Walther, 33, 127
Rationalism, 52
Reason in Common Sense (Santayana), 141, 162
Rebellion, 132
Rebellious barons, 10, 11, 34, 71, 77, 95, 133, 138, 150, 151, 229
Recognition, 209–210
Reconstruction, 71
Red Army, 148, 250
Reichstag, burning of, 39
Reichswehr, 250
Rejection, 104, 105
Renaissance, 27, 122
Renject Singh, 57
Reprisal, letter of, 206
Research Committee on Social Trends (U.S.), 120
Resistance, 106
Respect, 240
Reston, James, 228
Retribution, 206–207
Revolution, 8, 13, 16, 21, 24, 61, 63, 67, 72, 74, 77, 86, 88, 89, 98, 100, 101, 130, 132, 135–142, 154, 192, 199, 209, 244, 247, 254
see also specific countries
Rewards, 107, 108, 129, 250
Rhine Valley, 211
Richard I, King of England, 11
Richard II (Shakespeare), 7, 47, 48
Riegel, O. W., 46–47
Rights, 10, 54
Rise of American Civilization, The (Beard), 137
Roehm, Ernst, 147
Roles, 106, 107, 114, 126, 246, 250, 252, 254
Romagna, 19
Roman Catholic Church, 13, 27, 96, 146, 151, 185–186
see also Church
Roman Empire, 130, 148, 226
Roman law, 76
Rome, 27, 28, 39, 56, 66, 76, 148, 150
Rome, Church of, *see* Roman Catholic Church
Romulus, 27
Roosevelt, Franklin D., 18, 24, 47, 248
Roosevelt, Theodore, 248
Rosenthal, Joel T., 133
Rota, 56
Rousseau, Jean Jacques, 63, 91
Ruberto, King of Naples, 27
Rufus, William, 76
Runnymede, 11
Russell, Bertrand, 197, 247
Russia, 8, 38, 143, 197, 252
Bolshevik Party, 140, 186, 191, 244
and Cuban Missile Crisis, 186, 229–237
and Czechoslavakia, 199–200
economy, 18, 29, 179–180, 195, 196
and foreign aid, 179–180, 198
and Germany, 207, 210, 216, 223, 224
government, 56, 111, 122, 144
and Hungary, 215
ideology, 51, 54, 58, 59, 67, 109, 146, 182, 196
Manifesto of October 1905, 17

Menshevik Party, 191
peasantry, 13, 33, 72
political prisoners, 22, 147–148
Provisional Government, 155
Revolution of 1905, 17, 138
Revolution of 1917, 17, 71 n., 72, 100, 140, 155
Russo-Japanese War, 186
and Satellite Nations, 156, 172, 179–180
and United States, 176, 179–180, 186, 195, 202, 239
in World War I, 154, 222
in World War II, 188

St. Ambrose, 150
St. Augustine, 9, 91, 144
St. Optatus, 150
St. Paul's Epistle to the Romans, 149
St. Thomas, 94, 144, 194
Sakharov, Andrei, 53
Salic law, 10
Samuel, Books of, 37, 192 n.
Sanctions, 7, 11, 16, 25, 30, 59, 77, 125, 127, 129, 131, 141, 142, 204
Santayana, George, 135, 141, 162
Santo Domingo, 199
Scandinavia, 252
Scapegoats, 110, 112, 190
Schenck v. United States, 71 n.
Schlesinger, Arthur M., Jr., 229
Schopenhauer, Arthur, 73
Scott, James B., 201
Scutage, 12, 28, 32, 174
Secrecy, 189
Security, 107
Segregation, 38, 114
Self-esteem, 240
Self-interest, 203–208, 219
Sella curulis, 56
Sentiment, 220
Serbia, 222
Serfdom, 14
Servetus, Michael, 52
Servius, 27
Shakespeare, 7, 47, 48
Sherif, Muzafer, 64
Shogun, 198
Sicily, 131, 221, 226
Sino-Soviet dispute, 231
Six Day War, 156
Slater, Phillip E., 246
Slavery, 3, 4, 15, 17, 30, 49, 80, 136–137, 159, 163
abolition of, 137
Slogans, 45, 53, 134, 135, 137
Smith, Adam, 95
Social compact, *see* Compact, social
Social democracy, German, 145
Social influence, 240
Social mobility, 242
Socialism, State, 90, 121, 249
Socrates, 161
Solomon, 41
Sorensen, Theodore C., 229
South America, 154
South Vietnam, 172, 175
see also North Vietnam *and* Vietnam
Southeast Asia, 226
Sovereignty, defined, 5–6, 13
dual and plural, 153–159
and force, 128–133
and International Law, 201–204, 208–209
and law, 55–74
limits to power of, 8–13, 195–197, 198
and morality, 160–168
of nations, 171–193, 194–219
nature of, 4
and political processes, 115–142
popular, 79–91
and power, 115–117
and prestige, 128–133, 220–239
and revolution, 135–142
supremacy of, 5–15
territorial, 195

theme of, 4
and United Nations, 212–216
and unity, 143–152
weapons of, 14–19, 20–54, 171–193
see also Equality, Force, Law, Liberty, Power
Soviet Union, *see* Russia
Spain, 19, 147, 148, 188, 198, 206, 223
Spanish-American War, 188
Sparta, 221, 226
Spencer, Herbert, 99
Spinoza, Baruch, 144
SS, 147, 148
Stalin, Joseph, 18, 23, 39, 52, 109, 147, 182, 196, 199, 216
Stamp, Sir Josiah, 47–48
State, 9, 15, 22, 25, 28, 44, 59, 67, 70, 73, 74, 76, 85–90, 93, 95, 99, 101, 102, 115, 119, 120, 122, 123, 127, 143, 145, 146, 148, 150–152, 156–158, 160–162, 167, 195–218, 245–252
client, 178, 184
competitive position of, 177
political policy of, 178
sovereign power of, 178, 192
withering away of, 54, 79–81
State and Revolution, The (Lenin), 88–89
Stereotypes, 185
Stillman, Edmund, 196
Storr, Anthony, 243
Story, Joseph, 5, 6
Strength, 107
Stuarts, 71, 96
Subordination, 104
Sudetenland, 205
Suez Canal, 172, 199
Suez crisis, 215
Suffrage, 119
Supremacy of the Sovereign, 5–14
Supreme Court (U.S.), 6, 28, 56, 57, 62, 70, 84, 97, 98, 114
Supreme Court and Political Questions, The (Post), 62
Suspicion, 191
Switzerland, 227
Symbols, 37–48, 184–193
Syndicalism, 156
Syracuse, 221
Syria, 215

Tacitus, 79
Taiwan, 210
Tarde, André, 123
Tarquinius, Lucius, 39
Tartar invasions, 174
Teutonic law, 76
Teutonic tribes, 20, 21, 79, 167
Texas, 179
Thiers, Louis Adolphe, 24
Thirteenth Amendment, 15
Thirty Years' War, 34
Tholommeo of Lucca, 94
Thoughts on Progress, Peaceful Coexistence and Intellectual Freedom (Sakharov), 53
Three Faces of Power, The (Berle), 56
Tissaphernes, 188
Transjordan, 148
Treaties, 129, 192, 197, 202, 203–208, 211, 214, 217, 225
Tribute, payment of, 131
Triple Alliance, 222
"Trollope Ploy," 235 n.
Trotsky, Leon, 15, 17, 72, 96, 98, 118, 133, 135
Truman Doctrine, 197
Tudors, 96
Turgot, 137
Turkey, 235
Turks, 154, 186
Twenty-fourth Amendment, 28
Tyrannicide, 10

U Thant, 213
U-2 incident, 229
Ukraine, 141

UNESCO, 187, 190, 191
United Arab Republic, 238
United Fruit Company, 198
United Kingdom, 215
United Nations, 181–183, 191, 217, 219, 230, 232, 233
  and sovereignty, 212–216
  Assembly, 214
  Charter, 213, 214, 215
  Covenants, 218
  Educational, Scientific and Cultural Organization, *see* UNESCO
  peace-maintenance forces, 215
  Security Council, 210, 212, 214, 215
United States, 23, 24, 31, 47, 49, 85, 120, 212
  and China, 192, 224
  Congress, 137, 232, 233, 248, 252
  and Cuba, 179, 229–237
  economy, 35, 130, 178, 179, 243
  foreign aid, 180, 183
  foreign relations, 179, 198, 199, 210, 211, 238
  government, 6, 12, 15, 18, 139
  and Mexico, 179, 223
  presidency, 111, 133
  and Russia, 186, 195, 215, 239
  and Spain, 188, 223
  and Vietnam, 172, 173, 176, 191, 225
  and World War II, 207, 208, 251
  see also America, Civil War (American), Constitution, Supreme Court
United States Bank, 30
United States Steel Corporation, 144
Unity, 54, 143–152
Universal Declaration of Human Rights, The, 218
Universal Postal Union, 204
Upward mobility, 105
USSR, *see* Russia
Utilitarian Liberty, 102
Utilitarianism, 97, 99, 100, 139

Valentinian II, Emperor, 150
Valois kings, 5, 194
Values, 220
Vandals, 39
Vatican, 13, 56, 146
  see also Roman Catholic Church
Veblen, Thorstein, 163
Venezuela, 179
Vera Cruz, 179
Versailles Treaty, 205, 211
Veto, in United Nations, 215
Vichy government, 252
Vietnam, 119, 130, 173, 175, 176, 191, 197, 225, 236
  see also North Vietnam *and* South Vietnam
Villa, Pancho, 179
Violence, *see* Force
Von François, Kurt, 224
Von Hindenburg, Paul, 224
Voting, system of, 28

Wagner Labor Act, 18
War, as expression of national policy, 173
War crimes, 205–206
Wars of the Roses, 96
Warren, Chief Justice Earl, 98
Washington, D.C., 50
Weaponry, 175, 176
Weapons, political, 20–54
Webster, Daniel, 84, 119
Welfare state, 32
West Germany, 172, 175, 210, 223
West Indies, 29
Western Europe, 136, 180, 188
Western Powers, 202
William the Conqueror, 10, 76
Wilson, Woodrow, 13, 40, 59, 216
Win-lose expectations, 127, 191–193, 216, 253, 255
Winchester, Bishop of, 12
Wirt, William, 84
Withdrawal, 226

Withering State, *see* State
Witte, Count, 17
Words, 37–48, 184–193
World War I, 33, 42, 46, 83, 154, 174, 202, 205, 221, 227, 236, 251
World War II, 136, 139, 154, 156, 167, 172, 174, 180, 195, 202, 205, 223, 227, 251, 252
World Wars, 174, 227, 251
Wurzel, Karl George, 164
Wu-ti, Emperor, 21

Xenophon, 188

Yale Law Journal, 99 n.
Yugoslavia, 249

Zweig, Stefan, 116